AF522057

Hospitality
E-marketing

HOSPITALITY E-MARKETING

Ravindra Verma

CENTRUM PRESS
NEW DELHI-110002 (INDIA)

CENTRUM PRESS

H.O.: 4360/4, Ansari Road, Daryaganj,
New Delhi-110002 (India)
Tel: 23278000, 23261597, 23255577, 23286875

B.O.: No. 1015, Ist Main Road, BSK IIIrd Stage,
IIIrd Phase, IIIrd Block, Bengaluru-560085 (INDIA)
Tel: 080-41723429

Email: centrumpress@gmail.com
Visit us at: www.centrumpress.com

Hospitality E-marketing

First Edition, 2013

ISBN 978-93-81460-24-5

PRINTED IN INDIA

Printed at Balaji Offset, Delhi.

Contents

Preface

One of the first factors in Internet success is having a plan. Most businesses' do not have a strategy when it comes to their Internet presence. They build a website and hope people will come to it if it has neat graphics or they make a haphazard attempt to gain more followers on Twitter, but they do not establish a concrete plan designed to funnel people from their website to their restaurant or from their YouTube channel to their bed and breakfast. This is a serious mistake that can drain financial resources, not to mention employee time.

Another important factor in building a successful Internet presence is understanding which channels your customers are on and what constituents successful interaction on each channel. What works on Twitter, won't necessarily work on Facebook and vice versa. Understanding which channels really resonate with your audience will promote further engagement and a greater return on investment. Finally, your hospitality business' success on the Internet depends on you actually having an Internet presence. The fact of the matter is that 74% of all Internet users in the United States perform Internet searches which may be categorized as "local" in nature and 82% of those local Internet searchers follow up their online activities with an offline follow up, such as making a purchase or calling for an appointment. If you don't have an online presence, you are missing out on thousands of potential leads a month. Even if you feel that Internet marketing hasn't worked for you in the past, you should consider reinvigorating your campaign. Technology is constantly evolving and today's Internet users encompass a diverse range of individuals. One no longer needs to be tech savvy to enjoy all the Internet has to offer.

Internet marketing is considered to be broad in scope because it not only refers to marketing on the Internet, but also includes marketing done via e-mail and wireless media. Digital customer data and electronic customer relationship management (ECRM) systems are also often grouped together under internet marketing. Internet marketing ties together the creative and technical aspects of the Internet, including design, development, advertising, and sales. Internet marketing also refers to the placement of media along many different stages of the customer engagement cycle through search engine marketing (SEM), search engine optimization (SEO), banner ads on specific websites, email marketing, and Web 2.0 strategies.

In 2008, *The New York Times*, working with comScore, published an initial estimate to quantify the user data collected by large Internet-based companies. Counting four types of interactions with company websites in addition to the hits from advertisements served from advertising networks, the authors found that the potential for collecting data was up to 2,500 times per user per month.

This book contains the fundamental and basic information of subject and the selection of contents makes it an appropriate textbook for the students.

—Author

1

Internet Marketing Destinations in the Global Tourism

Introduction: Importance of Tourism and Online Travel

Tourism is not only the largest industry in the world but also the number one online segment, accounting for 11% of overall sales on the Net in 1998. E-business on tourism accounted for $13 billion in 1999. The online travel market is experiencing explosive growth, and is projected to go to $30 billion this year. It is already estimated that by year 2003 over 30% of online sales will be generated by online travel alone, including actual travel products as well as advertising earned by travel-oriented sites.

The number of travellers who use the Internet for travel-related and other purposes tops 70 million, half of which consult the Internet to get information on destinations or to check prices and schedules. The number of travellers booking online has soared by more than 80 percent to 11 million in the last year. Travel remains one of the most popular e-commerce categories, with 45 percent of online buyers saying they purchased travel online. This is outpaced only by books at 54 percent.

According to a recent survey by Biz Rate.com (1999), 85% of the respondents intend to use the Internet exclusively or in conjunction with off-line resources to schedule airfare (90% of those planning to purchase travel online), hotel (52%), and car rental (42%) reservations for holiday travel. More than 75 percent of respondents indicated that discounts would motivate them to purchase future travel reservations online. Thirty-nine percent said earning frequent flyer miles or points also would be a strong influence.

Cyveillance (1999) estimates that the overall universe of travel sites on the Web is 116,000. Based on analysis, it estimates that only approximately 6,500 travel sites (6%) are e-commerce enabled, i.e., offer the ability to execute transactions online. Internet start-up firms working as intermediaries and travel agencies will continue to fuel the online travel market. There is already fierce competition between intermediaries and hotels, airlines, and car rental companies.

Traditional offline companies, such as the Hotel Reservation Network (HRN), are shifting their telephone-based reservation system to the Internet to compete. HRN launched its Web site in 1995. In 1998 it booked 45 percent of its business online whereas in 1999 this figure reached 80 percent. Currently, travel agencies and intermediaries account for more than half the online travel revenue: 54% travel agencies, 25% airlines, 13% hotels, 8% car rental companies.

Tourism Destination Portals for Cyber Marketing

The literature suggests that the search for information used to plan travel is likely to take longer and to involve the use of more information sources than the search for information about most other consumer products.

The tourism industry is characterized by offering complementary business. This is similar to the computer industry, where a buyer often buys an assortment of goods made by different companies. For example, the manufacturers of the computer, printer, and software are often different. Similarly, a traveller will use air travel, a rental car, and a hotel room and purchase meals. Different companies provide these services. The goal of the traveller is to have an enjoyable experience. A properly designed Web site can facilitate the travellers' planning, helping to ensure they make the right choices and have an enjoyable experience. It can also serve as the distribution point for all the services they will need as they plan their vacation.

Tourism Destinations emerge as umbrella brands and they will need to be promoted in the global marketplace as one entity for each target market they try to attract. The emerging globalization and concentration of supply increase the level of competition and require new Internet marketing strategies for destinations. Hence, *destination marketing organizations* (DMOs) increasingly have to identify niche markets and develop their interactivity with tourists.

The distribution/allocation strategy of tourism products should follow a customer-oriented approach. A vertical marketing system should be in place bringing together a set of products related with each destination available for selection. This implies that each tourist destination must have a major portal Web site acting as a gateway to the destination rather than relying solely on a fragmented number of individual Web sites put online by the trade. Indeed, customers require one-stop shopping. The tourism destination portal site ought to be developed by the DMOs in partnership with the major market participants, through a contractual or corporate approach.

This would have links from and to the Web sites of the other organizations that have business related to the destination. Partnerships are important because by building relationships with other companies the DMOs get access to their consumers while helping those companies expand their product offerings. Moreover, the development of Web sites by main travel intermediary players is also important as these may allow the browser/visitor to access destination information provided by the DMOs' sites and to compare the services offered by competing destinations in order to make his/her travel decision.

A portal site for marketing tourism destinations should provide information on four core areas:

1. How to get there (e.g., air travel)
2. Getting around (e.g., car rental)
3. Places to stay (e.g., hotel accommodation)
4. Things to do.

All the items should come with availability and reservation facilities. These may be provided through links to other sites such as HRN, Internet Travel Network, or the World Res Company. The last is essentially a business-to-business site, in that it primarily serves other Internet companies. World Res provides a list of available rooms and prices at its 8,600 partner hotels to about 900 Web sites, including portals like Yahoo! and America Online, but predominantly travel sites. When a consumer visits one of those sites and makes a reservation, the transaction is reported back to World Res and, in turn, to the hotel that was booked. World Res takes a commission of between 3 and 10 percent of the cost of the booked room. The referring site gets up to 30 percent of the transaction fee paid by the hotel to World Res.

The investment bank Bear, Stearns Co. Inc. estimates hotel reservations made via the Internet will generate over $3 billion in revenues in 2002. In a recent market research study conducted by the NPD Group, 28 percent of visitors to hotel sites were found to actually book a reservation, and 84 percent of those were satisfied by the experience. Moreover, whereas it costs about 10 cents per dollar in revenue to book a reservation over the phone, a reservation booked online costs only 2 cents per dollar in revenue.

State of the Art in Web Design

The design of the Web site is one of the key issues to consider for achieving success in e-business. Successful sites are designed around the wants and needs of the targeted audiences. The Web presence must be designed not only to be visually appealing and user friendly, but also to be favourably indexed by search engines. According to a 1999 Jupiter Communications' research study, Internet users ranked "searching on the Internet" as their most important activity, rating it 9.1 on a 10 point scale. And most Internet users find information through the use of search engines and online directories.

Web sites have come a long way from the days of "brochure ware," those advertising-filled pages that flooded most organizations' first sites. Functionality has progressed to the point that the latest wave of Web technology even allows for personalization of content. Personalization technology now allows site designers to access demographic and psychographic information from the organization's own customer information files, other marketing data bases, and research derived from tracking the way visitors move around a site. Software automatically analyzes the profiles of site visitors, identifies what they are trying to do, and adjusts parts of the interface on the fly in an effort to enhance responsiveness.

But all this functionality comes at a price. As Web sites expand to accommodate additional features, customers may become confused by the plethora of choices and complex screen navigation trails. To avoid customer burnout and defection, managers need to strive for a balance between simplicity and functionality in their Web site designs to serve customers most effectively. The ideal state is referred to as "one and done." Customers visit the site, quickly find what they need, accomplish their tasks, and get out. Providers who cannot meet this standard risk losing business.

Since growth is an important part of the game, the technological underpinnings of the Web site must be set up to handle increasing transaction volume and transaction complexity. Experts advise building the site in a modular fashion so that the system can be expanded without having to change its primary architecture. The mentor for Web designers is "think big, start small, test quickly, and scale fast."

A site must be relatively simple and fast for the consumer to navigate. A site that limits the number of screens a person has to click through to complete and send a booking form is an important part of the equation. Thus, attractiveness, ease of use, and ability for consumers to quickly make a reservation are important Web design features. One of the contributing factors for ease of navigation is a limited number of elements per page.

Tourism organizations use their sites to post basic information — directions, prices, maps, and other brochure-type facts. But with sites evolving quickly, many need to institute truly innovative ideas: daily updates, real-time videos, snippets of music, e-mail feedback, and other interactive features. One major point of discussion is how sophisticated to make a Web site. Not every computer has the power, or the software, to take advantage of spiffy features. Some sites try to stay light on graphics to reduce download time. Others go heavy on graphics, thinking that is what makes the Internet fun and useful. The answer is to customize the Web site to the organization's target markets at the business-to-consumers (namely taking into account their level of sophistication) and business-to-business approaches.

Another important issue is that tourism organizations do not want to replace the experience by providing state-of-the-art Web sites on their destinations. Rather they want people to use their sites to maximize their visit.

There are a number of criteria a DMO must take into account when designing its Web site. The home page is the destination's "storefront" on the World Wide Web marketplace. It provides an index to the set of pages that describe the DMO and the tourism destination. The Web site should be organized in several main sections, including:

* *About the DMO* — this section may include a vision or a mission statement.
* *Tourism products/services* — using video-clips, audio, photos, and text to describe the benefits to the visitors of the destination's services. The Web is a great tool for market segmentation. Hence, the Home Page of the DMO's Web site should be utilized to immediately direct visitors to the most appropriate areas of information. An option of sending a CD-ROM through mail for less sophisticated users should be also considered. For example, a CD-ROM virtual tour of Las Vegas was created for the Las Vegas Convention & Visitors Authority (LVCVA) in conjunction with various corporate sponsors. The CD-ROM contains a vast multimedia directory featuring video clips produced by Vegas-area resorts and the LVCVA, stimulating high-resolution graphics, hot links to LVCVA member Web sites, valuable merchant discount coupons and extensive Las Vegas destination information.
* *FAQ* — providing a list of frequently asked questions.
* *Online ordering* — a site must provide, or at least have links to, booking and reservation facilities. In the former, situation shopping cart software has to be available so that

people can put multiple items in their cart from any number of product pages.

* *Interactive request form, guest book, or survey* — the DMO needs to connect with its visitors. This may be accomplished by enticing potential tourists to sign the destination's Guest Book and/or to fill out a survey — the DMO thus captures valuable consumer information for database development and later e-mail marketing actions. Getting users to sign up on an e-mailing list is a great way to stay in touch with current and potential clients.
* *What's new* — this section is where the DMO can put updates or new copies of a newsletter.
* *Giveaways* — a site may add further value to the visitor by giving away other free products and services like postcards, wallpaper, and screen savers.

The home page also needs graphics to look inviting. The best combination is a single sparkling *graphic* combined with text making the overall look of the DMO's "storefront" graphically balanced, pleasing, and informative. The *background texture and/or colour* used throughout the site should never overwhelm the text, but subtly complement it. The *page title* that is displayed at the top line of the Web browser is very important because it often shows up in search engines. The title should be descriptive using keywords that people might use to find the DMO page. A small graphic at the top of each page as well as texture and coloured backgrounds helps to unify the Web pages. Inadequate navigation design is probably the main failing of business Web sites. Getting visitors to information quickly and intuitively is the goal of navigation systems. The navigation should be designed from the customer's perspective, providing as many alternate and user-friendly ways to navigate the site as necessary, such as:

* *Menus* — the top-level menu should be kept to seven sections or less to avoid information overload. The use of left-side menus allow the destination's visitors to get deep into the Web site without clicking through a series of hierarchical linking pages, and displays the structure of the site more clearly. Another way to get the DMO's visitors

deep into the Web site quickly is to place a drop-down menu in the main page, with sections classified by indentations or spaces.

* *Image maps, buttons, and jump lines* – every page of the Web site must be reachable, either directly or indirectly, by a hyper text link from the main page.
* *Search engine* – installing a search engine in the Web site, offering information on attractions and entertainment, accommodation and transportation availability, so people can find what they are looking for quickly is another important design feature. Data bases are good for maintaining up-to-date information and allow a visitor to search both the static and the dynamic (Web pages built "on-the-fly") with a key word or date.
* *Hyperlinks* – the power of the Web is its ability to link to any other page in the world. Links from related pages as well as from industry index pages are very important. Thus, another key issue is to expand on the number of other Web sites that have hyperlinked with the DMO's site.

One can easily find numerous resources that teach the principles of good Web design. Sometimes, however, it is just as important to learn what not to do. Web designers should avoid making any of the following top 15 mistakes:

* *Using frames* – although users can now navigate through frames with fewer problems than in the past, frames still prevent users from e-mailing the URL (uniform resource locator) to other users and they also make the page more clumsy to interact with.
* *Gratuitous use of bleeding-edge technology* – instead of bragging about use of the latest Web technology, designers must realize that mainstream users care more about useful content and the company's ability to offer good customer service. Users who encounter as much as a single Java Script error usually leave a site immediately.
* *Scrolling text and looping animations* – it is extremely important for any content and navigation elements to

look very different from prevailing advertising designs since users tune out anything that they do not think will be relevant to their task. Currently, banner blindness (users never fixate their eyes on anything that looks like a banner ad due to the shape or position on the page) and animation avoidance (users ignore areas with blinking or flashing text or other aggressive animations) are two serious problems.

* *Complex URLs* – a URL should contain human-readable directory and file names that reflect the nature of the information space. Long URLs cause problems when users e-mail page recommendations to each other.
* *Orphan pages* – all pages should have a link up to the home page as well as some indication of where they fit within the structure of the information space.
* *Lack of navigation support* – users need support in the form of a strong sense of structure and place. Web designers should provide a site map to let users know where they are and where they can go, as well as a good search feature. Canonical navigation elements such as a site logo in the upper left corner (linked to the home page) or a clear indication of what part of the site the current page belongs to (linked to the main page for that section) are very useful.
* *Nonstandard link colors* – users rely on the link colors to understand what parts of the site they have visited. Links to pages that have not be seen by the user are blue, whereas links to previously seen pages are purple or red.
* *Outdated information* – with the growth in e-commerce, trust is getting increasingly important, and outdated content is a sure way to lose credibility.
* *Slow download times* – this is a very severe problem. Slow response times are the worst offender against Web usability. They often translate directly into a reduced level of trust and they always cause a loss of traffic as users take their business elsewhere at a distance of a click. Traditional human factor guidelines indicate 10 seconds as the

maximum response time before users lose interest. On the Web this limit may be increased to 15 seconds for a few pages.

* *Breaking or slowing down the Back button* – the Back button is the lifeline of the Web user and the second most used navigation feature, after following hyper text links.
* *Opening new browser windows* – this strategy is self-defeating since it disables the back button which is the normal way users return to previous sites.
* *Lack of biographies* – users want to know the people behind information on the Web. In particular, biographies and photographs of the authors help make the Web a less impersonal place and increase trust. For instance, it is particularly bad when a by-line is made into a "mailto:" link instead of a link to the author's biography.
* *Lack of archives* – old information is often good information and can be useful to readers. It is estimated that having archives may add about 10% to the cost of running a site but increase its usefulness by about 50%. Archives are also necessary to encourage other sites to link to the Web site.
* *Moving pages to new URLs* – anytime a page moves, any incoming links from other sites are broken.
* *Headlines that make no sense out of context* – headlines are actionable items that should help users navigate. They are often removed from the context of the full page and used in tables of content and in search engine results.

Design of Web Sites in the Tourism Industry: A Case Study

An in-depth fieldwork study has been conducted focusing on Web tourism marketing activities performed by public organizations, private companies, and dotcoms in Las Vegas. The findings are reported next.

Public Organizations

The Las Vegas Convention and Visitors Authority (LVCA) is the official destination marketing organization of Las Vegas. Went online on August 1997. The site includes information about conventions, lodging, and attractions in Las Vegas. Initially, the purpose was solely one of providing an online brochure containing over 500 pages of information. No e-mail facilities were embedded in the site. In order to respond to a number of requests, these were included at a later stage.

The Web site has been running separately / independently from the overall marketing strategy of LVCA. In other words, it is not integrated within the marketing strategy and communication plan. LVCA's goal in promoting Las Vegas as a tourist destination is to further develop its brand image as the entertainment capital of the world. Thus, this goes beyond gaming, by including other attributes such as dinning, shopping, shows, etc. With the redesign of the Web site currently under way there is also an intention to finally articulate it with advertising actions.

The LVCA collects e-mail addresses from its Web site visitors. It also conducts short online surveys from time to time on visitors' satisfaction with the Web site. It has built data bases for its three targeted segments: meeting planners, travel agents, leisure consumers. The Web site currently experiences over 7,000 daily users. LVCA hasn't developed any demographic profiles for its Web site users. Actually, this is a major concern which is to be put into practice along with the redesign of the site.

LVCA collaborates offline with organizations from other regions, promoting the Southwest United States as a triangle of complementary attractions: Las Vegas, Grand Canyon, and the Southwest Pacific Coast (San Diego, CA). It cooperates online with other organizations within the region through related links with major hotels, tourism agencies, and the Nevada Commission on Tourism. LVCA is also part of a community of 17 partners supporting a profit site operated by the Donrey Media Group which also owns the Las Vegas Review-Journal.

Las Vegas major competitive destinations may be grouped into three categories:

* Leisure — Orlando, San Francisco, Los Angeles, New Orleans
* Conventions — Chicago, Atlanta, Orlando, New York

* Gaming — Atlantic City, (and to some extent) Mississippi.

Three entities are involved in the design of the Web site: the LVCA, a Web vendor (which has been changed), and an advertising agency. Most of the data maintenance of the Web site is done in-house by the Web manager. The Web site is updated on a weekly basis, and the site is now being subjected to a major revision by the first time (once every two years). The most important features of a Web site for destination marketing are considered to be user-friendliness and usefulness, i.e., providing a good balance between graphics and functionality. The LVCA's revised Web site will strengthen these characteristics and will be more interactive. The LVCA's site has some unique features, such as:

* Keyword search and calendar search that are used by 75% of the visitors
* Hotel and motel search that is used by 60% of the visitors
* Weather page, which is also frequently used.

The Nevada Commission on Tourism (NCOT) is the state agency dedicated to promoting tourism in the Silver State. Its mission is to offer a composite view of the state, to emphasize the promotion of rural areas, underlining Northern Nevada. The official Web site of the NCOT. The purpose is to make available to the traveller an online visitor centre, providing more information and assisting him/her on planning a trip to Nevada. It aims to attract visitors to travel beyond Las Vegas or Reno, enticing them to extend their stay and go to other places.

The Web site has proven to help increase the number of inquiries about the state and to stimulate the growth in requests for the Visitors' Guide Booklet. Moreover, the site helped save some money on tele marketing, but not on print.

A research program for data collection is running which consists of sampling inquirers (telephone survey) in order to assess conversion ratios. Furthermore, the site has taken ongoing online surveys of its users. The NCOT collaborates offline with other organizations in the region as a member of the Western States Policy Tourism Council that gathers 11 western states of the United States.

The major competitive destinations for Nevada are:

* For the pleasure/leisure market — California (Anaheim-Disneyland), Florida (Orlando-Walt Disney World), Hawaii.
* For the gaming market — New Jersey (Atlantic City), Mississippi, other emerging states, including those expanding Indian gaming.
* For the conventions market — New York, Illinois (Chicago), Georgia (Atlanta), Florida (Orlando, Miami).

Both NCOT and an advertising agency have been involved in the design of the Web site. Its maintenance, updating, enhancement, and redesign is conducted through the ad agency. The site is redesigned once a year. This takes place when a new annual Nevada Visitors Guide / Booklet is published. Moreover, the site's Calendar of Events, which coincides with the publication of the Nevada Magazine, is updated every two months. In addition, there is a new overall theme every month which is also addressed by the Lieu Tenant Counselor.

The most important feature of a Web site for destination marketing is to have content-rich, updated, and very complete information. NCOT's site provides information on Nevada broken into six territories. It has a comprehensive hotel/motel listing as well as a calendar of events in the state.

Private Companies

The main purpose of conducting Internet/online activity is to provide information on the different properties/resorts, their services, and prices in order to entice users to make reservations and come to the resorts. The major players in Las Vegas are the Mirage Resorts Group (Bellagio, Mirage, Treasure Island, Golden Nugget), Mandalay Bay Group (Mandalay Bay, Luxor, Excalibur), Park Place (Paris Las Vegas, Flamingo Hilton, Las Vegas Hilton, Circus Circus), MGM (MGM Grand, New York New York), Boyd Gaming Corporation (Stardust, Sam's Town, Fremont), and Harrah's. Whereas the Las Vegas Convention and Visitors Authority's promotion gives more weight to conventions, the main resort groups emphasize the gaming/casino activity more.

It is generally agreed that the LVCVA should be the centerpiece of a Web site portal for Las Vegas as a tourist destination. However, in reality two other sites have been in that position – vegas.com and lasvegas.com. The former is part of a large regional media group that includes the Las Vegas Sun newspaper, Showbiz weekly, Las Vegas Life, Las Vegas weekly, and Las Vegas Golfer. The latter is operated by the Donrey Media Group that also owns a major Las Vegas newspaper, the *Las Vegas Review Journal*. This site is run with the support of 17 partners, primarily government agencies, including the LVCVA. Interestingly, vegas.com is given preference and considered more popular than lasvegas.com as a portal site to Las Vegas. The design of the Web sites is usually outsourced. A number of senior executives are also involved. The maintenance and information updating is mostly done in-house.

The most important features of a Web site are considered as:

* Being visually/graphically attractive
* Providing correct and up-to-date information
* Being interactive
* Enabling chat lines and stimulate consumer comments
* Providing availability and booking online
* Developing the right promotion online to entice the transient guest by providing attractive offers and interactive tools (e.g., weather information, driving directions, what to do) and using banners for brand image-building
* Offering a toll-free number
* Capturing data for conducting direct e-mail campaigns. Retail data bases are built with names and addresses of customers and prospects who visit the sites and inquire about further information.

Dotcoms

They usually receive over 300,000 visitors with more than 4 million page views a month. However, they are facing increasing competition from other sites such as (a Cox Communications interactive media city guide), and Microsoft's Side Walk. Actually, according to a recent research from Media Metrix (1999), a leader in Internet audience and digital media measurement, MSN Side walk has surpassed all competing online city guides in terms of consumer reach, achieving a reach of 7.3 percent, compared with other local guides like Digital Cities, with a reach of 6.3, and City Search, with a reach of 5.5 percent.

The dotcom sites are normally designed and maintained in-house. Major information updating takes place once a week (e.g., entertainment) whereas a lot of news is updated on a daily basis.

The most important features of a Web site for destination marketing are seen as providing quality content/information current and complete on the destination (e.g., resorts, restaurants, show listings, dining weather), ease of navigation/usability, and booking facilities. It is expected that in the near future the latter will be extended to also accommodate e-commerce on shows, restaurants, and sightseeing tours. Frequently asked questions and bulletin boards are also considered important characteristics.

Search Engine Positioning

Due to the clutter of sites available on the World Wide Web, DMOs ought to position themselves as the portals of their destinations. A sample search on the Yahoo! Directory as well as on the other major search engines by typing the name "Las Vegas" as a key word resulted in the following numbers. The Yahoo! Directory found 969 Web sites on Las Vegas. The Northern Light search engine found 1,313,971 pages on Las Vegas. In terms of search engine positioning, lasvegas.com is by far the best positioned. It consistently appears on the top 20 Web sites on Las Vegas: Alta Vista, Excite, HotBot/Lycos, Infoseek, Web Crawler, and Northern Light. Vegas.com comes ahead of lasvegas.com on Hotbot/Lycos and Northern Light but it does not show up on Excite, Web Crawler, and Alta Vista. The official Web site of the LVCVA, is visible only in Alta Vista and Infoseek.

Hyperlinks

Using the Alta Vista search engine the actual number of Web sites hyperlinked with each of the main dotcoms were found as follows: (8,570); . (1,938);. (1,212); and (1,017). Curiously, some hotel resorts have even more links such as the MGM Grand (1,235). Other national dotcom companies have most of the highest number of links: City Search (8,232), Virtual Cities (4,899), Cimedia (2,438), and MSN Side walk (2,319).

Table 1. Do's & Don'ts of Web Design for Destination Marketing Organizations

Do's	*Don'ts*
* Content/Information	* Content/Information
* About the DMO	* Outdated information
* Tourism Products and Services	* Lack of biographies
* Frequently Asked Questions	* Lack of archives
* Online Ordering	* Headlines that make no sense out of context
* Interactive Request Form, Guest Book, or Survey	* Complex URLs
* What's New	* *Navigation*
* Giveaways	* Using frames
* *Navigation*	* Gratuitous use of bleeding-edge technology
* Menus	* Scrolling text and looping animations
* Image Maps, Buttons, and Jump Lines	* Orphan pages
* Search Engine	* Lack of navigation support
* Hyperlinks	* Nonstandard link colors
	* Slow download times
	* Breaking or slowing down the Back button
	* Opening new browser windows
	* Moving pages to new URLs

Tourism is one area that can greatly benefit from a city's online presence as out-of-state and foreign residents visit a Web site and decide they want to travel there. Web sites of DMOs will continue to evolve into more marketing tools than just archives or information services. Their success relies heavily on the organization's ability to design effective Web sites, i.e., implementing the do's and avoiding the don'ts of Web design and Web usability. This paper addresses all these issues within the context of portal sites for marketing tourism destinations in the global market space.

Lessons from www Tourism Initiatives in South Africa

In Soweto, Johannesburg, in early December 1999, the South African Minister of Environmental Affairs and Tourism launched the "South Africa Welcome Campaign" as part of the process of educating South Africans about the importance of tourism in the country's economic development. According to Minister Mohammed Vali Moosa:

"Tourism follows manufacturing and mining in its contribution to our country's GDP [gross domestic product] and could quickly overtake mining if we continue to grow tourism both domestically and internationally. It is also the sector identified by the World Economic Forum as capable of rapid job creation." The purpose of the "South Africa Welcome Campaign" is to raise public awareness about the importance of building a culture that welcomes tourists to the country. According to the Minister, World Economic Forum statistics reveal that for every eight tourists that visit South Africa, one permanent job is created. Some of the important statistics which are provided include the following:

* Tourism is the world's largest earner of foreign currency;
* South Africa only attracts 0.2% of the annual estimated 300 million tourists in the world;
* South Africa was ranked 25th in the world's top tourism destinations in 1998 – up 10% on 1997 but was only ranked 42nd when it comes to top tourism earners in the world;
* Tourism brings an estimated 20 billion Rand (R) (US $3.1 billion) into our economy, second only to manufacturing and mining in its contribution to the gross domestic product (GDP); or in other words, it contributed 8.2% to South Africa's GDP in 1998;

* 75% of all South Africa's foreign arrivals are from Africa;
* In 1998 South Africa saw a 24.6% rise in American visitors to the country;
* Foreign tourists stayed 16.9 days on average in our country in 1998 and spent R842 (US $152) per day.

The catalytic role of tourism in South Africa cannot be underestimated. In a country where a significant proportion of the population is unemployed and underemployed, the need for economic transformation is urgent. It seems — at a superficial level — that tourism is the panacea for the country's economic woes. However, South Africa is a very complex country and the role of tourism is slightly more complicated than it seems from the Minister's speeches or World Economic Forum fact sheets. It is also widely recognized that South Africa has not harnessed her full tourism potential and several reasons are offered for this.

The typical one is that crime in South Africa is stifling the tourism industry's growth. Rising violent crime levels may deter many tourists, particularly North American, Asian and European tourists, from visiting the country but there are other less obvious factors that impact equally on the fact that South Africa is not optimizing its real tourist potential.

A less profiled reason is that of xenophobia which has only recently received some attention from the South Africa media and national government. Xenophobia is typically understood to refer to a pathological fear of strangers and strange places.

In South Africa, xenophobia assumes a more complex cultural and economic form in South Africa. Earlier in 1999, several African men working in South Africa and travelling on public transport were thrown from the train by an angry mob of supporters of the group known as the Unemployed People of South Africa. It was alleged that the *makwerakwera* (an impolite term for foreigners speaking African languages that sound like chirping crickets) 'stole' employment opportunities from South Africans. South Africa's economic hardships combined with the impact of years of isolation from the rest of the continent leads to a messy mix of distrust and disregard for other people from the African continent.

A third reason, and one with which we are particularly concerned, is that the proliferation of Web-based tourism initiatives in South Africa does not challenge the fundamental economic disparities between the vast majority of impoverished South African communities, the tourists who visit the country, and the tourism service providers.

The central purpose of our paper, therefore, is to look at some key issues of which we have been made aware through initiatives on which we have worked over the last 18 months, and to share these lessons with other developing countries, especially regarding use of tourism Web initiatives, particularly as it relates to commercial and to cultural tourism..

Commercial Tourism: Lessons from the Magic Tour Net Project

The Magic Tour Net project, the first case study to which we refer, is a commercial tourism enablement initiative on the Web and from which we have learned some critically important lessons. The focus of our reflections on this case study is an examination of commercial tourism and the related business implications when applied to the Internet.

The Magic Tour Net project was a European Commission (EC)-funded initiative aimed at addressing some of the concerns through the development of appropriate tools to enable the development and hosting of sophisticated tourism Web sites, supporting development of a tourism portal and addressing the availability of data for tourism Web sites. The development of the technical components was validated through the development of a pilot application focusing on the Western Cape province in South Africa. Details of the technical aspects of the project have been described in another conference paper — *Magic Tour Net: A Web based Multimedia and GIS Authoring System for the Development of Tourism-Oriented Web sites* by Laurens Cloete, Hina Patel, Maria Rita Nazzaralli of CSIR and Intecs Sistemi — and are not repeated here. The project also included a task focusing on the commercial exploitation of the project results, which incorporated a study into possible business models.

A key assumption of the Magic Tour Net project was that the Internet has the potential to overturn conventional business models and, by implication, to redefine the roles of different tourism actors such as travel agents, Tour Operators, and national and regional tourism authorities. As we progressed on this initiative, we had first-hand experience of the reality that new business models require new skills and tools. Theoretically, the Internet should allow tourism service providers such as hotels or restaurants or museums to offer their services directly to consumers.

There were, however, a number of considerations that prevented this from happening to the extent that we initially believed was possible.

The first of these was that the ability to design professional Web sites capable of competing with other distractions on the Web and ensuring Web sites were updated and maintained was (and still is) constituted by skills and resources not available to the majority of South Africans and to tourism service providers. The movement towards designing intuitive and user-friendly tourism applications was one step towards supporting a more dynamic and empowered tourism service sector in South Africa.

The second consideration was the need to stimulate and compel the virtual tourist. It is the case that potential tourists would like to get a sense of the place and the people they are intending to visit. Many tourists tend to use conventional media such as printed travel literature books containing visual images and maps of the places they would like to visit. Integrating images and static maps into Web site content is relatively easy but it offers little value over conventional media, and the Web site content remains essentially static. Overcoming this inertia of visual and other content was therefore an important consideration. During the course of the project, a survey was undertaken and the results confirmed a lack of dynamic, multimedia data that could be used to build tourism applications. We extrapolated further that finding accommodation or other tourism information presents a significant hurdle to the acceptance of the Web as the way to access tourism information.

The solution was able to address these two considerations in the following way. The solution consisted of building a tourism

Web site development and use system that would allow novice developers (i.e., the tourism service providers) to develop and publish professional Web sites with sophisticated functionalities that are not available on non-expert applications, and which, in turn, could be accessed effectively and efficiently by tourism users. From the tourist's perspective, it was possible to obtain — from a unique address — a large range of tourist information and to select a series of services to build his/her own tailored package. The added value to the tourist included the following:

* Information was available about an increased number of tourism actors in the tourism supply chain (e.g., service providers, travel agents and tour operators) in the host country thus enhancing the tourist's ability to choose; and
* Reservation and booking functionality was available at a potentially reduced cost to all players in the tourism supply chain.

These benefits are, however, obvious. A less obvious and more radical benefit is that the existence of comprehensive tourism Web sites highlights the changing roles of traditional media in the tourism supply chain. It is often assumed that the Internet is a threat to tourism but in fact, we argue, the Internet highlights the artificial distinction between the roles of Travel Agents and publishers. By combining the very valuable information that publishers own with reservation capabilities of Travel Agents and Tour Operators, a value-added service can be provided to tourists at a reduced cost.

Another benefit is related to foreign exchange. Although tourism is an important foreign exchange earner, a significant percentage of the money spent on tourism remains in the tourist's original country. For example, flight bookings are typically made in the tourist's home country and not in the host country. Through use of the Internet, service providers in countries that depend on tourism can offer their service in the tourists' countries and address this problem by offering some of the service over the Internet in the destination country. That assumes a more equitable distribution of the financial benefits across the home and host countries. And for South Africa, it is imperative that this happen.

The Magic Tour Net system was developed in recognition of some of the changes that are taking place in the tourism value chain. It addressed, in part, a third important consideration, namely the impact of the Internet on the whole tourism value chain as it applies to more than just the tourists and the tourism service providers. The Magic Tour Net system does have a potential to address the problem of maintaining up-to-date data about the service or the host country. Through the tools provided by the system, it is possible for data to be maintained by people that have the greatest interest in having their data up-to-date. For example, restaurants may be able to own a part of a larger Web site dedicated to a city or region. A common and professional look of the Web site can be built into the system through the design of templates and style sheets, but data can be maintained by many different entities in whose interest it is to keep their data updated.

What it did not address directly was the impact of the Internet — and related tourism supply chain transformations — on the people of the host country who engage in informal and opportunistic economic activities within the broader tourism supply chain. In a developing country, informal and opportunistic economic activity (e.g., informal traders of crafts or 'car guards') are real and necessary survival strategies for the vast majority of unemployed and underemployed South Africans. The mentor of the Internet Society (ISOC) — the Internet is for Everyone — takes on a more subtle significance than just having all South Africans seated in front of personal computers with modems. Instead, virtual tourism content should be developed in recognition of the fact that the broader tourism supply chain can be transformed and that the benefits of an enhanced tourism supply chain should allow for accrued benefit to the widest range of South Africans, formally and informally employed.

Cultural Tourism: Lessons from the Culture ware Project

The second case study to which we refer in this paper is the culture ware project and our specific focus is on the lessons we have learned about cultural tourism initiatives as applied to the Internet's tourism supply chain. This project is a multi-million rand state-funded project on which we are working within a consortium made up of a historically disadvantaged university, a state tourism marketing body, and a Section 21 Western Cape tourism company. The project has several aims but one of the most important is to develop proof of sustainability of digital multicultural consumption in tourism, education and public awareness. The project is currently in its second year.

One of the research activities undertaken within the framework of the culture ware project was the creation of a virtual tourism experience. The chosen environment was a 'non-traditional' tourism and cultural site, namely an informal settlement on the eastern seaboard of South Africa. The virtual environment consisted of, among others, a virtual *shebeen* or a beerhall in which users could interact with a shebeen queen avatar, an interactive radio digital object which allowed users to select music of musicians such as Hugh Masekela and Miriam Makheba, an interactive newspaper digital object which played video clips of shack destruction in the 1950s, and so on. The virtual environment was developed using appropriate virtual reality (VR) and multimedia software, and translated into VRML (Virtual Reality Modelling Language) for distribution on the culture ware project's Web site.

The specific residential site was chosen as a potential tourism experience because it currently is a high-profile presidential project and has several cultural and economic programs under way to reclaim the township's potential and its past. And tourism is regarded as an important enabler of its reconstruction and development. The experience designed consisted of a nostalgic / retrospective experience into the township's vibrant community life of the 1950s. This residential site is part of a larger group of cultural spaces — including Sophia town and District Six — which receive local attention because of South Africa's process of reclamation and political and cultural restitution. A story board was conceptualized in which a narrator (in this case, a nine-year-old boy called Mandla) 'talked' the viewer through the experience to enhance the realism of nostalgia for a potentially 'alien' cultural and historical experience (alien, that is, to the viewer). A list of curatorially and historically authentic artifacts were presented, and the structures and landscape in the environment were closely examined and redesigned to depict textural and historical integrity (e.g., the shack home polygons were re-angled away from 90-degree verticals to 80-degree verticals while roof polygons were manipulated to appear 'mangled').

The development of this virtual tourism experience created several important challenges. Some of these challenges were obviously of a technical nature and included translation of a virtual reality model into suitable format for consumption via the Web. We do not wish to address these here but instead focus on two other challenges – namely, designing culturally sensitive interfaces and Intellectual Property Protection (IPP).

Interfaces are often regarded as technical elements only but there has been a significant rise in awareness of the context and content-specific requirements that impact directly on the conceptualization and design of interfaces, whether they be for the Web or other means of distribution.

We begin our discussion of this issue by referring to an important argument by Barbara Kirshenblatt-Gimblet in *Destination Tourism: Tourism, Museums and Heritage* that had direct relevance to the content and context design issues in our project. Kirshenblatt-Gimblet argues that the current mechanisms we use to display culture and art demand that we ask questions about the meaning behind 'displaying' these items. Her argument is that there is a technology that has developed which guides how we use objects and artifacts to 'display' their meaning to us and to others. The meaning behind design in cultural tourism Web sites is, we argue, of critical importance in a developing economy and there are several reasons for this, which we will examine in turn.

The first is that cultural tourism experiences enabled through Internet technologies and Web-based initiatives are part of a much broader process of commodification of knowledge in society. Jean Francois Lyotard in *The Post Modern Condition: A Report on Knowledge* emphasized this point several years ago when he argued that in an era of rapid growth of computerized information technology, technology is both a product and hastener of change. In the Information Age, knowledge is 'legitimate' because of two things: the effects of that knowledge and the efficiency of the effects of that knowledge. Leotard calls this 'performativity.' Knowledge has become a commodity and can be controlled and sold with the intention of achieving more for the purposes of securing a market edge. Our concern, here, is that in efforts to promote cultural tourism in South Africa, the Internet is obviously increasingly used to attract foreign tourists to South Africa's shores but these efforts often occur outside — or ignorant of — questions about the unintended consequences of this form of commodification of cultural tourism content.

There is, and will continue to be, an inherent triviality to Web content of cultures and people. A Web-mediated or virtual-life experience of a culture is not intended to replace the real-life experience of that culture and place — including the annoyance of long queues or lost passports! However, as Sherry Turkle has argued in *Life on the Screen*, 'we construct our technologies, and our technologies construct us and our times.' According to Turkle, the Internet provides us with opportunities for cultural appropriation through manipulation of specific objects and hence, people's knowledge of cultures develops through those things with which they have become actively involved. Turkle argues that in today's era while we know that computers are not sentient yet, the way in which we interact with them — and through them — blurs the boundaries between things and people. In the age of computer-mediated communication, Turkle asks what impact will this have on our commitment to other people? The Internet, she argues, is a social laboratory for experimentation with self, identity and post modern life. The Internet is an 'easy fix' to providing a substitute to face-to-face interaction. It is part of a move toward virtuality which tends to skew our experience of the real in several ways:

* it makes denatured and artificial experiences seem real (obviously, we build our idea of what is real and what is natural with the cultural materials available);
* it lends itself to what Turkle refers to as the 'artificial crocodile effect,' an effect that makes the fake more compelling than the real; and
* the extent of how compelling it is makes us believe that we have achieved more than we really have.

Cultural tourism experiences consumed via the Internet – unless intentionally designed to do otherwise – run the risk of presenting context and content about a host country, at best, in inherently trivial ways and at worst, in paternalistic ways. Data and information used in a cultural tourism Web site or application are often presented as sufficient unto themselves rather than – as should be the case in South Africa's tourism imperative – as sufficient information to help the virtual tourist transform into a *real tourist.*

Cultural tourism content can also be presented or displayed in such a way that the subject (e.g., an indigenous rural Nguni culture) becomes the object of someone else's gaze. The relationship between tourist and host is a complex one and it should not be the case that cultural tourism Web sites are designed only for the benefit of the tourist or for the service provider. Benefits should accrue, too, to the host, in the broadest sense of that term. And that issue raises directly questions about whether or not the conceptualization of the Web site was sufficiently participative of the people on whom the gaze of the virtual and real tourist will fall.

In participative conceptualization and consultation processes with communities, the assumption is that members of that community have an active role in accruing benefit and adding value to the entire supply chain and the relationship with the tourist. In that sense it is possible to argue that cultural tourism Web content will reflect the economic models on which they are based. And if it is the case that tourism is central to the human and economic growth of a developing country, then progressive tourism management approaches are critical considerations in the conceptualization and design of tourism interfaces. The Internet does not, in and of itself, result in these progressive tourism management and transformative economic approaches – instead it reveals the need for them more clearly.

The second lesson learned relates to Intellectual Property. In cultural tourism Web sites, obviously, the cultural artifacts which are on display should be culturally authentic. No cultural tourism initiative – virtual or otherwise – can be sustainable if it is premised on inauthentic content and context. And obviously in Web-based cultural tourism experiences, authenticity is particularly important as a way of making information about a people or a culture sufficiently compelling to get the virtual tourist transformed into a real tourist. However, culturally authentic artifacts — particularly in postcolonial countries — are particularly at risk of exploitation because the resources required to preserve those cultural heritage artifacts are often channelled into more immediate concerns such as housing, health care and (unfortunately) often weapons of war.

IPP should be of higher import to African countries because of the legacies of cultural artifact, natural resource and human plundering that constitute the colonial legacies of those countries. Unfortunately, it does not always and consistently receive the same attention. South Africa, however, has recently developed legislation on cultural heritage resource management and is addressing issues of IPP as it relates to digital facsimiles of those artifacts.

Securing the intellectual property rights of a particular cultural artifact obviously embraces a technical component — and these issues are addressed in another conference paper by culture ware project researchers, Johan Eksteen and Dr Louis Coetzee — but also legal and curatorial components.

In South Africa, the design imperative to make cultural tourism Web sites compelling and attractive to the virtual tourist has been brought into direct conflict with the IPP imperative and specifically the legal and curatorial aspects of digital reproductions of culturally authentic artifacts. As the virtual cultural tourist's need for heightened and unique stimulation increases, the need for content and context authenticity is enhanced. But this, however, assumes that someone, somewhere, has taken care of the IPP of a digital artifact. South Africa is unique in its dilemma. What we mean is that it has a vast array of multicultural communities and artifacts which when combined with the legacy of cultural hegemony and sophisticated institutionalization and organization of English- and Africans-speaking cultural groups implies that the majority of our cultural artifacts are at risk from a new form of technological colonialism. The Internet ushers in real risks of having the IPP of a digital reproduction of an indigenous South African cultural artifact being held by a non-South African agent. And in that relationship, a South African agent would be expected to, for example, pay for the right to use a digital reproduction of a particular photograph of an indigenous bead work design, on a South African cultural tourism Web site. Obviously, that is not to the economic or cultural benefit of an emerging South African cultural tourism industry.

State intervention may seem anathema to many developed countries which actively support little or no state intervention in the free market global economy but in South Africa, state intervention in matters of this nature is critical. Progressive cultural heritage management legislation as well as provision of support to cultural groups to ensure IP on their own cultural artifacts, whether those artifacts be tactile, oral or foodway artifacts, becomes one of the most important preventative mechanisms against a new era of (technologically enabled) colonialism.

In our paper, we have presented some key lessons that we have learned from two quite different Web-based tourism initiatives in which we have engaged.

The first case study, the Magic Tour Net project, examined the impact of the Internet on more equitable distribution and facilitation of the skills and resources required to develop and publish suitable commercial tourism Web sites. And it also attempted to highlight the importance of developing commercial tourism Web site applications that are cognizant of the obvious and hidden changes that the Internet has upon the tourism supply chain. We believe that we are only now beginning to understand some of these impacts and are progressing slowly towards being able to ensure that our tourism Web initiatives are able to ensure that tourism enhances the economic and human development imperatives in South Africa. In our second case study, the cultureware project, we have learned some critically important lessons about the impact of the Internet on cultural tourism as a phenomenon and enabler of human and economic development. We highlighted only two issues among the many we encountered. The first was about the consequences of commodification of tourism information in the content and context of these Web sites. And related to that was the second lesson about IPP of postcolonial countries' cultural artifacts in a potentially increasing technologically enabled neo-colonialism.

Our specific country's dynamics and realities require solutions and approaches that may not be appropriate to all countries engaged in Internet-based tourism but we do believe that what we have uncovered will be of increasing importance to other developing countries' increased access to and use of the Internet in their economic activities. We hope not only that the lessons we have learned will enhance the activities in which we engage but also that the application of these lessons will ensure that other members of the developing world engage in Web-based activities in a more empowered way, such that Web-enabled communication and commerce benefits them and their people.

Challenges and Opportunities Facing Canada's Tourism Industry

The world has changed dramatically over the past 10 years, but some of the issues that faced the tourism industry in the early 1990's are still here today. The environment in which the industry operates requires tourism stakeholders to fundamentally shift their strategic approach not only to resolve long-standing issues but more importantly to effectively address current challenges and capitalize on new opportunities.

Changing demographics, shifting travel patterns and volatile economic conditions are increasing the pressure on industry stakeholders to develop effective campaigns and business strategies. More recently, health and safety issues such as pandemics and global security concerns as manifested by WHTI have increased the urgency for industry action.

The challenges facing the tourism industry are complex and numerous. Addressing these challenges will require a high level of coordination and cooperation to marshal resources more effectively. Fiscal pressures and competing priorities among all F/P/T partners and tourism stakeholders will require new and innovative partnership arrangements to respond to growing competition and global opportunities.

Opportunities exist for governments and the private sector to seize the extraordinary opportunity afforded by "mega events" occurring in Canada and abroad. For example, Canada can learn from Australia's experience with the Sydney Games in 2000 as it prepares to host the 2010 Olympics in Vancouver. The Sydney Games demonstrated that strong public/private partnerships and cooperation result in widespread incremental benefits. The challenge confronting governments and tourism stakeholders will be to establish the necessary linkages to ensure the development of collaborative strategies in conjunction with major international or domestic events so that lasting benefits will be created across the country.

The analysis of domestic and international arrivals and spending patterns indicates that if Canada is to continue to be a pre-eminent destination for leisure and business travel, investments will have to be made to enhance and tailor tourism products and services according to the needs of a highly competitive marketplace. Further analysis of niche markets and specific strategies to position the industry within those niches will have to be undertaken by both public and private sector tourism stakeholders. It is in this context that Building a National Tourism Strategy will be developed and refined.

The consultations with industry stakeholders confirmed many challenges that were identified in the November 2003 Consultation Framework and the key challenges listed below represent priority areas for collaboration. However, since then, changing circumstances may have altered stakeholder priorities. At the time of the consultations, the U.S. had yet to announce the WHTI. Following the announcement in April 2005, it became increasingly clear that this measure could be highly detrimental to the Canadian tourism industry.

WHTI is a national, industry-wide concern affecting every region and most sectors of the tourism industry. As such, it is an issue that could be effectively addressed in the context of a National Tourism Strategy.

Provincial/territorial governments will continue addressing particular issues and challenges in their jurisdictions but increased collaboration is required so that their strategies and action plans can help strengthen the tourism industry by enhancing its international competitiveness. Whether competing with new and emerging destinations or responding to world "shocks," addressing the challenges facing the industry in a collaborative manner will be key to growing tourism in Canada.

Key challenges raised during industry consultations include:

1. Comprehensive research to better understand the expectations of travellers;
2. More cohesive marketing and promotional campaigns while reflecting provincial/territorial realities and diversity in Canada;
3. Further development of Aboriginal tourism;
4. Human resource strategies to attract and retain employees in the industry;
5. Investments in tourism infrastructure;
6. Efficient and integrated transportation systems; and.
7. Broadening and adopting sustainable tourism and best practices.

Understanding the Expectations of Travellers

Research has shown that as demographics shift so do travel patterns and demand for products and services. The advancement of technology has also had a significant impact on the tourism industry. Continuing to upgrade and modernize visitor information services will be important in providing visitors with quality, user-friendly and consistent year-round information. Being able to understand and adapt to these changes will be increasingly important.

An Aging Population

What was once a relatively homogeneous market for international tourism products is now fragmented into a number of highly specialized niches. As the baby-boom generation advances through middle age, industry stakeholders recognize that customer needs and expectations are changing. There will be rapid growth in the seniors market segment as the baby-boom generation begins to reach 65 years of age in 2011. It is estimated that seniors will represent 25 percent of Canada's overall population by 2026, compared to the current 12 percent. Similar aging trends are forecasted in most developed countries. Trips by foreign residents in the older segments of the population have been increasing more rapidly than trips taken by other age groups. This slow but steady shift is forcing the industry to adapt its services and products in order to appeal to a growing, mature clientele.

The Government of Ontario's report "Impacts of Aging the Canadian Market on Tourism in Ontario," states that "if the new generation of [mature] Ontario residents displays similar tourism activity preferences to their 2000 counterparts, the impact of an aging population will result in a shift away from outdoor activity such as canoeing and fishing, towards non-strenuous warm weather activities and indoor cultural events and attractions." This reinforces the importance of conducting research on travel patterns to be able to tailor tourism products, and be more responsive to present and future preferences.

Changing Travel Patterns

According to a survey conducted by the Western Australia Tourism Commission, an emerging market referred to as the "children of the information age" is developing. This segment is characterized by increasingly sophisticated travellers who are experienced, well-educated and discriminating consumers who are more aware of what the competition has to offer.

They are becoming less destination-oriented and more experience-oriented. This transformation into an "experience market" is based on personalized services and customized holidays that allow visitors to play a more active role in their travelling experiences and search continually for new tourism products, such as the increasing variety of spa vacations. The CTC has identified a similar trend in Canada and research in this area will help better position the country.

Visitor Information Services: Increasing use of Technology

Increasingly, the knowledge economy is having a significant impact on the tourism sector and the travel industry is one of the most connected in Canada.

According to the 2004 Conference Board Consumer Internet Barometer, two-thirds of consumers are now using the Internet to make travel arrangements and the level of satisfaction reported among users is very high.

In 2003, 26 percent of Canadian businesses made travel-related purchases online, up 18 percent from 2002. Combined private and public sector online travel sales reached $19.1 billion in 2003, an increase of almost 40 percent on top of a 27 percent jump the previous year. The Economist referred to online travel as being one of the most successful forms of e-commerce. Americans presently buy 20 percent of their total travel online, but many in the industry believe this proportion could reach 50-60 percent within a decade.

The International Federation for Information Technology and Travel and Tourism reported in January 2005 that convergence of the Internet, wireless applications and inter-active objects are increasing the importance of smart business networks. Additionally, pervasive computing applications will provide new services and greater convenience for customers. The last decade has seen Internet business solutions transform consumer behaviour and business practices resulting in a rapid growth of new business models such as the low-cost airlines and their online reservations systems and 'smart businesses'. Smart businesses are flexible, dynamic, collaborative, and able to move swiftly to leverage market opportunities.

Internet business solutions are not only affecting business models, they are also driving market changes. In 2004, online bookings in Europe increased by more than 50 percent and 10 percent of total revenues in travel and tourism came from online business.

Three consumer trends are e-business driven: readiness to spend more on trips, more frequent vacations but shorter stays, and an increasing importance of the mature segment of the market. Internet business solutions are increasingly used to improve visitor information services but their application to reduce costs and increase operating effectiveness and efficiency can have a substantial impact on business viability.

The F/P/T partners will need to collaborate in working with their tourism industry to ensure that they fully capitalize on the advantages provided by IBS.

Cohesive Marketing Campaigns that Reflect Provincial/ Territorial Realities

Canada's cultural, geographical and language landscape makes the country a highly appealing tourist destination. Diversity is one of Canada's major differentiating characteristics and capitalizing on it must become a tourism planning priority. The tourism industry's maturity or level of development varies among provinces and territories. Some areas of Canada are still emerging destinations, while others are better established with thriving tourism businesses.

Southern Canada is characterized by major cities, events and gateways, relative ease of access and a wide variety of well-established and emerging products. Maximizing the potential of festivals and events (i.e.., sport, culture, and heritage events) will require new horizontal approaches for the tourism sector. Northern Canada is characterized by emerging destinations based on nature tourism, niche products, Aboriginal attractions and wilderness. Access to these areas and their sustainable capacity are an on-going challenge facing tourism development. Research requirements and product development and marketing opportunities vary across provinces and territories and among rural and urban areas. The CTC leads Canada's national marketing campaigns in collaboration with those of the provinces/territories.

However, there is a need to keep developing collaborative approaches to increase the cohesion, effectiveness and efficiency of national initiatives, while at the same time, recognizing the different priorities and needs of all provinces and territories. Strengthening the collaboration of tourism marketing between the provinces/territories and the CTC will not only serve to better coordinate existing initiatives but it will improve their complementarity, potentially leading to innovative partnerships.

The F/P/T partners need to collaborate on research initiatives to identify growth opportunities for all provinces and territories of Canada. Improving overall coordination of research, product development and marketing strategies will better enable F/P/T partners to capitalize on new and emerging opportunities both domestically and internationally.

Developing Aboriginal Tourism

Aboriginal tourism is one of Canada's unique strengths, in both the domestic and international markets. However, the growth of this segment of the tourism industry faces significant challenges. Tourism represents about one quarter of the Aboriginal economy in Quebec, the North and the West.

According to the 2003 National Study on Aboriginal Tourism in Canada, demand for Aboriginal tourism is outpacing capacity. There are relatively few market-ready products in the Aboriginal tourism sector, particularly near gateway cities and major tourism routes.

Many businesses do not have sufficient tourism market awareness, business skills, product development and marketing expertise to successfully compete. The Virtual Tour of Aboriginal Canada, a web portal, was developed in response to the perceived need to generate a higher level of public awareness regarding Canada's Aboriginal tourism industry.

There is great potential to increase Aboriginal tourism activities and at the same time contribute to the wealth creation, economic development and self-reliance of Aboriginal people and communities in all provinces/territories in Canada. The Quebec Declaration clearly recognizes Northern and Aboriginal tourism as an emerging and important sector. Improving partnerships between Aboriginal stakeholders, industry and government will require a better understanding of Aboriginal aspirations and Aboriginal culture in relation to market realities in an effort to evolve the Aboriginal owned product offering.

Developing Northern Tourism

Canada's northern tourism products offer a truly unique experience. While the North is renowned for its nature and wilderness adventures and aurora tourism, it also offers history, distinctive culture and festivals as well as some innovative emerging products such as 'diamond tourism' in the Northwest Territories. The number of tourists travelling to the North is slowly rising. In 2004, the Yukon had over 250,000 arrivals, an 8 percent increase over 1999.

The Northwest Territories saw arrivals increase by almost 4 percent between 2002 and 2004 when the number surpassed 61,000. While Americans represent over three quarters of the Yukon's tourists, more than half of the arrivals in the Northwest Territories are Canadian.

Increasing the number of tourists that visit the North is challenging because it is a product with a narrow market segment. Other issues include access, both in terms of availability and cost, receptive capacity and sustainability. Transportation infrastructure is expensive. Long distances with low traffic result in high costs to individual travellers. These key considerations must be taken into account when endeavouring to develop northern tourism. The northern environment is remote and highly fragile; its natural beauty is part of Canada's heritage and wealth.

Attracting and Retaining a Workforce

The Conference Board of Canada estimates that there will be a shortfall of close to one million workers in the Canadian economy by 2020. According to the Canadian Tourism Human Resource Council, Canada's overall labour force is expected to decline from a growth rate of 1.4 percent in 2005 to 0.4 percent in 2016, due to an aging population and lower birth rates. To compound the problem, labour demand continues to increase across all sectors as a result of strong economic growth.

The tourism labour market is characterized as a seasonal, fragmented, multi-faceted service industry, with a large number of entry-level jobs. The seasonal nature of the tourism industry is contributing to the development of dual labour markets, comprised of core workers and peripheral ones. In many cases, employees view tourism as a gateway into the labour market.

Approximately 60 percent of tourism employment is within the food and beverage, and accommodation sectors. These are the areas most in need of a stable and skilled workforce.

In light of potential labour shortages, it has become increasingly important to enhance the quality of jobs in the tourism industry and to facilitate the entry of those who are under-represented in the labour force. Canada needs to study what other countries are doing to address similar challenges. For example, some Organisation for Economic Cooperation and Development (OECD) countries are currently undertaking efforts to enhance the employability of foreign workers. An opportunity exists to examine how Canada can adjust current immigration policies to better reflect the tourism industry's needs.

Although the tourism industry offers the first work experience for many people, the sector is sometimes ill-perceived as a career choice. At the same time, the ability to attract skilled employees is critical to the industry's growth. There is a need to promote the wide range of long-term career opportunities and prospects that tourism offers, particularly in the operation and management ranks, as well as general hospitality. Attractions, hotels, airlines, auto rentals, and entertainment are but a few areas that offer rewarding, long-term careers.

Investing in Tourism Infrastructure

Typically tourism infrastructure is viewed as consisting of museums, cultural institutions, heritage sites and parks, but the enjoyment and success of tourism experiences also requires quality public infrastructure. All governments are committed to work collaboratively to restore infrastructure in Canada. As such, they have invested more than $30 billion in infrastructure since 1993 in numerous projects across the country.

Despite the substantial investment that governments have made in infrastructure, Statistics Canada reports that the growth in value of public infrastructure assets in Canada has been significantly lagging behind the economy as a whole. In the mid-1970s, public infrastructure as a share of GDP was 23 percent, but declined to 16 percent by 2001.

However all governments are making substantial investments in public infrastructure that benefits the tourism sector directly and indirectly. The significance of tourism interests in infrastructure projects must continue to be communicated to the various jurisdictions responsible for infrastructure development. The strategy will be instrumental in championing coordination and cooperation between governments, particularly in providing policy direction on tourism and related infrastructure projects.

Ensuring an Efficient Transportation System

As the second largest country in the world, Canada's vast territory and diverse geography pose an ongoing transportation challenge for the tourism industry. During the stakeholder consultations, concerns regarding the impact of an inadequate transportation system were raised.

The high cost of air travel in Canada's remote areas and limited transportation options, especially by rail and ferry, affect the ability of tourism operators to promote their products. At the same time, recent shifts and growth in the low-cost carrier segment of the airline industry is helping the domestic tourism market. The cheaper, more flexible price structure of these airlines has enticed more people to travel. They provide affordable air access to many provinces and territories in Canada that were once considered too costly to serve.

In this context, there is a need to continue seeking opportunities to ensure that accessibility, affordability, and service quality are facilitated by a liberalized international air policy, and that tourists' entry into Canada is not impeded. Efforts to seek opportunities for new international bilateral agreements with other countries need to continue.

In addition, the updating of existing agreements, such as the recently concluded liberalization of the Open Skies bilateral agreement with the U.S. should be encouraged. As changes to air liberalization are primarily related to federal transport policy, the CCTM will collaborate with key transportation departments and other stakeholders, as required, in achieving the key results and outcomes.

There is also a need to better integrate the national transportation system to allow passengers to connect easily between modes of transportation, whether they are travelling by bus, boat, plane, train or automobile to or from other points within and outside Canada.

As part of this, particular attention should be paid to ensuring the efficiency and security of the Canada-U.S. Land border, since the U.S. is our main source of international travellers. To this end, Canada and the U.S. signed the Smart Border Declaration in 2001, agreeing on a 32-point action plan to address border processes, invest in border infrastructure, and identify technological solutions to speed movement across the border while ensuring security.

The Border Infrastructure Fund was established to support border infrastructure projects at Canada's busiest land border ports of entry. Furthermore, as part of the 2005 Security and Prosperity Partnership of North America, Canada, the U.S. and Mexico are committed to a number of initiatives that promote border efficiency and security.

The Government of Canada is committed to pursuing integration of the national transportation system and to investing further in new infrastructure at the border. Budget 2006 provided an unprecedented level of support for infrastructure of various types across Canada. This includes support for small and larger scale municipal infrastructure projects in communities across Canada, and improvements to land border crossings and highways.

The fluidity of our major international gateways and trade corridors is crucial not only for the tourism industry, but for the economy as a whole. Through the Asia-Pacific Gateway and Corridor Initiative, Canada seeks to boost commerce with the Asia-Pacific region to integrate investments in transportation infrastructure and improve the efficiency and reliability of the regional transportation system.

Adopting Sustainable Tourism Development and Quality Practices

Sustainable tourism enhances and preserves our natural and cultural heritage and improves Canadians' quality of life. Tourism development needs to balance economic viability, environmental conservation and social impacts. Sustainable tourism endeavours to minimize environmental and cultural impacts while contributing to economic development. The long-term success of the industry depends on business owners and operators being stewards of the environment and adopting quality practices.

In A Manual for Sustainable Tourism Destination Management by Walter Jamieson and Alex Noble, 2000, it states that increasing evidence shows that an integrated approach to tourism planning and management is now required to achieve sustainable tourism. The document goes on to identify some of the most important principles of sustainable tourism development which include:

* Tourism should be initiated with the help of broad-based input that involves all stakeholders, including the community where the development is taking place, and the stakeholders should maintain control of tourism development.
* Tourism should provide quality local employment and a linkage between the local businesses and tourism should be established.
* A code of practice should be established for tourism at all levels—national, regional, and local—based on internationally accepted standards. Guidelines for tourism operations, impact assessment, monitoring of cumulative impacts and limits to acceptable change should be established.
* Education and training programs to improve and manage heritage and natural resources should be established.

F/P/T governments and the industry must work together to develop a cohesive strategy for tourism sustainability in Canada. In spring 2004, the Tourism Industry Association of Canada (TIAC) undertook an update of the Code of Ethics and Guidelines for

Sustainable Tourism developed in 1992. The update, prepared in consultation with industry, was released in February 2005. The Code provides a common basis and framework for the industry to move forward effectively in support of the shared responsibility for sustainable tourism. The aim is to enhance the quality and sustainability of natural and cultural heritage-based experiences. The Code could provide the basis for F/P/T partners to develop a collaborative approach to a sustainable tourism.

Tourism Marketing Strategy

The Accidental Tourist

"For Newfoundland and Labrador, there's no such thing as an accidental tourist. It takes deliberate planning and determined effort to visit here, compelled by curiosity and the promise of what's unique and different in our people, culture, lifestyle, and dramatic scenery."

Barriers & Opportunities

Travel distance, access, and cost continue to be significant barriers for visitors, and a competitive disadvantage for the tourism industry in Newfoundland and Labrador. A short peak season, capacity constraints during peak season, and increasing problems and delays at border crossings and in airports make increasing tourism visitors and revenue even more difficult. Competing with well-known tourism destinations that are well-funded and heavily advertised makes the job even tougher. Despite these barriers, there are opportunities open to Newfoundland and Labrador Tourism.

Baby bloomers are entering the empty nest stage of the family lifestyle. They have money, time, and keen interest to explore destinations that are off the beaten track, unusual and unspoiled places where few have gone before. Places like Newfoundland and Labrador. Ontario, our largest non-resident market, still remains largely underdeveloped for Newfoundland and Labrador tourism. Our greatest opportunity may lay in the launch of the new Tourism brand positioning and personality for Newfoundland and Labrador – and the creative strategy which we use to express it. Our coastline, rich history, unique culture, people, and natural environment remain our key strengths.

Marketing Objectives

The marketing objectives for Newfoundland and Labrador Tourism are to increase non-resident visitation and expenditures from our core markets, thereby increasing the tourism industry's annual contribution to the economy. The strategies and campaigns created to achieve these marketing objectives will also be guided by the desire of government and the Tourism Board to extend the tourism season beyond the core summer season in order to increase the economic benefit and the long-term viability of the industry.

Marketing Strategy

Newfoundland and Labrador Tourism will take a growth-strategy approach to marketing Newfoundland and Labrador as a tourism destination. Advertising will reach and persuade visitors to come to Newfoundland and Labrador, rather than to other destinations in their evoked set. Public and media relations will reinforce the key messages, delivering a consistent and relevant brand image of the province, while sales and online initiatives will "close the loop." The tourism product – in the form of attractions, experiences, and infrastructure – has a larger role to play in increasing length of stay, amount of money spent per trip, and overall tourism revenues.

To be successful in attracting customers from competitors, it's essential that we focus and concentrate our resources on the best opportunity – and create programs and campaigns that are fully integrated.

Target Markets

Newfoundland and Labrador Tourism will focus and concentrate its resources against the target audiences and markets which offer the best opportunity and the highest return on investment. The target market is the non-resident touring and explorer market with concentration in Toronto, Ottawa, Calgary, Halifax and Montreal. Additional geographic markets include the Mid-Atlantic Region of the United States, California and the UK.

Activity-based markets include Meetings, Convention and Incentive Travel market, the Hunting and Fishing market, the Hiking market and partnerships in Outdoor Adventure and Cruise markets.

Touring & Explorer Market

The touring and explorer group is a broad leisure market seeking sightseeing and soft-adventure experiences – from nature viewing to cultural experiences to hiking, birding, and whale-watching. Demographically, research reveals them to be singles and couples in the pre- and post-full nest stage of the family life cycle. Not surprisingly, they tend to be in two age groups: 25 to 34 and (skewed) 45+ years of age.

They also tend to be well-educated and have a higher than average proportion who are university-educated and have higher than average household incomes.

Psychographically, they see themselves as increasingly sophisticated and experienced travellers, seeking more unusual places and experiences 'off the beaten track'. They are looking for an antidote to the stress and plastic composition of urban life and modern times. They're interested in discovering and experiencing the unspoiled natural environment. They are curious people, more interested in unexpected and intriguing experiences than repeat trips to conventional 'tourist' destinations: "been there, done that."

Marketing efforts in the United States will shift from the New England region to the Mid-Atlantic region for Newfoundland and Labrador. These travellers are seeking adventure and cultural experiences in new destinations. To maximize our efforts, Newfoundland and Labrador works cooperatively with the Atlantic Canada Tourism Partnership (ACTP).

ACTP is a nine-member, pan-Atlantic partnership comprising of the Atlantic Canada Opportunities Agency, the four Atlantic Canada Tourism Industry Associations, and the four provincial departments responsible for tourism. The international market is developmental for Newfoundland and Labrador, with low penetration but with long-term potential and high-spend per visitor. Newfoundland and Labrador Tourism will continue to pursue this market in partnership with its Atlantic Canada Partners (ACTP), with primary focus being on the United States and the United Kingdom.

Marketing activities include travel trade partnerships, familiarization tours, trade shows, media relations, and joint marketing with the Canadian Tourism Commission (CTC). The CTC and its industry partners have launched a new global advertising campaign in the UK, Germany, and France. ACTP is a partner in this UK program to build more consumer awareness of the region.

Meetings, Conventions & Incentive Travel Market

Newfoundland and Labrador Tourism provides consultation, materials support, and mailing assistance to international, national, and regional conference organizers hosting conventions and meetings in Newfoundland and Labrador.

Incentive travel is a global management tool that uses an exceptional travel experience to motivate and/or recognize staff for increased levels of performance in support of organizational goals. Newfoundland and Labrador Tourism provides consultation, marketing, and product development support to industry suppliers in this lucrative market. Trade shows and marketplaces are available through partnership opportunities in North American markets.

Outdoor Adventure Market

Outdoor and nature activities such as hiking, birding and kayaking are core to our tourism experiences. These experiences appeal to outdoor enthusiasts and have a broad appeal to our touring and explorer market. Newfoundland and Labrador Tourism partners with the Newfoundland and Labrador Adventure Tourism Association at consumer and trade shows.

Hunting & Fishing Market

Newfoundland and Labrador offers hunters and sport fish enthusiasts some of the most amazing and rewarding outdoor recreation experiences in the world.

Newfoundland and Labrador Tourism partners with the Newfoundland and Labrador Outfitters Association (NLOA) to develop a fully-integrated marketing program for the hunting and fishing market.

Newfoundland and Labrador Brand

Brand Positioning

Most tourism brands are positioned on tangible products and features. Not surprisingly, most advertising presents an inventory of 'products' – places to go, sights to see, and things to do. But people don't buy 'products', they buy benefits. The real benefit lies several layers below the tangible tourism 'product' – in the emotion of the brand, and the feelings it evokes.

Newfoundland and Labrador will stand for 'creativity'. 'Creativity' is true to the brand of Newfoundland and Labrador. Creativity – natural, spontaneous, and uncomplicated – defines who we are, what we do, and the place around us.

We express it in everything we do and say. It will differentiate the Newfoundland and Labrador brand and become our strongest unique selling point. 'Creativity', as the brand positioning, will be expressed and supported by three pillars:

People: The very real character of our people, their attitude, and way of life. Real, genuine people – warm, friendly, welcoming, uncomplicated, witty, humorous, and fun-loving. All the more powerfully felt because of the historical undercurrent of an unrelenting and unforgiving environment, mastered only through a fierce independence, steeped in self-reliance, quiet pride, and creative ingenuity.

Culture: Our history, heritage, music, art, language, architecture, folklore, traditions, values, and the vitality of colour and texture in everything we touch. It links our past with our present and expresses our spiritual and creative and intellectual qualities.

Natural Environment: This place of fierce beauty that lives by the sea. A rugged land with 29,000 kms of coastline, rich icons of whales and wildlife and icebergs, and a sensuous magic light that pours over the landscape and into the art and culture, and hearts of our people.

Brand Personality

A tourism brand personality is the feeling or image that people have about a place. Newfoundland and Labrador's brand personality will personify the creativity of our people and our culture and guide all marketing programs. The Newfoundland and Labrador Tourism brand personality is the natural and spontaneous expression of who we are:

* Natural and uncomplicated.
* Warm and friendly.
* Genuine and authentic.
* Quietly and proudly independent.
* Spontaneous, rather than practiced or self-conscious.
* Witty and funny, with a natural spontaneity.
* Creative – not only in art and culture, but in our natural ingenuity and inventiveness.
* Comfortable in our own skin.

Touring & Explorer Marketing Activities

Canada Market (Newspaper Campaign)

Online Campaign:A series of online advertising including leader boards, big-box, skyscraper, and banners on a variety of business/ news-related websites such as The Globe and Mail, travel-specific websites including Air Canada, Expedia, Travelocity & Yahoo and interest/activity websites dedicated to activities such as birding, hiking, whales, and nature viewing.

Ontario Market (Television Campaign)

Ambient Campaign: Newfoundland and Labrador Tourism is finalizing its ambient marketing activities for the upcoming campaign. Ambient marketing is also called guerilla marketing or place-based marketing; it is marketing or advertising that occurs wherever customers happen to be, it is memorable because it is usually unexpected and unconventional.

Newspaper Campaign: A combination of full-page ads and 4-colour preprinted inserts in Ottawa Citizen.

Radio Campaign: Sponsorship of weather and air quality reports on selected radio stations in Toronto.

United States Market: Marketing efforts in the United States will shift from the New England region to the Mid-Atlantic region for Newfoundland and Labrador. These travellers are seeking adventure and cultural experiences in new destinations. To maximize our efforts, Newfoundland and Labrador works cooperatively with the Atlantic Canada Tourism Partnership (ACTP).

ACTP is a nine-member, pan-Atlantic partnership comprising of the Atlantic Canada Opportunities Agency, the four Atlantic Canada Tourism Industry Associations, and the four provincial departments responsible for tourism. In 2009, Newfoundland and Labrador will continue to focus its efforts in the United States with an emphasis on the hiking and walking activity markets.

Magazine Campaign: Newfoundland and Labrador Tourism advertisements in Audubon, Harpers, National Geographic Traveller, and Smithsonian.

Online Campaign: A series of online advertising including leader boards, big-box, skyscrapers, and banners on websites such as Audubon, Smithsonian, Yahoo, Google, National Geo and activity websites such as Backpacking Light.

Overview: The international market is developmental for Newfoundland and Labrador, with low penetration but with long-term potential and high-spend per visitor. Newfoundland and Labrador Tourism will continue to pursue this market in partnership with its Atlantic Canada Tourism Partnership (ACTP), with primary focus being on the United Kingdom.

Marketing activities include travel trade partnerships, familiarization tours, trade shows, media relations, and joint marketing agreements with Overseas Tour Operators/Wholesale and with the Canadian Tourism Commission (CTC).

International Travel Media Program

The Travel Media Program plays an integral role in maximizing consumer and trade awareness of Newfoundland and Labrador through unpaid media coverage in key overseas markets. Travel media includes freelance journalists, travel editors, broadcasters, producers, and travel trade media. Newfoundland and Labrador Tourism, along with our International counterparts, estimates editorial value from travel stories is four times that of paid advertising. In 2008-09, Newfoundland and Labrador received in excess of $45 million in media coverage and was featured in numerous international newspapers and magazines.

Editorial

Help us keep media informed of what's new in Newfoundland and Labrador. We welcome your information on new travel products, events, personalities, folklore, and regional descriptions for unique travel story opportunities. The information you give us is used to pitch unique story ideas to media and to initiate and plan media tours to Newfoundland and Labrador for qualified journalists. You are also encouraged to submit articles on new tourism products and attractions for the CTC and various media outlets.

Media Tours and Press Trips

Co-host travel media at your business as they tour Newfoundland and Labrador to experience our tourism products first-hand. You may participate by sharing costs or providing in-kind contributions for these tours.

Sales Activities

Media events, promotions, and sales calls in our key international markets are crucial elements in our travel media program. Many of these activities are undertaken in partnership with the CTC and the Atlantic Canada Tourism Partnership (ACTP).

In-Province Resident Marketing Activities

Newfoundland and Labrador Tourism will continue a season extension program for the in-province market. The program covers all four seasons and provides opportunities for tourism operators to promote seasonal packages and create partnerships with other operators in their region.

The objectives for the program are:

* To increase resident in-province travel and expenditures by motivating residents to travel at home.
* To increase resident knowledge of activities and attractions that occurs during fall, spring, and winter seasons as well as the summer period.
* To increase frequency of travel by motivating residents to take additional and more frequent short trips during the shoulder seasons as well as their annual summer vacation. Increase focus on the shoulder seasons.

Resident Direct-Mail Campaign

The Resident Direct Mail Campaign consists of direct mail brochures and a multimedia advertising campaign.

It is an excellent opportunity to get your vacation package delivered to every household in Newfoundland and Labrador through the brochures mailed each summer, fall and winter.

Your involvement in the In-Province Direct Mail Campaign is automatic and free when you participate in the Packaging Marketing Program.

2

E-Business and Hospitality Market

Introduction

Information technology has always an important part in much of the travel and tourism industry. However, perhaps the most significant and exciting development in the sector in the last few years has been the emergence and development of the Interned. The Internet has grown from a small network of computers, set up in the USA the late 1960s for defence purposes, into today's global network linking millions of computer users around the world.

Private users and small companies can connect to the Internet via the phone line using a mode and by opening an account with an Internet Service Provider (ISP), whist larger companies or organisations will have dedicated connections provided by telecommunications companies.

Digitised business or managerial information can be disseminated throughout the network and specially designed computer applications can analyse this information and respond accordingly, thereby interacting with customers, other businesses and organisations. This activity is now known as eBusiness of eCommerce.

The purpose of this chapter is to preview of the role of eBusiness in the tourism sector and, in particular, to consider how it is affecting both industry players and customers. It also on to look at some future developments in eBusiness technologies and the implications that these may have for those involved in tourism. It does not, however, delvin to Internet engineering and communication technologies but, nevertheless, assumes that the reader understands basis Interment concepts, terminology and, indeed, jargon. Examples of interesting or useful web sites are given in parentheses throughout.

Definitions

eBusiness is business or management activity conducted by electronic means over computer networks. It is more commonly referred to as eCommerce; however, eCommerce tends to focus on the transactions between customers and suppliers, whereas the term eBusiness can encapsulate the total business process, both within and without the firm, including the relationship between customer and supplier. eBusiness, then affects a variety of business activities, such as marketing, human resource management, procurement and distribution, as well as having implications for the state in terms of the law, taxation and government regulation. Most notably, however, it is changing consumer behaviour whilst, at the same time, providing the consumer with increased power and choice.

Therefore, the scope of eBusiness extends well beyond the popular view of web pages being used to advertise and sell things. The components of eBusiness will include email, internative websites, mobile phones, television and, possibly, other household appliances!

Characteristics of eBusiness

Global reach

The Internet is a global network which means that eBusiness has, theoretically, a global reach. However, although this characteristic is true as far as communication is concerned, the picture is more complicated when the distri-bution of tourism products in considered. It is not practical, for example, for a Brities travel agent to sell a Spanish holiday to a customer in Australia because the customer would, of course, have to come to the UK to take the holiday.

Global reach is also constrained by consumer protection law and other kinds of regulation both of the tourism sector in particular and, increasingly, of eBusiness generally. This will affect the ability of tourism firms to market their products on global basis and may mean that companies engaged in eBusiness will have to adapt their activities and procedures in order to comply with such regulations in different parts of the world. At the same time, consumers are ways of buying from sites overseas because consumer law has not yet caught up with the new legal situation being created by the Internet. For example, if a consumer in Brazil arranged to rent a country cottage from a web site in Sweden and a dispute over the transaction arose, to which country's consumer protection law could that customer appeal? In other words, in the age of the Internet, an important yet unresolved question is which counuy's laws protect the consumer when they are making purchases across national boundaries?

This is one reason why some companies have localised domain names as well as the more common international dot.com (.com) suffix. An example of this is *eBookers,* the online travel agency that has a main site at www.ebookers.com as well as various international sites, including www.ebookers.com/fr for France, and www.ebookers.no/ for Norway. Indeed, some sites' computers advise surfers that they should go to their 'national' site. *Expedia,* (http://www.expedia.com/) does this, reminding customers that they cannot buy American air tickets if they are browsing form outside the USA.

Of course, different rules and regulations may not be the only reason for a firm to have a variety of localised domain names- there are good marketing reasons for them as well. Potential customers may feel more confident interacting with a web site presented in their own language and with one that appears to be based in their own country.

In some cases, government regulation may lead to companies leaving particular geographic locations precisely because they can set up and conduct business anywhere by using the Internet. For example, in 1999, the large bookmakers *coral* and *William Hill* threatened to move their operations overseas to reduce the tax burden imposed on those who bet. A private bookmaker, *Victor Chandler International,* had set up an offshore operation on Gibraltar and was able to reduce the tax on betting.; The big bookmaking companies were beig squeezed by the rival operation's success. In late 2001 the taxation rules on betting were changed and taxes that were imposed on the customer are now levied on the bookmakers' profits. The change was largely as a result of the increase in betting on the Internet (BBC 2001).

Disintermediation/Reintermediation

It was believed that one of the consequences of the growth of the Internet and the development of eBusiness would be the elimination of intermediaries between supplier and customer, a process that has been termed 'disintermediation'. This potentially occurs because the Internet allows customers to communicate directly with the supplier or producer of a product. Thus, a potential package holiday customer can buy place tickets from an airline, accommodaton from a hotel, car-hire from a hire company, and so on (in effect, creating their own package) and this can all be carried out if the suppliers have a 'web presence'. This means that, in theory, the need to have travel agents based in the high street is unnecessary. However, this process of disintermedication has not yet happened, for several reasons:

- It is very difficult for individuals to buy components of their holiday by surfing the Internet-it is time consuming and, in the long run, usually more expensive because individual consumers cannot benefit from the economies of scale that are available to travel agencies and tour operators.
- New intermediaries have emerged that specialise in marketing travel products on the Internet. Companies such as *Travelocity,* (www.travelocity.com), *Expedia* (www.expedia.com) and *Lastminute* (www.last-minute.com) new allow customers to search, select and buy tourism products in one place.
- Sometimes the new intermediaries get it wrong and do not provide the customer with the best deal.

- The development of the new intermediates, referred to as 'reintermediation', has meant that many of the traditional travel agencies now also have web sites to market their products. Originally, these sites were advertisements for their high street shops and had no interactive facilities at all. Many, indeed, directed surfers to their branches by providing phone numbers. However, they have now developed into sophisticated sites from which to market their products (www.lunnpoly.com and www.firstchoice.co.uk).

It does seem likely that there may be a slight fall in the number high street travel agencies over the coming years, in much the same way that the UK banking sector closed unprofitable branches during the late nineties. However, the traditional agencies that are now trading on the Internet appear to be seeing this as complimentary to their marketing strategy in respect of their 'bricks and mortar' presence, rather than as a replacement. This begs the question, though, of whether the Internet is allowing these particular companies to reduce costs. Indeed, the setting up Internet operations as well as having shops may, in fact, have the opposite effect and actually increase costs.

Virtualisation

The Internet allows companies to contract out business activities to other firms more easily. An airline, for example, could outsource its aircraft, catering, in-flight and ground services, and so on, to specialist firms. Whilst this has always been possible in the past, the Internet makes this much less difficult and it can be much more efficiently organised. This is because all the suppliers could be locked into the airline's computer network where communications and operations between all the parties can be managed electronically. In some cases, the contracted company could even be based in another country.

Automation

eBusiness is ideal for automating business processes. Costly manual processes involving paper, telephones and the staff to carry them out can be, to a large extent, eliminated or redeuced.

Storage efficiencies can also be achieved because most information can be held on electronic databases for easy retrieval, comparison and manipulation. This, in turn, allows companies to obtain information at a very detailed level both in terms of its internal processes and its customers. This all leads to cost reductions and to other benefits both for the supplier and the customer.

Cost Reduction

As already mentioned above, eBusiness technologies allow companies to reduce costs, primarily because the physical requirements of information collection, manipu-lation, analysis and storage can be radically reduced. Furthermore, because customers interact with web sites in order to collect much of this information, human interme-diaries, such as telephone sales staff, can also be reduced in number. Thus, 'cost reduction in service is largely achieved by moving towards customer self-service, with the help of technology. Part of the cost reduction can be passed on to the customer'. Indeed, some corporate customers are already switching from using traditional travel agencies to book business travel arrangements, to booking online (Rice 2001).

Collaboration

The Internet allows companies and their suppliers to be electronically linked via 'subnetworks' called *intranets* or *extranets.* An intranet is a closed network which a particular company or organistion. An extranet is a network that may link a company with its suppliers or other stakeholders. In other words, suppliers have access to a particular company's network to exchange information-the general public would not, however, have access to this network. Three major areas where the internet is making an impact in collaboration are in product development, procurement and joint marketing.

Product Development

Companies can involve their suppliers in the development of new products through network technology. Being, the aircraft manufacturer, has, for example, engaged a specialist company, Aeronet, to build it a wide-ranging intranet that allows suppliers and subcontractors to obtain technical information about its planes.

Boeings's suppliers and subcontractors to obtain tecchnical information about its planes. Boeing's suppliers and customers can now directly download information, such as maintenance manuals and customers can now directly download information, such as maintenance manuals and engineering drawings, that used to be distributed in 'hard' form.

Keeping and supplying information in this way means that, when updates are necessary, the company does not have to order another print run of documentation- it just updates the digital information on its server. Again, this information would be available only to authorised individuals or organisations like the maintenance staff of airlines that fly Boeing aircraft and would not be accessible to casual net 'surfer'.

e-Procurement

e-Procurement is the procurement and tendering of goods and services using electronic means. Many airlines now do business with their suppliers electronically. For example, a company in the USA, *Free Markets,* has recently signed a contract with the *One world* airline alliance of 31 airlines. The company, which has been working with airlines and other aviation related industries since 1998, believes that it has saved an estimated $2.7 billion for its customers (www.ebizchronicle.com).

Joint Marketing

The Internet allows tourism principals, such as airlines, to jointly market their products, thereby avoiding other travel intermediaries. The Orbitz site, which was established by five US airlines, (www.orbitz.com), promotes itself as offering 'access to the most low airfareson the Internet, plus great values on rental cars, hotel rooms and more.

In addition, Orbitz brings you the latest in fare-finding technology, so you can be sure that you're getting the most complete list of available airfares.' The is just one example of how airlines are moving into areas that were once the preserve of the travel agent. Furthermore, some of the new start-up companies are now collaborating with older, more traditional companies in their marketing strategy. For example, in 2001, *Lastminute* and *Thomas*

Cook established an arrangement whereby Thomas Cook would be the preferred supplier of airline tickets.

Marketing and eBusiness

The most immediate effect of the growth of the Internet in the tourism sector has been its using marketing. Many early web sites acted as promotional tools for tourism enterprises, whether they were large tour operations companies or small rural hotels. To use the Internet for marketing is relatively simple, inexpensive and extremely cost effective. A bed and breakfast business can, for example, design its own web page, arrange with an Internet Service Provider to put it online and, after registering it with a few search engines, wait for the customers to make enquiries. Many of these sites still exist but, as Internet technologies and software applications have developed, larger tourism businesses have been looking for more than just a means to promote their products and interactivity, multimedia presentations and page customisation have become commonplace (www.thomas-cook.co.uk).

Interactivity–getting the Customer Close to You

Before the advent of the Internet, consumers were largely passive recipients of promotional information provided to them by the tourism industry. The Internet, in contrast, allows customers to interact with the medium, actively seeking out the information they desire. This also means that the companies providing this information can react to this activity by identifying what the consumers' interests and needs are. More tailored information can then be sent back to the surfer and the cycle of information exchange is repeated. A simple example of how a web server can interact with a surfer is at *'Ask Jeeves'*, a search engine (www.ask.co.uk). If an enquiry is made about a specific country or destination, the results page will include advertisements for that country. It is likely that regular surfers will revisit the same sites, thereby allowing the companies to further refine their knowledge of the customer. This has several implications has far as interactivity is concerned:

- Sites must be available constantly as, nowadays, customers may want to buy products at any time of the day or, indeed, night. This has implication for staffing and servicing-especially if a site is complemented by the human touch through help lines and so on.

- Sites must be easily 'navigable' so that interactivity can be made as straightforward as possible. This means that web site design and site 'stickiness' becomes critical.
- Companies need to try to enter into closer relationships with customers once they can identify who they are. This entail, for example, encouraging customers to give more information about themselves through the completion of forms or the 'Personalisation' of their own version of the company's web site.
- Customers can now seach for tourism services much more quickly and efficiently on the Internet. This means that comparisons can easily be made between companies and the competition between them in intensified.

Market Research—getting Closer to the Customer

Interactivity is one way in which tourism companies can obtain information about their customers but other eBusiness technologies can also provide sophisticated tools for carrying out market research. When surfers browse web sites, information can be obtained regarding their interests and activities either overtly or surreptitiously. This information can then be stored, retrieved and analysed, although any eBusiness operation that does this is still subject to the Data Protection Act, 1998.

Some techniques that are commonly used to gather information on customers are given below:

- Electronic order forms.
- Electronic registration.
- 'Cookies'.

Order Forms

An obvious and open way of acquiring information is for companies to ask surfers to provide them with information. If a customer is looking to book a holiday they will have to provide information about himself or herself to the operator in question. This is normally done by completing a form online. The form itself can ask questions that are not directly related to the ordering of the holiday and the customer can, if he so wishes, provide this additional infor-mation. The details on the form can then be processed to complete any order that has been made by the customer. However, the information, because it is provided electronically, can be analysed and stored for further market research.

Registration

Sometimes, web sites encourage surfers to register themselves with the web site and this, again, helps firms obtain useful information regarding their wants and needs. Once registered, users will be offered additional benefits over and above those offered to casual surfers. For example, page customisation might be available where customers can adjust the 'look'n 'feel' of the page to suit their own testes, or regular emails will be sent to those registered regarding special offers.

Cookies

A less transparent way of obtaining information on surfers is to send a 'cookie' to the surfer's computer after they have loaded a web page. A cookie in a small file that is stored on the users computer by the company's web site. It will contain information regarding the consumer's activity on the web. This may be information about what the customer has ordered on the Internet in the past, or about which advertisements have attracted his attention. When the customer revisits the web site in question, the cookie is accessed so that the customer and his web activity, can be identified. The web page can then be 'personalised' for that customer.

In some cases, the management of cookies can be highly sophisticated. For example, information can be contained in the cookie regarding the frequency or likelihood that a customer may place an order. This means that, when a regular customer returns he, or rather his surfing activity, is directed to much faster computer servers so his order can be processed more quickly. Causal browsers, identified by their cokies, are directed to slower servers.

Cookies and similar software are giving rise to some concern about privacy on the Internet and many surgers object to the idea of outsiders placing files, however small, on their computers. Some browsers now allow surfers to choose whether to accept cookies before they are downloaded (www.opera.com); however, if cookies are refused in this way, it may mean that the customer is unable to access the site.

The new capability to gather large quantities of information about customers using customer interaction, and the processing of it using electronic databases, means that companies can develop both the ability and the flexibility to be able to offer customised products to individual customers-one-to-one marketing.

Promotion-getting the Message to the Customer

Early web sites concentrated almost entirely on promotion. They were effectively little electronic posters or brochures-'brochureware'. One major advantage over physical promotional tools like brochures, is that tourism suppliers are able to rapidly update their information regarding prices, timetables and product attributes etc. online. Some consequences of how promotion has been affected and developed by the Internet are given below.

Web Page Design

As with all promotional devices, design is critical. Too many pages look cluttered and confusing and this detracts from the promotional effect. Clean dsign with a logical navigation system is critical if a page is to be effective as a promotional tool.

Corporate identity and branding can also be reinforced using the web page. As noted above, existing travel and tourism companies are already presect in cyberspace. Their web sites will have been designed so that their corporate identities are highly visible and integrated into their overall real world brand image.

Advertising

Soon after the emergence of the Internet as a marketing tool, 'banner' advertising developed whereby tourism companies could buy space on more generic Internet portals. Banner advertising consists of a small advertisement or *banner,* usually placed at the top of a web page, where a firm can promote its products. If a customer clicks on the banner, he gets taken to the site advertised. It is thought, however, that the 'click through rate' for banner advertisements is only about 0.5 per cent. Another form of advertising is 'interstitial advertising, where a small additional window opens when a web page is accessed. However, a reading of the popular computer press indicates that these forms of advertising are extremely irritating and software now exists to prevent them loading on to a web page, thereby defeating the purpose of the practice. Any company thinking of using this form of advertising needs to think carefully about whether more people may be put off the product than be attracted to it.

The Internet also encourages 'affiliate' advertising. This is where a firm with a complimentary product places small advertisements on another company's web sites. A car hire company might buy some space on a tour operator's site, for example, or an airline might use a hotel site to promote itself. (http://berlin.hyatt.com/bergh/).

Finally, technology is now becoming so sophisticated that 'geo-location software' has been developed that enables companies to identify where a particular surfer lives. This means that advertisements and other promotions can be targeted at people's browsers based on their location, and of course, location can be an indicator of age, lifestyle and class. This targeting can be further refined depending on the time of day or day of the week. For example, an airline could promote discounted tickets for weekend travel to potential customers within a defined radius of a particular airport. The advertisement would only appear on those customers screens—it would not appear on screens outside the designated zone even if those surfers were looking at the same web page.

Email

Email can also be used to promote goods and services on the Internet. Unsolicited emails, however, are viewed with suspicion surfers. Therefore, companies that want to use email as a promotional tool will ask site visitors to register their interest with a particular site, thereby inviting emails about special offers, late availability, on new products (www.klm.com and www.britishairways.com). Email can also be customised to reflect a particular company's corporate identity: however, this does not seem to have caught on and most emails still appear to surfers as plain text. This may be because some email programmes have difficulty hanging such content.

Text Messaging

Text Messaging (SMS) is now increasingly being used as a promotional technique. It is especially useful when used tactically, In the summer of 2000, a company called *Worldpop* (www.worldpop.com) began promoting clubs, and other products, in Ibiza using text messaging, Clubbers needed to register to receive the SMS service and about 800 did so. The SMS system was also used to control capacity at certain clubs, advising clubbers where the longest queues were. This kind of promotional strategy is likely to grow in the future as it offers firms the ability to target carefully selected audiences with specific information while at the same allowing them to measure the response. *'Mobiles offer marketers the aluminate direct, personalised, time-and location-sensitive method of advertising'* (Day 2001).

Market Development—getting more Customers

As the Internet makes international markets more accessible it allow organisations in the tourism sector to attract customers and visitors from far and wide. A country house hotel or a National Park can use the Internet in this way; for example, both the Langley Castele Hotel in Northumberland (www. Langleycastle.com) and the Dartmoor Natonal Park (www.dartmoor-npa.gov.uk) have web sites that can now be used to market both organisations around the world.

The Internet has enabled companies reach parts of the market that might once have been difficult and expensive to attract. For example, a specialist firm that offered walking holidays would, in the past, have probably concerntrated on reaching its target market through specialists magazines and the weekend leisures supplements in newspapers. By going online the company has the ability to reach a much wide market-especially if it makes sure it has registered with several search engines. (www.nzwal-kingcompany.com). 'If you run a small travel agency or tour operation, it is very important to realise that it pays to specialise on the Web. Specialist operators and agents will not only be sought out by travellers for their specific expertise, but there is actually less competition' (Travel Trade Gazette 2001a).

The Internet has also allowed new business models to develop. One of these is the online auction. Instead of an auctioneer gathering together a lot of potential customers in one physical space, an online auctioneer gathers them together in cyberspace. Surfers can long on to dedicated web sites and make offers for the products that are for sale. The web based travel site *Priceline* (www.priceline.com) offers customers the chance to bid for air tickets online. Other generic sites like *eBay* (www.eBay.com) also offer this facility for all kinds of tourism products.

Product Characteristics and Distribution

The characteristics of a particular product are crucial when considering whether that product can be sold and distributed over the Internet. 'Digitsed' products, like software, or 'digitisable' products, such as music, can easily be delivered through computer networks to customers' computers. Small products, such as books or CDs, can be transported via conventional delivery system like the post or courier services. In both these sases, distance is not a particular issue. However, with some services it might be. For example, if a plumber used the Internet to advertise and promote his services he could still only operate whitin the geographical area in which he did before. A plumber in London, however stylish and sophisticated his web page, could not relay offer to carry out repairs in Los Angeles. So how does this affect tourism products?

Tourism products are intangible yet they do have certain tangible aspects—an air ticket is tangible, the flight itself is intangible. This means that an air ticket can be ordered over the Internet and can be delivered to the customer by post, courier or at the departure airport itself. Interestingly, the function that the air ticket performs, that is, to show a check-in clerk that a customer has paid for a trip to a particular destination, can be now be digited. If the customer is sent a code by a computer instead of a paper ticket, that code can perform the same function of an ordinary ticket. The budget airline EasyJet used this system (http://easyjet.com/en/info/howToBook.html). This model extends to other to other tourism products like hotel accommodation or theatre bookings.

Digitising the tangible aspects of the tourism product, like a ticket or a hotel reservation, means that tourism companies will need build in added reassurance for customers who may not feel that they have bought anything because they do not have any physical evidence to prove that they have done so. Therefore, email, containing a unique reference number, is usually used to confirm that a purchase has been made.

Furthermore, the more complicated a product, the more difficult it might be to sell over the Internet. A air ticket, virtual or otherwise, is far simpler to sell through the Internet than a package holiday. A package holiday contains far more variables than a simple ticket—variables such as full-boards or half-board, bength of stay, type of hotel, transport from the airport, day trips, insurance, child prices, food, etc. Therefore, the customer may want the reassurance of a human salesperson with whom to discuss such things, as well as tangible objects like glossy brochures, complicated from and baggage tags.

Market Segmentation

The fact that the product can be digitised and distributed electronically may have implications for segementation in tourism marketing. Tourism consumers, as in all markets, can be segmented along certain lines based on behavour, culture and needs. Those who currently use the Internet tend to be from the more affluent and better-educated groups and they may have less fear about making eBusiness transactions.

This means that companies that traditionally target this kind of customer and able to make more of the Internet than others Youth market segments are also prime targets for tourism eBusiness whereas the grey market might be less so (www.gite.com).

eBusiness and Staffing

Touism businesses wanting to become ebusinesses will need to think about having to recruit new people to handle this new way of doing things.

Most of these staff are likely to come from the information technology sector but some may need to bring with them new skills in relation to marketing and operations. Firms can, of course opt to retrain existing staff but, given the technological nature of eBusiness, this may sometimes be difficult. An alternative, especially for a large operation, is to engage the services of specialist companies who can set up the appropriate web structures to do business online. In 1995, Japan Airlines contracted IBM to explore 'the opportunity to launch e-commerce services via the Web' (www-3.ibm.com).

eBusiness technologies also allow for more home working and distance working as working with the Internet means that workers do not have to occupy one building in a particular location. Furthermore, eBusiness is not constrai-ned by the traditional working day and the workforce will need to be managed so that 24-hour cover is given. This also means that opportunities for part-times may increase—maybe at the expense of full-time workers.

Restructuring and Redundancy

The development of an eBusiness may have the effect of 'flattening' the management structure. For example, if a travel agency company wanted to move out of the high street and sell its products on the Internet, it would want to close its high street shops down.

This would lead to redundancies, unless those staff could be easily relocated and retrained. It would also be likely that the network of shops would be replaced by a single operation in a large office with smaller number of workers.

There would be less need for these workers to interact with customers as most of the business, formally carried out face to face in the travel agencies, would take place electronically. These workers too would be managed by fewer managers. All the hierarchies that previously existed in the agencies would have disappeared, being replaced by a flatter, broader structures located in one place.

Finally, it might even be more cost effective to have this new operation based abroad. So, in this scenario, the dynamics of eBusiness have removed a travel agency's presence in the high street, reduced its workforce, flattened its management structure and moved its operations over-seas.

Public Sector Tourism

So far this chapter has dealt with eBusiness as applied to the private sector. However, the public sector can also benefit from eBusiness. Public Sector tourism is involved in the promotion of tourism in geographic areas usually to promote economic development. For example, in former industrial areas, many local authorities are keen to promote tourism to replace jobs and economic activity lost with the decline of older industries (www.durham.gov.uk), whilst others may be concerned with managing tourists within certain geogrphic boundaries (www.cumbria.gov.uk).

As with the private sector, public sector tourism can use the Internet to market tourism. Destinations and attractions can be marketed on the Internet and local authorities and tourist boards draw together many of the tourism operators and attactions in a particular area, and promote them on a single web site under one local or regional umbrella (www.zurichtourism.ch).

This allows small operators, like bed and breakfast operators and museums, organisations and firms that are never awash with money, to benefit from the power of eBusiness without having to invest in the technology themselves (www.wooler.org.uk).

The public sector, however, can do more with Internet technologies than just promoting a particular area. The large number of small businesses that make up tourism can be brought together by public sector bodies via the Internet. Local authorities can easily communicate with these businesses using the Internet. Tourism policy, marketing plans and other issues involving tourism can also be disseminated through the Internet to all those involved in tourism in a particular locality.

Other public sector bodies can also use the Internet to enhance their services. National parks, for example, can use the Internet to communicate with potential visitors about weather conditions or special events. They can augment their education and interpretation services (www.nnpa.org.uk) and they can manage the park more effectively in terms of communication with remote field offices, inventory management and so on by using the Internet.

Finally, public sector bodies can also use the Internet to disseminate information regarding tourism to those who have a professional interest like companies, researchers and academics (www.tourism trade.org.uk).

Future Developments

The eBusiness revolution started with access to the Internet via personal computes. While the personal computer will remain a key device for many tourists and tourism companies when engaging in eBusiness, new hardware is also being seen as crucial to the development of eTourism. Perhaps the most important of these will be the mobile phone but PDAs (Personal Digital Assistants) and other electronic devices, such as televisions, will also begin to play a role in eBusiness.

The personal computer allows surfers to browse at leisure looking for tourism products but the advantage with the mobile phone is that most of the time they are switched on. This means that those that can interact with the Internet are online all the time and when they are on the move.

This 'nomadicity' offers many opportunities for eBusiness, especially when it comes to engaging in short tactical communications with owners. 'Current uses of mobile devices take into account the limitations and focus on providing targeted information that frequently requires only short responses. Once the current limitations are overcome, increased sophistication of mobile applications is anticipated. Further application enhancements are expected in the areas of localisation, personalization and instant connectivity.' (www.dmreview.com). Telephones also have a familiarity that computers do not, thereby avoiding the fear some people might have when using 'new technology'.

The two areas where mobile phones will prove critical are text messaging (SMS) and third generation mobile telephony services (3G).

SMS

SMS is proving to be a very attractive way for suppliers to maintain contact with customers. This comparatively simple technology has achieved the same level of market penetration in three years that took email twenty years. Already, many airlines offer a mobile call service regarding flight schedules and other information that connects directly to subscribers' phones (www.china-airlines.com/us/index/htm). Furthermore, there are now companies that provide a price comparison service on the Internet for consumer goods (www.pricerunner.com). These sites can be assessed via mobile phones to carry out instant price comparisons based on product search criteria. It seems inevitable that this kind of facility will soon exist for travel products. SMS is also now being developed to handle more sophisticated information like simple graphics and sound.

3G

In the late 1990s, I-mode and WAP (Wireless Application Protocol) phones were introduced: These were the first attempts at providing internet access from a mobile phone. I-mode is however, confined to Japan and WAP to Europe. Although I-mode has proved popular, WAP has failed to take off in Europe, mainly because the technology is still an ineffective way of communicating with the Internet-it is slow and expensive and unable to handle much more than textual information. The real advance in Internet connectivity will come with 3G phones, which will be able to handle far more sophisticated information, including multi-media applications, at a much higher speed-expected to be 40 times faster than WAP.

In 2000, Swissair introduced a service for selected mobile phone users where the checking-in process could be done from a moblie phone using WAP technology.

This kind of service is likely to increase with the advent of 3G services where, for example, travellers will be able to make and adjust booking arrangements for air trips and accommodation from their mobile phones.

Payment for theses services will be charged on the basis of the service provided, or the quantity of bytes downloaded, rather than the time spent on the phone. Furthermore, with the development of 'agents' or 'bots' (http://botspot.com), tourists will one day be able to ask these software entities, via their computers or phones, to search for specific travel products online and report back with the results.

Related to these developments are biometric technologies, which might remove the need for passwords, boarding cards and even, one day, passports (http://webusers.anetstl.com/~wrogers/biometrics/). The technology is based around certain unique physical attributes of the human body, such as the iris or the face, some airlines have already begun to experiment with this when screening passengers boarding planes.

Conclusion

eBusiness in tourism has grown significantly in the past few years and looks to grow even faster in the years to come. This growth originated with simple web applications and has now developed to include mobile phone techonologies. Research carried out by Energies indicates that travel and tourism in believed by industry experts to the leading sector in eBusiness development in the future (Travel Trade Gazette 2001b). Moreover, Forrester Research (www.forres-ter.com), estimate that between '2001 and 2004 more than $212 billion of business and leisure travel services will be bought online in the US, Canada, and Europe,'

The Gartner Group www.gartner.com) sees eBusiness as going through four phases (Leemakdej 2001). These are :

(*i*) The 'cyberspace placeholder' phase, where businesses used the Internet to advertise their products;

(ii) The Common Gateway Interface (CGI) phase, which saw the beginnings of interaction between surfer (customer) and server (supplier);

(iii) the transaction phase, by which time firms were creating 'virtual stores' and began to integrate their online presence with existing information systems; and

(iv) The transformation phase, whereby companies' web resources will connect with their suppliers information systems to improve supply chain management, while at the same time integrating the management of human resources, processes and production.

The nature and characteristics of each of the myrlad of organisations that make up the tourism sector will determine how fast each one goes through these four 'phases'- some, like major airlines, are nearing phase for. It seems inevitable, however, that those companies that fail to understand the potential offered by eBusiness will struggle to survive today eBusiness is business.

3

E-Business in the Hospitality Sector

Introduction

As hospitality industry executives contemplate the launch of the new millennium, they need to recognize the huge changes that are occurring in the way business is being conducted and begin planning in earnest as to how they will respond. For those operating within the physical world, the concept of electronic business or "e-business" may appear to be of limited significance. But such an assumption could be costly. E-business and its applications are undoubtedly the No. 1 topic in the boardrooms of most of the world's largest companies. The financial markets are making massive investments in the companies that deliver Internet technologies, content and related products and services, and the corporate world is now moving toward e-business offerings at a rapid clip.

On the business-to-business (b-to-b) front, e-business is projected to grow enormously in the United States over the next several years, with business-to-consumer (b-to-c) trade not as big, but growing just as fast. The McKenna Group estimates that the b-to-b marketplace could grow in value to US$500 billion in 2003. But those estimates may be low. General Motors Corporation, Ford Motor Company and Daimler Chrysler, for example, have just announced that they plan to combine their efforts to form a b-to-b integrated supplier exchange through a single global portal. Meanwhile, on the retail front, the race is on to win the Internet consumer, whose ranks are growing rapidly.

Traditional retailers have much to be concerned about as retail sales over the Internet skyrocket. And while such activity has yet to grow to the same extent in Europe and Asia/Pacific where the cost of phone calls remains an issue, it surely will over time. In the meantime, travel is one of the more popular online products for sale and over the next several years, it is projected in the United States alone to grow to US$12 billion.

E-business is rewriting the economic rules globally for every industry-including hospitality, travel and leisure. Indeed, it's important to recognize that we are now operating in what has been described as the "new economy," as global trends drive change, including globalization, consolidation, convergence, technology and communications. Even more, it is clear that the underlying sources of value are also changing. Use of intangible assets such as information, brands, customers, relationships and networks distinguish the most successful companies in the world.

The Impact of the Internet

It is clear that the Internet is having a huge impact on how we conduct our lives and our businesses. And it arrived virtually overnight. In the United States, for example, it took 38 years for television to get into 50 million homes. For the Internet, it took just five years. And for those U.S. consumers that are online, four out of five believe that the Internet is a more important invention than television. Of these same online consumers, close to six in 10 prefer e-mail to paper mail for business correspondence and over one in four check their e-mail while on vacation.

The Internet is also changing the customer relationship-undermining and redirecting customer attention to new sellers of products and services and away from their traditional relationships. And as this occurs, the traditional approaches that hospitality businesses have taken to distribution are all being affected. From reservations taken over the Internet, which are projected to more than double to 9% of volume over the next year, to the declining role of the travel agent.

This occurs as so-called "infomediaries" provide information and access, and software robots troll the activity online to develop matches between buyers and sellers, analyzing complex patterns and looking for trends for marketers to capitalize upon. As for the infomediaries, we can expect some of these to move into the transactions business and continue the process of disintermediation. For some hospitality companies, it may be best to join this new competition, particularly if it cannot be beaten at its own game.

The reality today is that the balance of power is shifting from sellers to buyers and in so doing it makes the importance of delivering high-quality service, convenience and value for money ever more compelling. The Internet has clearly levelled the playing field by making price information broadly available to the consumer. Internet business models affect product and services offerings, pricing, distribution and customer service, as well as long-term information capabilities. As a consequence, some hospitality suppliers will inevitably feed different tranches of their inventory through the various channels at their disposal-including the Internet, travel management organizations, destination packagers and the like.

Convenience and Consistency

In the end, customers want both convenience and consistency. They don't have all the leisure time that futurists once predicted they would have by now. In fact, they have less. Today's fast-paced world produces ever more stress, and consumers want information and they want it fast. And if hospitality companies and travel providers don't deliver convenience, somebody else inevitably will. They also want to be wired up to the rest of the world-at home, in their office and especially when they travel. And for hoteliers trying to cope with in-room technologies and the delivery of high-speed Internet access, we will soon be seeing more integration of network communication and entertainment products to further complicate or liberate our lives, depending on your point of view.

Customers are also looking for consistency-a simple concept, but central to whether a brand has value or not. And in the emerging networked world, aligning the value propositions of alliance partners and ensuring a seamless and consistent experience will only be as good as the weakest link in the chain.

New Business Rules are Emerging

Within this new economy, the operating environment for hospitality companies is changing. There are new rules of conduct, new relationships and new criteria for success, along with a new set of metrics.

The revolution that we must now confront is therefore no less significant than the one that our forebears had to deal with as the Industrial Revolution changed how people lived, worked and dealt with each other. And like our distant relatives of centuries ago, there are boundless opportunities and countless risks, most obscured within an environment of great uncertainty. In such an era there are certain traits to business behavior that will distinguish success from failure. At this stage in the new economy's evolution, these traits would appear to include speed, agility and flexibility.

Speed is necessary to get to market early with a first-mover advantage that assures early adoption by an increasingly fickle, restless and frequently disloyal customer. Such speed is imperative as so-called "start-up" companies come to dominate their chosen niche in extremely short periods of time, frequently preempting the opportunity for those too slow to react.

Agility is required to be able to respond to competitive threats by not only those we know and can monitor, but also unseen competitors. These latter competitors may not even exist as yet, but as they emerge, they may quickly disintermediate established customer relationships.

And, finally, flexibility is needed to reorganize the established models of business and all of the related processes, and adapt the organization in organic fashion to a new environment in whatever form it takes.

From Place to Space

For business executives at large, one of the most compelling changes that has confronted them in recent years is the potential for e-business. But while the significance of these new media are all too apparent, the business solutions required to capitalize on opportunities they offer are unfortunately not. For most hospitality executives, the essential frame of reference has been a geocentric one where real estate and geography have been the big drivers in a physical world-buildings, dots on maps, markets served, chains. In tomorrow's world, these concepts will require some fundamental adjustments to provide for market "spaces" rather than "places" as the nature of relationships between hotel businesses, their customers, their suppliers and their alliance partners go through rapid and constant change.

As these changes occur, the new economy's business leaders must quickly learn the new rules of the game and adjust their approaches accordingly. And the most successful among us will align key processes around the Internet, build corporate intelligence automatically, create integrated value chains and develop new processes to deal with an ever-changing set of circumstances.

The Human Capital Challenge

Supporting the changes in the new economy will be a vast pool of talented human capital anxious to bring new ideas and new technologies to bear on the traditional ways of doing business and, in doing so, steadily increase the pace of productivity improvement. And if the hospitality industry is to respond to this coming reality, it will need to address some of its most vexing challenges-particularly those relating to the recruitment, training and development of human capital.

The human capital inventory for an e-business will require entrepreneurship, as well as visionary leadership, strength in sales and marketing and commitment to customer relationship management. The organizational bias will need to be toward creativity and risk-taking, and away from dependency on analysis and procedures.

In addition to the human capital challenge, many of today's legacy organizations are better structured to work in the old economy, but are considerably less aligned for many activities in the "new." The cultural challenges may in fact be no less daunting than those presented by some of the technological ones. For large organizations attempting a major shift in orientation, the presence of a significant culture may turn out to be quite a hindrance.

Redefining the Hospitality Business

In some industries, profits are made on spare parts and maintenance rather than on mainstream products. In the new economy, we may see this business model replicated in the hospitality industry. And for those companies that discount or give away products such as hotel rooms in order to sell linked services, they surely will be redefining the meaning of hospitality. They will also be marketing an array of hospitality and leisure products and services to a customer base that is no longer satisfied with the traditional ways of making such purchases.

Hospitality businesses that traditionally provided room, board, management and marketing may need to rethink their roles in the new economy, particularly as services become more valuable than products. With the rapid growth of "infomediaries" and their facilitation of transactions, hospitality businesses may need to redefine themselves in order to prosper in an increasingly electronic world where one-to-one customization is the order of the day. But for those contemplating repositioning their companies in an e-business environment, it will be necessary to focus on the current value proposition of the business and determine how it might be reformatted or enhanced to ensure success in the new setting.

Is the Industry Prepared?

But just how prepared is the global hospitality industry to capitalize on some of the opportunities afforded by the emerging new economy? In Arthur Andersen's recently published global survey of technology, Hospitality 2000: The Technology, we addressed some of the issues that the industry is facing. These included the closed nature of our technology architectures, the way in which we collect information on our customers, our investments in Internet, intranet and extranet technologies, and our adoption of electronic commerce. The results are not especially encouraging and suggest an industry still relatively slow to adapt to e-business. Only 39% of the industry's Web sites, for example, can handle reservations on a real-time basis, and even fewer still (19%), collect customer information. At the same time, just 22% are using "push" marketing programs and a distinct minority (just

19%), have extranets to suppliers or customers. But these adoption rates are nonetheless projected to grow and we should, therefore, expect our industry's leaders to be far more attuned to the needs of an e-business environment in the years to come.

As information technology (IT) is used to facilitate a company's entry into the world of electronic commerce, our industry's leadership will also need to overcome a natural tendency to be disappointed by the role of IT in achieving competitive advantage. For many years IT was seen as a mechanism to support back office finance and accounting functions. In the future, it inevitably will be one of the principal drivers of value creation in the new economy. But we should not be mislead by IT-in e-business, it will be the strategy, not the technology that will make the difference between success and failure. But having the strategy in place is only the first step. It must be linked to every part of the business.

Planning for e-Business

With the costs of playing in the e-business world escalating rapidly, hospitality executives should consider the four phases of what might be called the "E-Business Lifecycle." The first of these-E-Business Strategy Development and Planning-must address the market and competitive context, articulate the vision and opportunity, outline the strategy and the business case, and identify the risks. In recent years, we have frequently seen hospitality businesses put up a Web site on the Internet and consider this an e-business strategy. But without a strategy for this new form of commerce and the business planning process to drive it, such reactionary approaches stand little chance for success.

Once the plan is in place, an e-business design phase can commence to address site design, lay out the business architecture, identify the technical infrastructure, plan for performance, availability and capacity, and deal with tax issues and enterprise security.

Following the design phase, E-Business implementation will prepare for the launch with training and change enablement, implementation and integration, testing and roll-out. Once in place, E-Business Operations will need to be supported by IT and audit services, Web site activity analysis and Web site maintenance. Finally, measurement systems will need to be established to monitor performance.

As industry executives embark on this e-business lifecycle, they will need in the first stage to clearly establish the business case for investing in new technologies, systems and organizations by addressing both the cost reduction and revenue enhancement benefits. On the revenue side, there are a number of factors to consider. These include the company's ability to identify and recruit the most valuable customers; the ability to seamlessly cross-sell the company's products and services, as well as those of alliance partners; the ability to retain valuable customers and reduce attrition (especially relevant in a world of questionable brand loyalty); and finally, when and how to eliminate costly and unnecessary discounts through revenue optimization.

In this kind of environment, the property management system will no longer hold sway as the centre of the hospitality universe, but will become just one in a series of customer touch-points that will increasingly include the Internet. These touch-points will ultimately need to be fully integrated into a customer information system supported by sophisticated data warehousing and data mining technologies.

Adding to the industry's costs in this portrait of the future is the cost of grafting e-business technologies onto the industry's legacy systems. At a certain stage, it may make sense to start from scratch and ensure that every system is Web-enabled. This would allow a total interface for a high-growth e-business, thereby maximizing the customer relationship management opportunities that it presents.

Success on the Internet

As to the role of the Internet, its comprehensive reach and ubiquitous nature has already ensured its central place in the new economy. But how should we evaluate whether an Internet application is deserving of our attention? Firstly, productivity on the Internet in the years to come will be vastly improved by much higher bandwidth than is currently in place. And with higher bandwidth will come applications that can benefit from such extra capacity delivering tightly focused and reliable content to an increasingly sophisticated and demanding e-customer. If an Internet application is to succeed in the future, it will therefore need to be designed to capitalize on this coming reality.

Secondly, an Internet application needs to form a community of some sort because without a sense of place, albeit of the virtual sort participants will not have that all-important sense of belonging. And as with the industrial revolution, which drew a disparate population to centers of economic activity, so will such "intranet communities" grow in value as their populations increase in size and their economic product expands. For larger businesses that form such communities, they are developing new revenue sources and are reinventing their relationships with customers, employees, suppliers and partners. Smaller companies intent on participating in this new environment, may need to be content as a participant in an established community, rather than trying to take on the creation of a community itself. It is better, perhaps, to be one of many players in a successful space than struggling to establish an identity in a world surrounded by also-rans.

Whether large or small, community developers and marketers of the virtual sort will have to recognize that what may have appeared cool in the physical world to generations brought up in the old economy will not work in the world of e-business. Being cool and staying that way in order to get and keep attention will remain a constant challenge, especially for those keen to nurture a younger generation of travellers brought up on MTV and the Web.

Finally, the successful Internet application needs to improve service while reducing transaction costs, particularly as the balance of power in the buy/sell relationship continues its inexorable migration from sellers to buyers. Service improvement strategies will be nothing new for hospitality businesses, but it is noteworthy that service (rather than on-time delivery, price or other concerns) is the top factor that encourages return e-business.

This must be an area of focus since the current growth of e-business appears destined to outpace the supporting infrastructure and its related service at least over the short term. But as hospitality executives know, delivering good service can be expensive. Scaling the types of service response to the circumstances is a growing need, but one that can be modulated if the value of each customer can be distinguished and the response adjusted accordingly.

In considering the opportunities in hospitality e-business, industry leaders should take stock of the dynamics that are occurring in the new economy and plan accordingly. It is probably easy to dismiss the e-business world as a playground for others with products and services that are more obviously applicable. But our industry is changing, as is the world around us. And as alliance partners, vendors, customers, employees and systems all become Web-enabled, hospitality companies must adjust their strategies, organizations, processes and technologies accordingly.

Bottom Line Rules with Extended Stay

The demand for extended-stay lodging has existed since travellers with a little money in their pocket have had both the time and the inclination to spend time away from homes and businesses. The extended-stay concept dates back to 19th century England when visitors arrived at rooming houses in horse-drawn carriages, and travel was a more leisurely affair than it is today.

Today, the extended-stay lodging sector offers diverse products that vary widely throughout the world to serve the needs of modern leisure and business travellers. And while product offerings differ on the two sides of the Atlantic, there is some consensus on the definition of extended stay. This hotel sector in a variety of forms is made up of commercially run lodging properties with suites or apartments comprising one or more rooms.

As the hospitality industry enters the 21st century, extended stay represents a significant opportunity for hotel companies, developers and investors. Interest in extended stay has been spurred by high net income margins and occupancy rates that typically surpass hotel industry averages. Indeed, extended-stay lodging can be seen as a "win-win" situation for the hotel owner and investors. Higher occupancy rates, lower construction costs and shorter periods of stabilization paint an attractive picture for hoteliers in Europe and the United States. In London, for example, occupancy levels for extended-stay properties are actually better than the already strong levels posted by conventional hotels. In the United States, extended stay was reinvented as a commercial enterprise when Marriott opened its first Residence Inn in 1974. Now, the economics of the extended-stay sector have made it a magnet for real estate investment trusts (REITs) and other investment groups in hospitality.

This article draws a profile of the extended-stay lodging sector as it has evolved in the United States and Europe, with the focus on its current state of development and economic opportunity in the future.

What is Extended Stay?

Extended-stay properties operate under several banners, but generally fall into one of three categories:

- all-suite hotels;
- apartment hotels or aparthotels; and
- serviced apartments.

The traditions and definitions of extended-stay lodging, however, differ from country to country. All-suite hotels, featuring the full range of services available at a first-class hotel in the United States, are typically not considered a part of extended-stay lodging in Europe. The apartment hotel (or aparthotel) is primarily a European term. They are popular with tourists in resort areas. Serviced apartments, which are known as corporate housing in the United States, are described as boarding houses in Germany. In Eastern European cities, the term also identifies single apartments found in various buildings that are marketed and serviced by an operator.

The lexicon of extended stay in its many variations can be attributed in part to its history of development. In the United States, extended-stay lodging has been adopted by the hotel industry as an extension of hotel lodging. Hotel companies such as Marriott have begun to penetrate the corporate housing sector with extended-stay properties for business use.

As extended stay was reinvented as an extension of the hotel industry, it has continued to be identified as a complementary commercial enterprise annexed to U.S. hotel development. In contrast, the sector in Europe has grown as a separate business concept, particularly in Great Britain and France. And in Germany, the segment emerged as a product diversification among real estate developers in the early 1990s when hotels and housing were not too attractive to investors, but the combination of the two seemed to hold a potential for good returns.

Varying definitions of extended-stay lodging in Europe and the United States are also reflected in the type and volume of performance data available. In the United States, data has been developed on this segment of the hospitality industry. In Europe, however, the prevalence of serviced apartments with widely varying sites, locations and contract terms, as well as the limited supply of apartment hotels and the small markets in some cities, make it hard to obtain performance statistics and even harder to compare cities or countries from market to market.

Location

The development patterns of extended stay are also distinctly different in U.S. and European markets. European serviced apartments have traditionally been located in city centers with strong, all-season tourist and business demand. Catering mostly to leisure travellers, apartment hotels were initially unbranded. The easy availability of transportation was of primary concern. Establishing extended-stay lodging in major cities meant that many properties were converted, rather than purpose-built, offering fewer and smaller units than comparable properties in the United States. The major European aparthotel brands, Orion and Citadines, began to expand domestically in France in the late 1980s, and internationally in the early 1990s when they opened properties in Belgium, Spain, Portugal and the United Kingdom. In many cases, the bulk of supply is in the capital cities.

In the United States, however, preferred extended-stay product locations are often suburban areas, usually close to suburban office parks, hospitals or senior residence communities. Southern locations fare better, mainly due to the high volume of relocation, both by companies and their employees, and by senior citizens. Although used by leisure guests, most extended-stay accommodation is located so as to be convenient to business travellers. Moreover, it has taken U.S. operators much longer to build up the domestic market and move to international locations than their European counterparts.

The difference in location types between the United States and Europe relates to the varying patterns of settlement and the level of dependence on cars. The general preference for urban locations in Europe has important implications for the economics of the projects, since land prices will typically be much higher in central areas and available plots tend to be smaller. In general, the downtown locations have meant conversions and nontraditional solutions to space and configuration problems, rather than new construction.

The greatly varying development patterns and economics in the United States and Europe will, undoubtedly, continue to translate into varying risks and rewards for developers of extended stay properties.

U.S. most Highly Developed

The U.S. extended-stay market, the world's most developed, is primarily comprised of three extended-stay products: (1) all-suite hotels; (2) limited-service hotels, and (3) serviced apartments, the corporate housing market.

The all-suite hotel is relatively common in metropolitan areas and refers to full-service hotels with two-room units, usually with a bedroom and living room. These hotels have limited public areas and services. The apartment hotel, as its name implies, is equipped with a kitchen or kitchenette and may have one or two rooms. These hotels are often in the budget or economy class. They are typically described under the limited-service concept because they usually have fewer staff on site with food and beverage limited to a breakfast room, and they do not report food and beverage revenue. Serviced apartments-intended for the corporate housing market-are generally considered separate from the extended-stay lodging sector. Properties in this category vary widely in size, even in the same location. They have fully equipped kitchens and service is limited to daytime reception and weekly or biweekly cleaning. Typically there are no public areas such as lounges and breakfast rooms.

Supply. In the United States, there is a clear segmentation of extended-stay products among upper-, mid-and lower-tier properties, based on servicing and pricing. The pioneers in extended stay developed first-class properties. But with the increased mobility of middle-class travellers, the volume of business travel and the entry of franchise companies into the market, new brands and operators have emerged in the lower price/service tiers. The largest U.S. extended-stay hotel operators, such as Marriott and Extended-Stay America (ESA), commonly have multiple brands in each segment. In 1998, the extended-stay supply in the United States comprised 137,500 units. Of those units:

- Thirty-nine percent were in the upper tier; Marriott Residence Inn dominated that market with 303 properties.
- Twenty-nine percent fell into the mid-tier with ESA's Studio Plus at the top with 86 properties.
- Thirty-seven fell into the lower tier, with ESA leading with 222 properties.

A short history of extended-stay in the United States offers insights into the market's expansion with mid-and lower-tier properties leading in that growth. According to Smith Travel Research, upscale room supply increased by 75% between 1994 and 1998, compared to 600% for lower-category stock. The growth trend continued in 1999: by mid-year there were 179,300 rooms in extended stay properties, a 25% increase over mid-1998. Of the 30,300 rooms in the pipeline in late 1999, 37% were in the budget and economy segment, and 31% in the mid-price segment. Analysts estimate total extended-stay supply to increase to 300,000-320,000 rooms by the end of 2002, or 8% of projected hotel room supply.

Growth has been especially rapid during the last two or three years in areas with high population growth, technology industries and rapid rates of immigration. As a result, extended-stay lodging comprises up to 13% of total rooms supply in some southern cities and 9% in metropolitan centers, in contrast to only 3% of total lodging supply on a national basis.

The economics of success. Analysts expect the supply of extended-stay products to continue to grow by some 40,000 to 50,000 units per year until 2003. The interest in the sector is spurred by high net income margins and occupancy rates that typically surpass hotel industry averages. In 1998, extended-stay upper-and lower-tier properties achieved 78% and 67% occupancy, respectively. This stands in sharp contrast to the industry as a whole, which averaged 64% occupancy.

Major players that once dominated the extended-stay market are being joined by REITs and franchise companies, which have been lured by the attraction of the bottom line. Higher occupancy rates, lower construction costs and shorter periods of stabilization have caught the eye of these new entrants. Construction costs are lower because no money is spent on common area design and construction, plus the initial land costs are lower. The stabilization period tends to be shorter than hotels of comparable quality because of lower operational costs, reduced payroll, and the elimination of low-profit centers such as restaurants. Net operating income (NOI) margins of 50% are not uncommon.

More Players: the Corporate Housing Market

High mobility in the U.S. business sector has created a strong corporate housing market. Oakwood Corporate Housing, founded in 1969, is the world's largest serviced apartment agent and operator with more than 20,000 units in the United States, Thailand, the Philippines, China, and Britain. Large U.S. agents include CRS Corporate Housing, Preferred Living, Apartment Connection, and Corporate Housing Connection. On the Internet, two major search directories for U.S cities are now provided by Rent Net and Showcase Suites.

Some U.S.-based agents market properties worldwide. The largest are BridgeStreet Accommodations (4,000 units in the United States, Canada, Britain, France), Barclay International Group (Europe, the United States, Mexico, Israel) and Global Home Network (London, Paris, Prague).

The Extended-Stay Concept Dates back to 19th Century England

The extended-stay concept dates back to 19th century England and a more leisurely approach to travel than today. Now, this diverse sector primarily caters to the corporate executive needing a suite or apartment with one or more rooms.

Great Britain's Market Thriving

In the United Kingdom, serviced apartments are the most common extended-stay product, but aparthotels are increasing in number. Initially the units were designed for the corporate executive or the affluent traveller, but a growing number of mid-level properties have become available during the past few years.

Supply. London represents the most highly developed corporate market in the United Kingdom, as well as Europe at large. Extended-stay supply includes 54% high-end accommodation, while 46% are mid-level properties, which are overwhelmingly located in the West End areas of Mayfair, Kensington and Knightsbridge. The aparthotel market is primarily identified by two brands: Orion and Citadines, both part of Westmont Hospitality. The largest serviced-apartment players are Park Lane Apartments with nine properties and the Cheval Group with four properties. As chain operators enter the market, consolidation and attention to branding may be expected.

Extended Stay in London

London	*Units*	*Properties*
Apartment Hotels	300	4
Serviced Apartments		
High-end	1,600	44
Mid-level	1,100	12
Total	3,000	60

Source: Arthur andersen estimates.

Market segmentation in the United Kingdom is not based on price, as is often the case in the United States, but rather more on the size and services required by the predominant group of guests.

For instance, there are properties that cater specifically to guests from the Middle East who spend the summer in London with their families and prefer finely appointed apartments with multiple bedrooms.

The economics of success. Extended-stay occupancy levels in the United Kingdom are typically between 80% and 90%. As in the United States, those levels are somewhat higher than the already strong occupancy levels of hotels in London. Serviced apartments have prospered because of stable tourist and business demand for the product. The high quality of furnishings and spaciousness of the apartments have resulted in high rental rates. Hotels have also recognized the increasing market interest in serviced apartments and several have converted rooms into apartments for extended-stay use. Additionally, operational and marketing synergies make the construction of serviced apartments adjacent to a hotel good strategy.

Marketing. U.K.-based agents, such as Foxtons typically have international operations. The locations covered vary in scope from just a few properties in European capitals (Holiday Serviced Apartments) to offerings around the globe through partner affiliations (The Apartment Service). Some agents, however, are still concentrating on the domestic market and have only limited international offers (Regency Apartments).

Canada's Hospitality Sector: Consolidation

Canada marks the millennium with celebrations spanning the country, from the Atlantic coast to the Pacific islands of British Columbia. In fact, the Millennium Foundation of Canada was the world's first organization dedicated to creating legacies to mark the year 2000.

Moreover, Canada's hospitality sector is enjoying a strong run up to the millennium, with solid occupancy rates and a robust domestic economy-a 3.3% annual growth rate-fuelling business travel.

With the Canadian dollar hovering about US$0.67 for most of the past two years, Americans and other international travellers have discovered that Canada is a great bargain. Domestic travellers, whose spending power abroad has been significantly diminished, agree.

The result has been healthy occupancy rates in the lodging industry in many major markets across the country. In Toronto, for instance, average annual occupancy has reached a 75%, and tourist and convention spending was more than C$6.4 billion during the past year.

These positive fundamentals have not been lost on the major industry players, who through the driving force of consolidation are beginning to dominate Canada's hospitality market. During the last year, Canadian Pacific, Westmont Corp., Intrawest and others have made significant moves in their attempts to lead their industry sectors:

Canadian Pacific: In May 1998, Canadian Pacific acquired Delta Hotels, which managed or franchised approximately 10,000 rooms at 34 properties. In the deal, Canadian Pacific Hotels acquired the management company and the Delta brand, as well as leasehold interests in three properties for C$93 million. This was followed in late 1998 with the acquisition of the seven warm weather resorts of Princess Hotels from Lonrho Plc for US$540 million.

Canadian Pacific then entered into an agreement with Fairmont Hotel Management LP, creating a new hotel management company called Fairmont Hotels and Resorts Inc.

This new company will manage 69 hotels, including trophy assets such as The Plaza Hotel in New York, The Fairmont in San Francisco, and The Fairmont Copley Plaza in Boston. Canadian Pacific also continues to add prestigious domestic properties to its portfolio. These include a purchase and renovation of Le Manoir Richelieu in June 1999, which recently re-opened, as well as a new Fairmont Vancouver Airport Place, which opened in October 1999.

Based in Toronto, Canadian Pacific is Canada's largest owner-operator of full service hotels, with approximately 26,000 rooms at 69 properties and 21,500 employees across Canada, the U.S., Mexico, Bermuda, Barbados and Asia.

Westmont Corp.: Industry consolidation continued into the spring of 1999, when UniHost Corp. was acquired by Westmont

Corp. At the time, UniHost had the second largest multi-brand hotel operation in Canada and was among the top 10 globally, with a portfolio of 12,000 rooms at 122 properties–102 owned and the balance managed. This would be added to Westmont's existing portfolio of 8,500 rooms at 45 properties across Canada. The group now manages a wide variety of brands, including Comfort, Crowne Plaza, Holiday Inn, Holiday Inn Select, Marriott and Quality.

Westmont Corp. is operated in partnership between the Westmont Hospitality Group, which owns and operates more than 300 hotels in Canada, the U.S. and Europe, and Whitehall Street Real Estate Funds, which is managed by Goldman, Sachs & Co., New York.

Intrawest Corp.: In mid-1999, Vancouver-based Intrawest Corp., the owner of 10 mountain resorts, including Mammoth and Squaw Valley in the U.S. and the Whistler/Blackcomb all-season resort in British Columbia, purchased 50% of Blue Mountain Resorts Ltd., the largest mountain resort in Ontario. In other skiing niche-related news, ClubCorp Resorts, the world's largest owner and operator of private clubs and golf resorts, sold Mont-Sainte-Anne, a ski resort just north of Quebec City, to Resorts of the Canadian Rockies.

Other major deals would soon follow. In June 1999, Canadian Hotel Income Properties (CHIP), a real estate investment trust (REIT), received an hostile takeover bid from another REIT, Royal Host, which has an asset base of C$300 million, which includes 3,500 rooms at 33 hotels. CHIP, Canada's first hotel REIT, owns and operates nearly 8,000 rooms at 36 hotels across Canada. Participating with Royal Host in its bid is Westmont Corp., which stands to gain a few more hotels for its new Canadian operations.

Meanwhile, activity also is occurring in other niche sectors of Canada's hospitality industry. In mid-1998, Canada's Vinings Franchise Systems and Atlanta-based U.S. Franchise Systems, reached an agreement to bring the Microtel brand concept to Canada. Microtel Inns & Suites is a growing, franchised chain of newly constructed budget and economy hotels.

Continuing this trend to bring quality budget lodging to Canada, Cendant Corp.'s Knights Franchise Systems, Inc. signed its first international master franchise agreement for the development of Knights Inn brand hotels in Canada with AFM Hospitality of Toronto. AFM, which already holds the master franchise for Cendant's Ramada and Howard Johnson brands in Canada, expects to add more than 100 Knights Inns during the next five years, recently opening its first in Niagara Falls, Ontario. AFM also recently signed a deal with Seattle-based AST Brands LLC to bring the Aston brand to Canada.

Largely attributed to Canadian "snowbirds" escaping the winter for a warm-weather holiday in the U.S. or Caribbean, Canada has long suffered a tourism trade deficit. But with tourism spending growth rate within Canada expected to top 4% annually coupled with a declining rate of growth in tourism spending by Canadians abroad, a trade balance is projected within two to three years.

Indeed, this new strength in the hospitality sector has not been lost on the industry's major players in Canada, where consolidation is not only the major trend in the industry, but also the driving force behind change as we enter the new millennium.

The Risks in Computerization and Information Management

Hotel managers awakened in the early morning hours to news of an earthquake, fire or explosion are unlikely to think first of saving the hotel's AS400 information system or retrieving computer data tapes from off-site locations. Evacuating guests and employees is paramount. Disaster plans put people first. Nevertheless, loss of a property's information technology (IT) functions can plunge any company into operational disarray, triggering revenue losses and negative publicity that may take years to overcome. Technology systems rendered inoperable in one location can ripple through an entire hotel organization, forcing the company to fall back on manual operations. Reservations, property management and communications systems must be quickly replaced and guest data recovered to avoid major losses.

A case in point involved the bombing of New York's World Trade Centre in 1993. The terrorist act inflicted physical damage to a large area of downtown Manhattan, including an adjacent hotel. Although the hotel was evacuated in less than fifteen minutes with no fatalities, the telephone and computer system was damaged. The hotel could not account for guests and employees. Communications failures prevented management from communicating with emergency services. The loss of heat could have caused further damage to existing systems from the bursting of frozen water pipes. The hotel's experience points to one of the key elements in a technology disaster recovery plan-maintaining critical operational and financial data at an off-site storage facility. Following a disaster, off-site facilities that maintain reservation and accounting information would be available immediately for retrieval of in-house guest records, financial documents, guest history and sales information, minimizing a disaster's effect on a hotel's data and information.

Prompted by insurance companies or experience, most companies have addressed the need for a disaster recovery plan (DRP), if not put one in place. Few, however, create and maintain written plans on IT disaster recovery. In a survey conducted by Comdisco, Inc., one of the largest disaster recovery companies, it was estimated that only 45 percent of companies maintain a formal plan in the event of computer disruption.

The survey addressed the level of corporate readiness for disaster recovery, concluding that only 12 percent of enterprises have an effective disaster recovery plan. Another 6 percent were partially prepared. Fully 82 percent of companies were ineffectively prepared for a technology disaster. The survey measured: 1) data centers, 2) local area networks, and 3) enterprise wide area networks. While the survey itself was cross-industry, hospitality companies rely heavily on all three of the technology components measured. A disaster recovery plan specifically addressing technology is essential to any hotel's risk management programs.

Threats to Technology Systems

One of the most destructive events for hospitality companies occurred in September 1992 as Hurricane Iniki unleashed winds up to 200 miles per hour on the Island of Kauai, Hawaii. The damage amounted to $1.6 billion and resulted in 85 percent of the island's hotel rooms shutting down for at least two months. With 30-foot waves and complete power outages, all hotel technology systems on the island were lost. Particularly in areas with potential for destructive weather, the need for disaster recovery and off-site back up systems cannot be overstated. Hotel properties without technology disaster recovery plans may be closed for much longer periods of time than other companies.

Of the 320 technology recoveries supported by Comdisco since 1985, hardware failure was the largest cause at 24 percent, followed by hurricanes and power outages at 16 percent each, and floods accounting for another 15 percent.

The seeds of major technology failures may occur within the systems themselves. One of the largest providers of global distribution of airline and hotel reservations experienced an outage in mid-1998 due to a software error, resulting in the complete cessation of new reservations bookings for more than five hours. An outage on a system that processes an hourly average of 45,000 airline and hotel reservations can cause major service disruptions and customer dissatisfaction.

Even a supplier with a system that is 99.9 percent reliable must expect and plan for a system failure. Senior management may be unaware of the need to maintain detailed back-up plans for systems and data. Only a select few in the if department may consider systems recovery as a primary function in the event of a disaster.

Disaster Categories : 320 Recoveries Supported

Hardware Problems	24%
Power Outage	16%
Hurricane	16%
Flood	15%
Miscellaneous	12%
Fire / Explosion	7%
Bomb	5%
Earthquake	5%

Source: Comdisco

Almost all hospitality companies have one main database for reservations and guest history. Both are at risk if a disaster occurs.

In addition, the industry's reliance on technology and communication creates several less traditional risks.

The global distribution system, the importance of customer data, productivity heavily reliant on terminals and information, and the long-term effect on loyalty of a single negative experience, are additional risks particularly present in the hospitality industry. In addition, companies are racing to build information about customer and spending patterns, investing millions of dollars in systems to institutionalize this knowledge. Loss of these systems and databases is analogous to organizational memory' loss. While rebuilding physical property may take several years, guest loyalty and behavioral history' may often require more time and money.

Creating a Disaster Recovery Plan

Clearly, the development of a technology disaster recovery' plan is an essential part of any company/s risk management program. Its development and documentation at a minimum will require the following steps:

Take an Inventory: Include items critical to the business, including the reservation system, database and the systems that support it. Telecommunications (dial-up lines, frame relay, dedicated lines and the Internet) can be included as support systems.

Assess Unavailability: Assess what will occur if critical systems are absent over specific periods of time. Ask key questions for each system. What foreseeable impact exists if accounting functionality is down, for example, or the property management system applications are non-responsive? Determine the maximum amount of downtime for these critical items before there will be a significant impact on the business.

Identify Alternatives: Identify disaster recovery alternatives for critical functions. Hospitality companies might decide that a "hot site" is a reasonable alternative with the loss of a reservation system. A hot site is a computer and data processing centre with computers in place and waiting to be used by a company experiencing a disaster. Most hot sites are permanent facilities where the company can recreate its computing environment.

Determine Alternative Requirements: Identify what is needed for an alternative to be implemented. Minimum requirements may involve telecommunications with certain bandwidths or dial-up lines. A specified level of power redundancy may be required for servers. Agreements with hardware vendors or vendors who provide disaster recovery sites may also be an option.

Identify Costs: Gain an understanding of the total cost for each alternative. Examples of common costs include arranging hardware agreements with vendors or the cost of having a disaster recovery site available for use. Installation fees, purchase of redundant telecommunications, and the purchase of upgrading telecommunications (i.e., increasing bandwidth) are other common costs. Some hospitality companies may have additional costs relating to reservation system development time as a minimum alternative requirement.

Estimate the Recovery Period: Estimate the amount of time until the critical systems become available. Each alternative should have a specified recovery period.

Define the Limitations: Determine the limitations of each system back-up or alternative, including vendor agreements or hot sites. The plan needs to address questions of hardware replacement, especially if it is rare, discontinued, or a lag time exists between the purchase order and its delivery. The cost of an alternative or the length of time until availability may also be limitations.

Determine the Benefits: Weigh the benefits of each alternative. Use the benefits of a faster recovery in the event of a disaster as a competitive advantage.

Test the Plan Annually: Document the test and test results as a best practice to provide a record of any problems encountered and their resolution.

IT Training in Disaster Recovery: Provide proper training of IT personnel for implementation of the disaster recovery plan.

When a disaster or hardware failure does occur, planning rigor will make all the difference in the speed of recovery. A completed disaster recovery plan for technology systems allows companies to realize large returns on a relatively small investment-minimizing what may otherwise be an unnecessary and costly outcome of disasters.

Hotel Companies Plan Future Strategies after Consolidation

The pace of consolidation within the global hotel industry has quickened in the last year. The resulting organisations are now concentrating their resources on how to develop and add further value to their existing and inherited brands. The strategies of Bass Hotels and Resorts, Starwood Lodging and Patriot American Hospitality illustrate the priority that hotel companies give to increasing brand awareness in a competitive marketplace.

Bass Hotels and Resorts

At a recent conference in New Orleans, it was confirmed that Bass Hotels and Resorts (BHR) will continue to focus on brand preference and the distribution of each chain in its relevant market. BHR is also planning a significant investment and aggressive expansion. Some US$1 billion is destined for the Inter-Continental brand, whilst increased advertising and promotion of loyalty schemes will enhance the market's awareness of the company 5 other brands, in particular Holiday Inn Express and Staybridge Suites. The company is also focusing on boosting its presence in the Middle East with several major projects under construction in Egypt, further expansion in Saudi Arabia, and a number of developments in Lebanon and Jordan.

Starwood Lodging

Following the acquisition of Sheraton and Westin, Starwood has invested US$400 million in its portfolio. During the first half of 1998, 49 management agreements were signed with a further 20 scheduled for the latter part of the year. Twenty-two hotels have been converted to the Westin or Four Points brands. For the new brand, sites under construction include five in North America, three in New York, one in Seattle and one in San Francisco. Starwood also announced that it will be combining its REIT and Starwood Hotels and Resorts to create a single C-corp with the REIT as a subsidiary. This allows the corporation to work around the change in federal law that precludes "paired share" REITs from growing through future asset acquisitions.

Patriot American Hospitality

During the third quarter of 1998, 19 hotels were converted to the Wyndham brand, and Patriot predicts that the brand will have grown from 78 units at the beginning of the year to 185 owned or managed properties by December 1998.

During the second quarter, nine former Grand Heritage hotels were repositioned as part of the Wyndham Grand Heritage brand. In the meantime, the luxury hotel division, which currently consists of 11 properties, will be branded Grand Bay Hotels and Resorts. The existing Carefree Resorts, Grand Bay Hotels and Golden Door Spa will he folded into this new operation. The roll-out of this brand will be limited to between 25 and 30 hotels in the next five years to maintain the exclusivity of the product.

Gambling in the Las Vegas

Whilst the rest of the world looks cautiously to the future and development plans are put on hold or scaled down, Las Vegas is once again breaking the mold.

During the next two and a half years, 20,000 new rooms will be added. A large percentage of these are in the form of "mega-hotels" such as Hilton's "Paris' property with replicas of the Eiffel Tower and Arc de Triomphe. The scale of this new building boom is significant in itself, but the fact that it is occurring at a time of such global economic uncertainty, has raised questions about the scale of development.

There is also the added worry that the local hotel market has softened somewhat, with occupancy rates now at 86 percent compared with more than 90 percent two years ago.

These levels are, of course, still extremely high, but when companies operate on the assumption of full capacity it becomes a significant drop. The turmoil in the Asian market is also taking its toll, especially with the intentional high rolling gamblers. In addition, Las Vegas 10 years ago had a monopoly in legalised gambling; today additional jurisdictions have legalised gambling.

The competition is getting tougher. In an attempt to attract more families to Las Vegas in the early years of this decade, the city introduced Disney-style entertainment, but gambling and other forms of themed entertainment do not always combine well and the results have been somewhat mixed. ... and for the rest of the world?

In spite of concerns over current and future trading conditions, many hotel companies are considering further investment and expansion across the world. Recent announcements include.

Following a 22 percent increase in profit for the six months to June 1998, U.K.-based Millennium & Copthorne Hotels has announced expansion plans. These are said to include continental Europe and gateway cities in the United States, such as Chicago, Los Angeles, Washington DC, Dallas and Atlanta.

Paris-based Accor SA is undergoing an aggressive expansion plan in Europe and South America. In Poland, the company is seeking to establish subsidiaries and joint venture partners to assist them in their development plan in central Europe. There are to be over 25 Ibis properties within the next two years. The company hopes to establish a network of over 30 Etap budget hotels during the next five years. In Brazil, Accor aims to have developed 5,500 rooms in 40 cities by the year 2002 with an initial investment of US$21 million.

Accor is also continuing its interest in expanding into Asia. Speculation continues over their interest in bidding for Century International. It has been reported in the French press that Accor is interested in expanding via the partial acquisition of Hong Kong-based Regal Hotels International.

For the first nine months of 1998, Starwood announced a 7 percent increase in revenue per available room (RevPar) for their owned hotels worldwide, with increases in Europe, Latin America and North America of 14 percent, 8 percent and 6 percent respectively.

This resulted in a 14 percent increase in EBITDA. The casino operation faired equally well with an increase in revenues of 28 percent. Starwood's development plans not only include the hotels division, but also the casino group. By the year 2000 there will be a Caesar's riverboat in Indiana, USA with 90,000 square feet of casino space and a 500-room hotel. A joint venture in Johannesburg, South Africa with Guateng will create 75,000 square feet of casino space and a 200-room hotel.

For the lodging brands of Marriott International in the United States for quarter three, RevPar grew by 5 percent compared with the previous year. Results for the international properties were moderately lower in 1998 due to the difficult trading conditions in the Asia-Pacific region. This dip was partially offset by profit growth in Europe, the Middle East and Latin America. However, the company expects to increase its portfolio by more than 150,000 rooms during the next five years, 30,000 of which are to open in 1998 within 200 hotels. Utilising US$500 million of equity, Swissotel is eager to increase its current portfolio of 24 hotels to 60 properties by the year 2000. Currently the portfolio covers five continents with hotels concentrated in the main business centres and resort areas. For the future, Swissotel is seeking a presence in Los Angeles, San Francisco, Miami, London, Paris, Singapore, Hong Kong and Tokyo. One may be surprised to learn that hotel companies are seeking developments in Asia, but Swissotel management reportedly believes that the economic situation in that region provides a good opportunity for growth.

In Jericho Peace Prevails on the Gaming Tables

The Oasis Casino opened in September 1998 and is situated in the Jordan valley, close to the ancient town of Jericho. Operated by Casinos Austria, the recently opened US$150 million Oasis has been attracting large numbers of Israelis. According to reports, in the first weeks after opening, at least 1,000 people each day could be seen waiting to enter the casino, which had already reached capacity. Frustrated crowds even tried to enter the premises through the staff entrance to gain a chance to try their luck at one of the 45 gambling tables and 220 slot machines.

This dramatic exposure of frustrated demand has spurred Israeli politicians to revive a governmental committee, which was appointed by late Prime Minister Yitzhak Rabin, to establish two casinos in Israel on a trial basis. The Gavish Committee has previously had to deliberate over the possible pros and cons of developing a casino in the highly popular Red Sea destination of Eilat. The initial decision on opening a casino was postponed but remains eagerly awaited by local hotel operators who are expecting strong increases in demand from visiting gamblers. The Oasis Casino is expected to generate positive side effects for the local economy, supporting the 30,000 population resident in Jericho. The casino employs some 1,000 locals, and the economic spillover from the traffic created by gamblers who come from Jerusalem and even as far as Tel Aviv is having a positive effect on the local population's attitude towards the casino. Spending in Jericho has increased considerably, which in turn has had a positive impact on a number of critics who had previously rallied against the casino prior to its opening.

U.K. Travel Industry Consolidation to Set a Global Trend

Consolidation of the U.K. travel industry has progressed at a rapid pace during the past six months. The greatest level of activity has been witnessed by the major players, as they aim to fight off competition by increasing market share and the number of distribution channels in existing markets, or obtain footholds in new markets.

Some examples of major deals in recent months include:

- Acquisition of Unijet and Hayes & Jarvis by First Choice for £134 million in June 1998;
- Purchase of Direct Holidays by Airtours in July 1998 for £80.7 million;
- Acquisition of Crystal Holidays by Thomson for £66.2 million in August 1998; and
- Announcement of the merger between Thomas Cook and U.S.-based Carlson in October 1998, which, if approved by the Monopolies and Mergers Commission, would create one of the world's largest leisure travel companies.

The high level of activity by the leading U.K. tour operators has forced other companies to take a closer look at their distribution channels. In October 1998, First Choice, Britain's third largest tour operator, unveiled its new distribution strategy. In addition to purchasing retail travel agent Bakers Dolphin for £12 million and acquiring minority stakes in the regional chains Hays Travel and Holiday Express, it is also planning to open 533 new shops within the next two years.

Simultaneously, First Choice is buying a 25 percent stake in Holiday Hypermarkets. Holiday Hypermarkets is a pioneering new concept in retail travel, and it is estimated that the 10,000 square foot shops will generate fifteen times the number of bookings of an ordinary travel shop.

At the same time, U.K. companies have begun to diversify geographically through acquisitions in Northern Europe and North America. In October 1998, Airtours announced the acquisition of US-based tour operator Vacation Express for US$24.3 million. In Europe, operators are very keen to gain a foothold in Europe's largest outbound market, Germany. Airtours was the first U.K. tour operator to gain entry, with the purchase of a 29 percent stake in Frosch Touristik (FTi) and a further option to purchase the remainder in 2002. Thomson is also pursuing foreign expansion, having almost reached its maximum allowable market share in the United Kingdom. Under U.K. law more than 25 percent market share would technically make it a monopoly and consequently in breach of the rules of the Monopolies and Mergers Commission. According to Travel Industry Digest, Thomson is reportedly believed to lie interested in a potential alliance with Neckermann, Germany's second largest tour operator.

The current activity from the major U.K. tour operators is likely to continue, as they remain eager to gain a foothold in foreign markets. The Thomas Cook/Carlson deal indicates activity will most likely move away from takeovers into formal alliances and share swaps as a means of consolidation..

4

The E-Business Agenda

E-business (Electronic Business) is the convergence of communication and information processing technology within core business process and culture. It is an enabling *business* process made possible with technology that provides more information and faster information delivery.

It is neither a separate technology for business nor a separate business process. To most people, E-business incorrectly conjures an umbrella of radical initiatives for doing business on the Internet—rather than for efforts at enabling business as usual and extending marketing, sales, and support opportunities merely through a new channel.

The E-business umbrella comprises other indistinct terms lacking exact meanings and context, such as *I-business, E-commerce,* and *I-commerce,* where "I" and "E" refer to "Internet" and "Electronic" integration. Recognize that E-business is not *E-technology* nor even *E-computing*. Even I-business is still *business* with its emphasis clearly on commercial acumen rather than technical skills.

E-business is first and foremost business requiring experience in money flows, deal-making, sales and marketing, fulfillment, business responsibility, and the hot seat of making weekly payroll. Technology is only a supporting player, not the leading actor. Technology enables or inspires E-business innovation. It makes or breaks implementations. It opens doors for contracts, new business, or integration assignments where competent skills seem limited.

However, success with e-business is judged in the language of business—not of technology. The role of business is one empowered by sharing information and making deals. Instead, the power of technology roles is enhanced by hoarding information or purposely misdirecting its application.

There is a stark contrast between the business skills of who you know, what you know, and how you broker complex deals and the technical arts with magician-like penchant against revealing secrets to the uninitiated. It not only hobbles traditional information technology roles but also undermines pure E-business initiatives. The agendas are different, so much so, that they reverse each other. Until the business culture of sharing meshes with a technology culture inbred in withholding, the success rates and returns for E-business initiatives are likely to fail at the same rates of existing technology—at about 90% through problems of scope creep, not what the user wanted, inability to scale, mismatches in expectations, and poor usability.

Most people misjudge E-business equating it to the purely American model of Internet-driven catalog sales supported by virtual shopping carts and credit card payment processing. Yes, the E-business umbrella does include Internet schemes, the so-called I-business, but garners a miniscule market share. American models for E-business are mostly based on evolutionary concepts that leverage the Internet for distribution, delivery, and global access. I-business remains unproven, a segment epitomized by the still-as-yet-unprofitable Amazon.com and Ebay. E-business, on the other hand, is profitable, but it is a different from the high-profile I-business; it really is a nuts-and-bolts business. It is driven by finance, multiple languages, multiple currencies and payments, and manipulated by exchange rates, current balances, taxes, tariffs, and governmental incentives. While I-business schemes are proving compelling (or at least cannibalistic of existing channels) if not yet profitable, smarter innovators are seeing I-business as a necessary lost-leader presence within a new and larger E-business sales and marketing channel transcending the Internet.

Specifically, E-business includes EDI (Electronic Data Interchange), ERP (Enterprise Resource Planning), manufacturing supply chains, CRM (Customer Resource Management), health care billing, automotive supply, global customer support, anywhere/anytime banking and brokerage, and business-to-business integration.

These focused solutions demonstrate positive returns on investment. It includes the electronic notification of orders through such time-proven supply chains as EDI, wire transfers, facsimile ordering, telephone ordering, catalog sales, credit card payments, extension of business credit, voice mail, and e-mail. E-business sibling, e-commerce, which like it is just vague term, generally refers to business-to-business initiatives, such as the integration of backend systems with customers and vendors.

In aggregate, business-to-business communications and transaction processing represents more than 99.9% of all E-business transactions. In contrast, greater than 90% of E-business is EDI, which is unlikely to vanish. It is likely to transition into new forms of end-to-end integrated transaction processing, including XML (Extended Markup Language, which is just a presentation method) and EDI performed using XML. At the least, EDI will not disappear although it might get a new name just as Information Technology (IT) is transforming into E-business.

About 9% of e-business is transacted as banking and credit card events through clearing houses, payment transfer systems, check reimbursements, and proprietary channels. I-business (Internet catalog sales) represents 1% of US retail sales, a blip in the E-business statistics, which are 0.06%. Equating Internet-driven sales with E-business misrepresents the potential for any other global E-business agenda and downplays proven IT skills thereby undermining a successful business agenda.

Although Intel, Dell, Compaq, and other companies—independently—have announced Internet and E-business sales volumes in excess of $1 US Billion per month (June 1999), it is misleading to view these efforts as successful I-business ventures at this time. Two important business assessments remain fuzzy. First, these sales are cannibalizing existing direct, wholesale, and value-added sales, creating high-profile channel conflicts and fulfillment dislocations in preexisting structures and relationships.

For example, Levi Strauss upset Federated and its other wholesale buyers by competing for retail share.

Second, although these I-business sales volumes are enormously large, the companies and their auditors have yet to justify the margins against the fully-burdened Internet site and marketing costs. Few retail pure I-business ventures show profits at this time, less than 1%, as reported by the U.S. Department of Commerce (recently broken out as a new statistical tracking category) or by many independent research organizations.

However, other E-business ventures are enormously profitable, without financial transactions of any kin d.

For example, National Semiconductor, in particular, as a low-cost manufacture competing against worldwide labor and currency markets, benefits by forecasting exact preproduction sales levels with 3O (sigma) accuracy.

The logistics for global E-business require multiple languages and multiple currencies. The point is that E-business is not purely an Internet play, not even a pure sales transaction process, but rather business enabled through integrated communications and processing.

E-business reflects a substantial and explosively growing component of business. Information technology has transitioned to E-business, even if the terms seem different. Communications has transitioned to E-business. Wide area networking has transitioned to E-business.

Local area networks, desktop computing, and Internet-distributed processing is becoming part of E-business and losing any standalone importance apart from IT or E-business.

If anything concrete, E-business is the convergence of communication and information processing technology supporting the core business. To represent E-business as anything else, such as a technical tour de force or a radical business method, overvalues technology and deflates existing business skills. The agenda for profitable E-business is to enable traditional business and financial decision-making, sometimes with greater efficiency and faster speeds.

How Banks Fit in an Internet Commerce Business Activities Model

The Internet commerce arena has become a very complex world. Millions of sites wait for visitors offering a vast number of products, services and information. The dynamic and flexible nature of the medium as well as its ubiquitous reach have leveraged a great variety of business activities. New intermediaries have appeared in the virtual value chains and new types of business, e.g. the virtual organizations, have arisen as a result of the innovative business models that emerged at the early dawn of the net economy era.

The plethora of business activities exploiting the capabilities of Internet as a global, cheap, multimedia distribution/delivery channel may confuse the newcomers and prevent those willing to enter it due to the lack of a market chart that shows clearly what is happening in this area.

Banks and financial institutions, in general, have established an Internet presence with various objectives. "E-banking will soon mature into an offensive business strategy rather than a passive 'must-have'" [Hirst 1999]. Some banks are there because their competitors have been.

Some others prefer a 'wait-and-see' practice. Some are using it as a banking channel, being part of their distribution/delivery management. Very few, however, have set a strategy for exploiting the opportunities offered by Internet. To do this, they need some sort of e-business activities chart, showing the structure of the Internet market in order to decide which business is relevant to theirs and where to invest on. Moreover, decision-makers would like to know what are the Internet business activities in which other banks have been engaged in.

This is exactly the purpose of this paper. To provide a concise, comprehensive way of modelling the Internet commerce market, because its business activities have not been systematically chartered, and, second, identify the role of banks in the Internet commerce world. Examples of current initiatives of banks are given and suggestions are made for possible new areas for differentiation.

The Role of Banks in the Internet World

Initially, banks promoted their core capabilities, being products, channels and advice, through the Internet. Then, they entered internet commerce market as providers/distributors of their own products and services. "The trend toward electronic delivery of products and services is occurring dramatically in the financial service industry (something we call "e-Finance") where the shift is party a result of consumer demand, but also of a ruthlessly competitive environment" [Geyer 1997]. More recently, due to advances in Internet security and the advent of relevant protocols (e.g. Integrion, OFX, SET etc.), banks discovered that they can play again their primary role as financial intermediators and facilitators of complete commercial transactions via electronic networks and especially via the Internet.

However, "financial service organizations are implementing multiple styles of electronic financial services" [Schiller 1997]. Some have chosen a 'direct web presence', others have opted either for 'owners of an financial services organization-centric electronic marketplace', or for 'participants in a non-financial services organization-centric electronic marketplace' [Schiller 1997]. However, this scheme is very abstract and vague and does not support any decision-making process for the banking institutions to define a niche market for them to invest on and compare with their rivalries.

An Internet Commerce Market Structure Model

The following model charts the Internet commerce market, by distinguishing the types of business activities of the Internet commerce and, thus, categorizing the role that they various participants, including banks, play in this market.

Technology Providers

The technology infrastructure is an integral part of the Internet commerce edifice. Telecommunication organizations, Internet Service Providers, Web hosting services organizations, Web development software houses and IT integrators are technology providers who have flourished by the presence of the Internet commerce business. A few banks are considering to spin-off their web technology resources and start-up a new business as Internet technology providers.

Content Providers

The richness of the medium's content has been a critical success factor in attracting a sharply growing number of web sites visitors and commercial users. Content providers are the source of the raw material that flows through the medium and upon which intermediators offer added value. Four major categories of content providers have been identified. For example, banks feed their web sites with their content which usually includes a corporate profile, product and pricing information, rates, some application forms etc.

- *Producers, owners, manufacturers, retailers.* They possess a good, service, piece of information that want to advertise, promote, sell, distribute over the Internet. Most banks operate a web site with a catalogue of their products and services for promotion and communication purposes. A growing number of banks worldwide offer e-banking/ web banking/internet banking, whereby their customers manipulate their personal finances and execute transactions via the internet.
- *E-brokerage.* Activities or firms that offer an interface to the end-user/customer for access to various products/services. An e-brokerage activity may be an agent that presents a variety of products (e.g. loans), rates them, makes suggestions and facilitates purchasing. Or it can be a means to trading.

A special type for e-brokerage is *information brokerage.* Web sites that give access to databases of special interest topics are information brokers. Downloading can be free-of-charge or not. Some banks' sites act as information brokers because they provide access to rates, indices, economic information and reports pertaining to the whole sector in which they operate in, rather than giving information pertaining to their own organization only.

- *E-services providers.* These business activities are not carried out in brick-and-mortar premises, but they are realized in the virtual world. Usually they provide services for participants of the Internet commerce world.

Virtual banks can offer cheaper rates due to the lack of labour and premises costs. The comfort of remote, self-service banking that virtual banks offer augments the quality of service perceived by their customers.

- *'add-on' material providers:* In this category fall the advertisers and infomediaries ("sole or main source of revenue derives from capturing consumer information and developing detailed profiles of individual customers for use by selected third-party vendors" [Hagel 1997]). Banks advertise their products, such as cards, loans etc. by using banners or other advertisement tricks on other's web pages, paying a fee to the owner of the advertisement space.

Context Providers

This type of Internet commerce business is about new intermediaries. They 'accommodate' context in a manner that adds value to its content components. Generally, context providers are e-marketplaces owners. The content scope of an e-marketplace may extend vertically or horizontally, addressing the interests of an industry sector, a user community, a special purpose or it may aggregate material from various general or related areas.

- *e-marketplaces:* "Marketplaces that connect buyers and sellers are up and running in many product categories, and are creating value by making trading more efficient. [...] There are three types of marketplace: those controlled by sellers, those controlled by buyers, and those controlled by neutral third parties [Berryman 1998]". In most of the cases, e-marketplaces are neutral, i.e. they are set up by third-party intermediaries which host sellers/merchants. Buyer-or Seller-driven marketplaces are often encountered in e-procurement, where products are asked for or offered, respectively. Specific applications include e-mall owners, e-auction houses, portal owners, and directory services owners. There are banks that host an e-mall putting forward their brand name as a guarantee for on-line shopping trust. A bank could also serve as an e-auction house because it can assure the securitization of the bidders, but, to the best of our knowledge, no banks have entered into this area yet.

Enablers

These are value adders that enable more transactions in the internet commerce market. Typical enablers are payment service providers, clearing houses, and trust guarantors. Banks are increasingly building payment infrastructure with various security mechanisms (SSL, SET etc.) because there is tremendous potential for profit as more and more payments will pass through the Internet.

The challenge for banks is to offer a payments back-bone system that will be open enough to support multiple payment instruments (credit cards, debit cards, direct debit to accounts, e-checks, digital money etc.) and scalable enough to allow for a stable service regardless of the workload.

Certification authorities enable secure transactions by managing the distribution and circulation of digital certificates, either SET certificates or not. Banks are qualified to play the role of a certification authority first at their customers and then offer it as a service. Security and trust infrastructures are obviously within the scope of banking in its broader sense. An example of such an infrastructure is Barclays' Endorse. "Endorse is a digital signature service enabling individuals and businesses to transact with trust over the Internet. The Endorse smart card creates the Members digital signature, which is used to guarantee the identity of the individual signing electronic data. The signature also protects the integrity of the data by detecting alteration during transmission". Based on the security and trust ingredients, other enabling services, such as copyright and intellectual property enforcement, can be offered by banks. "Magex secures the distribution of content and processing payments for digital information. Not only does Magex enable the delivery of digital content (music, films, agents, books, commercial information) but also offers persistent protection of copyright and collects the micro-payments" [SemaGroups brochure].

Open Governance: The Case for Unregulated E-Commerce

The Internet in it's current state represents a wild lawless frontier to large organisations afraid of liability risks but has proved to be a successful breeding ground for start up companies willing to face these risks in search of big rewards. The wealth of information and ease of use is proving to be irresistible to the consumer and larger organisations are keen to exploit this market but lack the legal framework required for protection.

Existing (UK) legislation covers E-commerce across three main areas: infrastructure (computer and communications law), information (data protection and intellectual property law) and commerce (contract law). These laws still present a large grey area to a business due to the question of jurisdiction; there is no uniform 'Internet law' rather local laws related to each trading location. This also raises the question of the definition of 'trading location', is this the country of product origin, country of destination, country of economic activity or of the server location.

Conventional laws in all countries struggle with issues such as the "jurisdiction question" largely due to the way in which legal systems (the world over) have developed. It has taken centuries for common law on contract to develop in England and Wales through disputes between aggrieved parties being taken to the courts and judgements then made providing legal precedent for future cases.

Over time laws have been challenged and developed to reflect society's changing standards. The problem with regulating E-commerce law is that of growth rate, E-commerce may be a relatively small concern at the moment (hence there is little in the way of case law) but it is predicted to grow at an explosive rate. To provide a legal framework a number of judgements are required unless a break is made from tradition and a predictive legislation defined. At the moment however no one organisation or body is in a position to define this legislation, certainly the UK government has shirked from this task.

The problems associated with implementing and interpreting legislation have been mentioned but what of the timing of implementation. If regulation is adopted prematurely there is a distinct risk of creating a rigid framework with potentially harmful laws restricting the growth of E-commerce. If these laws are adopted on a local, UK or EU for example, rather than global basis there is a risk that governments (law making bodies) may impose uncompetitive conditions in their regions of influence. But what if policymakers wait too long. A plethora of cases may eventually arise or 'non-wired' countries may be left in the cold due to the reluctance of their governments to conform to western moral and legal standards.

In defining a legal operating framework a variety of different party interests must be balanced. Businesses require clarity, governments require the ability to adopt their own interpretations of law and judges require a legal reference. It is clear at the moment that no one policy maker can define laws in an unbiased manner that can apply the world over, so why try. The OECD and UNCITRAL (United Nations Commission on International Trade Law) have begun to define high level guidelines for international contracts but these should not be developed into rigid law, rather left as operating principles. An 'Open Governance' system is required rather than procedural regulation. Virtual legal operating zones of mutual understanding will develop over time between industries and it is the cases these industries bring to the courts which will clarify the guidelines at the virtual interfaces between countries.

So where does that leave the current situation and the doubts I may have as a consumer about trust with dealing with potentially untraceable virtual operators who may be able to take my digital cash and move server locations in seconds.

The answer is simple and lies in the heart of open governance – autonomy and choice. Every decision involves risks and benefits and it is up to the buyer to choose whom to purchase from. If I have doubts about a virtual supplier's credibility then I may prefer to see evidence of their (products) existence, perhaps by visiting them and buying conventionally. If I would like more guaranteed legal protection then I may print of a 'hard copy' contract and have it signed physically not electronically. In doing so I would however incur the cost inconvenience and time wastage.

It is very easy to forget what business is taking place in the current hysteria surrounding E-commerce but both businesses and consumers must bear in mind that the Internet is merely a means of communication, the fundamental business transactions taking place have not been altered. The successful E-commerce businesses or suppliers of the next millennium will effectively answer both legal and consumer trust issues themselves by holding this principle to heart. Business to business trust will be built on open and honest communication as will effective consumer marketing strategies through the development of web links, recommendations and the exploitation of the Internet communication medium. Remember the words of one of Britain's most recognised scientists on being credited with revealing the molecular structure of DNA-'Communication is the Essence of Science' and apply this to the E-business situation.

E-commerce: In the Market or in the Marketplace?

Today, 44% of North American companies are selling on-line. Thirty-six per cent more expect to do so by next summer, according to Lucent Technologies. By 2003, International Data estimates that the 159 million people online world-wide will have mushroomed to 510 million. This community is made up of your usual mixed bag of surfers and legitimate customers. Exactly the sort of people that pass through your average retail outlet. Just how do you get passers-by to do more than kick the tires?

To start with one needs to be more than a little "Internet savvy": you need to be fully aware of the virtual community, how it is reached and how its dollars are captured.

You need to understand the consequences of business operations and service delivery in a near light speed environment. But the chances are you may be one of the 75% of CEOs that Price Waterhouse Coopers say don't regularly log on to the Net. Nevertheless, you could be approving large sums to establish an on-line presence.

Robert D. Hof wrote a whimsical piece on ecommerce in the March 10, 1999 *Business Week*. It was in the form of a memo to senior management on the implications of doing business electronically. In part he said, "We have to get off our butts and get wired. Not just E-mail. Not just Web browsers or a Web site. I mean the big kahuna: electronic commerce. Our future depends on nothing less than transforming our company into a full-fledged e-business. Now. Or else we're roadkill." His shock language was directed at that 75%.

But Hof's "roadkill" can also be experienced by those who *do* plunge in. Audits of system development exercises almost invariably discover that, even when project scope *was* defined, it seemed to become longer and wider as the project advanced. But often scope is not defined. Scope uncertainty is a principal reason why IT projects far too often end up costing more than anticipated, generating products that don't exactly reflect what senior management originally had in mind. The risks can be considerable.

The problem is requirements definition. Senior management may have a sound, and profound conceptual understanding of what it wants. The IT team may be highly proficient. Failure occurs in bridging business concepts, technical planning and development. Sometimes no one is all that clear on just what is trying to be achieved. In such cases, all parties struggle to convert a mix of needs, wants, ideas and options into a workable tool or utility, often under the guns of business expediency and other pressures. These pressures may be so great that the team leaps into development before sufficient time has been spent on the necessary preliminaries. The problem may be compounded when technical novices push their IS department to deliver before the business homework is done.

We need to know globally, conceptually and tactically just what it is we are dealing with here. Few would disagree that Amazon.com practices e-commerce. Airline on-line ticket reservations and purchasing are evidently candidates, as are eBay, Mbank and a host of others. But what of promotional Websites? What of ATMs? What about call centres that use telephony? And has all the Internet and Web hype really displaced the key functions of EDI?

Telephones, FAX machines and dedicated data lines are very much a part of today's business delivery infrastructure, and will continue to be so for the foreseeable future. Clearly "ecommerce" is a whole lot more than one technology and one user community. It is about the use of many technologies by many different individuals and organizations. The challenge is matching technology to need.

Let's start with some basic definitional issues. To begin with we are not all that clear about what "electronic" means. "Electronic" is not a synonym for "Internet". And we should not equate "ecommerce" with the World Wide Web. What is "commerce" in the electronic domain? Is it mere "presence"? Is it a transaction, or is it an event that by definition includes funds transfer? In my view "ecommerce" is an electronically facilitated business event.

These events may use technology in whole or in part. Importantly, activity on electronic channels must serve the corporate bottom line.

But serving the bottom line does not necessarily translate into immediate profit. For what could be a very long time, ecommerce involvement could be a loss leader. In effect, it may cost you to be there with no, or little, revenue assurance. In such cases, your corporate ecommerce strategy ought to be written around positioning yourself for future on-line business effectiveness. Either you, or your market, may not be sufficiently developed to make digital money.

There are many questions here but there is no denying that *whatever* ecommerce is exactly, it is big, and getting bigger. *CIO Canada* in August 1999 predicted that 1999 on-line retail revenue would be 145% over 1998.

The Boston Consulting Group, in its *State of Online Retailing 2.0* said that "online retailers in Canada and the US will collect US$36.6 billion during 1999". Amazon.com is said to be the third largest book retailer in Canada, having achieved this status without any apparent promotion. Their 1998 sales were a reported $600 million plus. Auto By Tel is the second largest auto dealer in the US. (There are related initiatives under development in Canada by Microforum Inc., Tim Dealer Services and National Bank called "e-FINCOM".)

Business Week notes that "e-commerce (activity) between businesses is five times as much as consumer ecommerce, or about $43 billion last year. And by 2003, Forrester Research Inc. figures it will balloon to US$1.3 trillion.

That's 10 times consumer ecommerce, constituting 9% of all U.S. business trade—and more than the gross domestic product of either Britain or Italy. Around 2006 or so, it might reach up to 40% of all U.S. business."

Further, *Business Week* notes that "the on-line superstore Buy.com undersells rivals, sometimes at or below cost, hoping to make profits off advertising. It hit $125 million in sales its first full year in 1998—more than any company in history." (Read the *Business Week* quote again. In the ecommerce world, business rules vary more than a little from the traditional).

The numbers are impressive, but they are no more dramatic than are the pitfalls. The ecommerce playing field is really more a minefield than a sportsfield. Many enter it without taking time to put on the proper gear or learn the rules well. Some appear to forget that in business the bottom line pervades all: there has to be a business case behind every initiative, even if that initiative is putting free cereal samples in 10,000 mail boxes. Consequently the Internet is full of commercial and institutional Web sites that do not support the enterprise; in fact, some sites are so poorly put together and infrequently updated that they telegraph negative impressions.

Ecommerce is rarely all or nothing. It is rare that one is either fully into it or not in it at all. Likely the "not at all" scenario is no longer an option. Even independently owned bed and breakfasts now understand that they at least need an e-mail address, if not a full on-line reservation system. But it is infrequently "all" as well, unless you are a dedicated "virtual company" selling insurance, banking services or books to connected customers.

What this means is that the enterprise of the present is, indeed must be, ecommerce active. The challenge for business managers is in defining what ecommerce is for them. Importantly, they need to define what elements of their operation will be on-line, in whole or in part. They need to determine where the value-add is in providing speed over person-to-person contact and vice versa. They need good development and management tools, and they need techniques for measuring results.

Companies frequently assign their ecommerce development activity to their IS shop, to communications or marketing with little or no direction. There is the assumption that this is a new vehicle, yes, but the rules are the same. Nothing could be further from the truth. Example: your very attractive corporate logo may look real good on a print publication, but the colours could come out frightful on a Web page. Also, staff who is not given quality direction will err on the side of quantity. Many managers believe that high volumes of on-line information are a success measure. Rather, it may send messages about your lack of focus.

More than a few organizations who have established a Web presence brag about the "hits" they are realizing. But these huge numbers don't seem to translate into business activity and revenue. Why would that be? The answer is that an Internet "hit" is no more than a customer glancing in your shop window as he walks by. Something may or may not register with this person but you have no easy way of finding that out. Effective on-line firms track very carefully what their electronic visitors do – where they go, how long they ponder a page, whether they go back and re-visit a site. Software is now available to allow you to measure just exactly what impression your site is making. This is equivalent, to a degree, to a shop owner being able to reach out of his store and sift through the short-term memory of a passer-by.

Far too little time is given to the client issue. The Internet, the Web and on-line services put the enterprise in a global community. A lot of that community is looking for something for nothing. Many of your enquiries and contacts will be, really, a waste of your time. But one never knows: your vision may have been firmly fixed on product vending in a 50 square kilometre area. You may be surprised to discover enquiries and orders coming in from other continents, many time zones away. Ecommerce will present you with a number of pretty serious risks and decisions. Do you re-engineer your operation to operate globally – as you must; or do you ignore those opportunities coming across your desktop and risk being panned by the on-line community?

Are you even emotionally ready to consider working in several languages and over 24 time zones? Do you have a reliable and current currency converter at hand? Are you licensed to vend in other countries? What happens if your customer is not satisfied with your product, or if you deliver and you do not get paid? If you offer "Excellent Customer Service", can you provide it at 4 AM on Sunday morning?

Imagine becoming *selective* about your customers. "Yes, I will deal with that person, organization, country, but not this one". I reckon few companies have established customer selection criteria that will serve to guide their front office workforce.

Here is the opportunity, and the challenge. Can you afford to ignore a global phenomenon that offers exposure to millions of potential customers and that enables transactions that could cost you less than a penny to process? If nothing else, on-line exposure can help you convey an image of progressive, informed, responsive enterprise. The challenge is in not losing sight of why you are there.

A useful checklist has been provided by John Sandala, Director of Internet and Electronic Commerce at AT&T Canada. He summarizes his "successful IP business plan" as based on:

A Senior Management Decision on a Clear Definition of Objectives

Application development initiatives that meet the needs of the new objectives while involving the input of end-users

Technology implementation efforts that identify the important technical considerations

User engagement programs to provide both inside and outside customers with the excellent service needed to keep them coming back to the site.

The gathering of feedback and constant measurement to develop continuous improvement plans.

The message for each of us is quite simply this: whether you are already *there*, that is in the market, or seriously considering going there – to the marketplace, you need to be very certain indeed that you want to be there, that you know what you want to do, and that you are architecting your presence so that you can get the very most out of it. And back home, you want to be sure that you are taking a fresh look at your business organization.....is it ready for on-line, real time activity in the global market? Have you automated as far as you can on-line help, database updating and order taking? Some of this will be necessary effectiveness conditions.

It's your choice whether you embrace electronic commerce. It is also your choice whether you make money at it now, later or never.

5

Role of E-Business in the New Economy

In context of the electronic revolution taking place in our economy we must recognize these changes take place in a larger economic context. Global competition, interest rates, laws and regulations, social concerns, industry traditions, consumer preferences etc., are all part of environment affecting business activities.

Besides, electronic and non electronic businesses share available economic resources including natural resources, equipment, telecommunication employees' skills etc. E-business, globalization and internet are interdependent. The more global players exist, the more business they want to do which will attract more people to get direct internet access. There are many categories of e-business such as e-commerce, e-marketing, e-mailing, e-auction, and e-supply and so on.

The integration of these categories through internet enhances existing business or to create new virtual business. E-business commonly referred to as "e-Business" or "e-business enable companies to link their internal and external data processing systems more efficiently and flexibly, to work more closely with suppliers and partners, and to better satisfy the needs and expectations of their customers.

In practice, e-business is more than just e-commerce. While e-business refers to more strategic focus with an emphasis on the functions using electronic capabilities, e-commerce is a subset of an overall e-business strategy. E-business involves business processes spanning the entire value chain: electronic purchasing and supply chain management, processing orders electronically, handling customer service, and cooperating with business partners. E-business can be conducted using the Web, the Internet, intranets, extranets, or some combination of these.

Benefits of e-Business

Expand Market Coverage E-Business eliminates these limitations of geography and time zones. The whole world is the available market, 24 hours a day, 7 days a week, 365 days in a year. Worldwide business professionals, buyers, and decision-makers have access to the Internet, spanning all time zones. The buyer conducts business "where" and "when" they want to without traditional limitations. So, with e-Business a firm creates a global, "365x24x7" availability to its customers.

The firms can offer complimentary and supplementary products, and add-on promotions as buyers make selections. This leads to a larger volume of ordering, creating a higher revenue stream at a marginally low cost per transaction. It makes previously uneconomical markets attractive. This increases the size of the available market by turning marginal segments into profitable ones. This ability to turn frogs into princes is powered by e-Business's low variable costs for addressing marginal segments. The power of the add-on products can also be sold into these previously unprofitable segments, turning them into substantially profitable ones.

Reduce Costs: The major cost-reduction benefit is the promise of changing the distribution of products and services to customers. Products requiring little or no experience in the buying cycle can be purchased by the customer on the Internet and delivered directly without intermediaries. The elimination of various layers of distribution is the major cost reduction benefit to the market.

The National Association of Purchasing Management outlines the following benefits:

- Reduction in process variations
- Reductions in costs and errors

- Vendor sourcing strategy support
- Improvements in process capability
- Procurement paradigm shift from passive to acti
- Elimination of unwanted paper trail
- Improved access to information
- Reduction in costs and cycle times.

Strengthen Customer Relationships

The purpose of a business is to find and keep customers. E-Business has the ability to deliver benefits that can address both aspects of this statement, by delivering better purchase experiences to the buyer. Buyers are migrating to Internet buying in situations when it's faster, better, and cheaper than traditional methods.

Faster e-Business assures faster delivery of products and services by speeding up order fulfillment, and delivering into just-in-time upstream processes, particularly in Business-to-Business environments.

Better Paper and client-server based systems with their "version control" limitations created problems that set limits to their efficiency. The "write-once, read-many" environment of e-Business assures that internal and external audiences see and work with the same up-to-date, accurate data. Additionally, where little customer-vendor interaction is required, e-Business creates an opportunity for virtual self-service counters.

Cheaper The Internet turns every vendor into an equal in a competitive bid. The customer now has more choice in suppliers. The customer has more alternate vendors, and lower prices are anticipated in all e-Business driven markets.

E-commerce is the process of buying, transferring, or exchanging products, services, and/or information via computer networks, including the internet, seeks to add revenue streams, build and enhance relationships with clients and partners and to improve efficiency. E-Commerce that is conducted between businesses is referred to as business-to-business or B2B. B2B can be open to all interested parties (e.g. commodity exchange) or limited to specific, pre-qualified participants (private electronic market). Electronic commerce that is conducted between businesses and consumers, on the other hand, is referred to as business-to-consumer or B2C. This is the type of e-commerce conducted by companies such as Amazon.com. E-Commerce is generally considered to be the sales aspect of e-business. It also consists of the exchange of data to facilitate the financing and payment aspects of the business transactions.

E-mail is a method of exchanging digital messages. E-mail systems are based on a store-and-forward model in which e-mail computer server systems accept, forward, deliver and store messages on behalf of users, who only need to connect to the e-mail infrastructure, typically an e-mail server, with a network-enabled device for the duration of message submission or retrieval. Email advertising becoming widely used as a means of distributing advertising messages to people on internet. Email advertising is being tied to the use of promotions and gimmicks. The main advantage of email advertising is that it is cheap to implement and can include feedback facility.

E-mailing Postal services and telecommunications companies are losing market share to the electronic communication, especially, e-mail. It combines the strength of a phone call is its immediacy and the letter has the advantage that everything is in written form. The internet enables instant communication in written form, either by e-mail or on line chat.

More and more businesses are talking digitally to each other. Other than a phone call, e-mails can contain more than just a text. It is possible to attach files like formatted documents, presentation, images or sound. Information can be shared much more easily-mail does also change the way to people communicate. Instead of writing down every aspect in a single letter; thoughts may be spread over multiple e-mails.

E-procurement The registered users look for buyers or sellers of goods and services. They may specify costs or invite bids. Transactions can be initiated and completed. Ongoing purchases may qualify customers for volume discounts or special offers. E-procurement software may make it possible to automate some buying and selling. Companies can control inventories more effectively, reduce purchasing agent overhead, and improve manufacturing cycles.

There are seven main types of e-procurement;

- Web-based ERP Creating and approving purchasing requisitions, placing purchase orders and receiving goods and services by using a software system based on Internet.
- E-MRO (Maintenance, Repair and Overhaul) same as web-based ERP except that the goods and services ordered are non-product related MRO supplies.
- E-sourcing Identifying new suppliers for a specific category of purchasing requirements using Internet.
- E-tendering Sending requests for information and prices to suppliers and receiving the responses of suppliers through Internet.
- E-reverse auctioning Using Internet to buy goods and services from a number of known or unknown suppliers.
- E-informing Collection and distribution of purchase information both from and to internal and external parties.
- E-market sites buying communities can access preferred suppliers' products and services, add to shopping carts, create requisition, and seek approval, receipt purchase orders and process electronic invoices with integration to suppliers' supply chains and buyers' financial systems.

The e-procurement value chain consists of Indent Management, e-Tendering, e-Auctioning, Vendor Management, Catalogue Management, and Contract Management. Elements of e-procurement include Request For Information, Request For Proposal, Request For Quotation, RFx (the previous three together), and eRFx (software for managing RFx projects).

E-shopping is the process of purchasing products or services over the Internet. An online shop, e-shop, e-store, internet shop, web shop, web store, online store, or virtual store evokes the physical analogy of buying products or services at a bricks-and-mortar retailer or in a shopping mall. The metaphor of an online catalogue is also used, by analogy with mail order catalogues. All types of stores have retail web sites, including those that do and do not also have physical storefronts and paper catalogues. Online shopping is a type of electronic commerce used for business-to-business (B2B) and business-to-consumer (B2C) transactions.

E-auction is a type of auction in which the roles of buyers and sellers are reversed. In an ordinary auction which is also known as a forward auction, buyers compete to obtain a good or service, and the price typically increases over time. In a reverse auction, sellers compete to obtain business, and prices typically decrease over time. A buyer contracts with a market maker to help make the necessary preparations to conduct the reverse auction. This includes: finding new suppliers, training new and incumbent suppliers, organizing the auction, managing the auction event, and providing auction data to buyers to facilitate decision making. Reverse auction is a strategy used by many purchasing and supply management organizations for spend management, as part of strategic sourcing and overall supply management activities.

The prices that buyers obtain in the reverse auction reflect the narrow market which it created at the moment in time when the auction is held. Thus, it is possible that better value-i.e. lower prices, as well as better quality, delivery performance, technical capabilities, etc.-could be obtained from suppliers not engaged in the bidding or by other means such as collaborative cost management and joint process improvement.

The buyer may award contracts to the supplier who bid the lowest price. Or, a buyer could award contracts to suppliers who bid higher prices depending upon the buyer's specific needs with regards to quality, lead-time, capacity, or other value-adding capabilities.

Reverse auctions are used to fill both large and small value contracts for public and private commercial organizations. Buyers, sellers, and market makers should adhere to auction rules and industry codes of conduct for the use of reverse auctions, if they exist. Problems arise when one or more parties fail to conform to auction rules. Buyers should not assume that reverse auctions will, in every case, deliver savings-either on a unit price or total cost basis. Reverse auction savings can range from negative to neutral to positive savings.

E-auctioning benefits include;

- Helps to reduce prices up to 35%
- Shorten the negotiation process
- Comprehensive dynamic pricing engine
- Multi attribute multiproduct, multi language and multicurrency
- Several auction timing models to fit our needs on an auction basis
- Full support of total cost of ownership calculations
- Free training support tools
- Customizable to suit our company image.

E-banking means any user with a personal computer and a browser can get connected to his bank-s website to perform any of the virtual banking functions. All the services that the bank has permitted on the internet are displayed in menu. Any service can be selected and further interaction is dictated by the nature of service.

Once the branch offices of bank are interconnected through terrestrial or satellite links, there would be no physical identity for any branch. It would a borderless entity permitting anytime, anywhere and anyhow banking. The network which connects the various locations and gives connectivity to the central office within the organization is called intranet. E-banking facilities include

- Access accounts round the clock, even on weekends
- See balances online and find out clearance of cheque deposit
- Transfer funds between accounts
- Download information directly into personal finance software
- Receive or pay bills online.

The Reserve Bank of India constituted a working group on Internet Banking. The group divided the internet banking products in India into 3 types based on the levels of access granted. They are: Information Only System General Purpose information like interest rates, branch location, bank products and their features, loan and deposit calculations are provided in the banks website.

There exist facilities for downloading various types of application forms. There is no interaction between the customer and bank's application system. No identification of the customer is done. In this system, there is no possibility of any unauthorized person getting into production systems of the bank through internet.Electronic Information Transfer System The system provides customer-specific information in the form of account balances, transaction details, and statement of accounts. The information is still largely of the 'read only' format. Identification and authentication of the customer is through password. The application systems cannot directly access through the internet.

Fully Electronic Transactional System This system allows bi-directional capabilities. Transactions can be submitted by the customer for online update. This system requires high degree of security and control. It comprises technology covering computerization, networking and security, inter-bank payment gateway and legal infrastructure.

- Automated Teller Machine (ATM) It is operated by plastic card with its special features. The plastic card is replacing cheque, personal attendance of the customer, banking hour's restrictions and paper based verification. ATMs used as spring board for Electronic Fund Transfer. It can provide information about customers account and also receive instructions from customers.It is capable of handling cash deposits, transfer between accounts, balance enquiries, cash withdrawals and pay bills. It may be on-line or 0ff-line.
- Credit Cards/Debit Cards The Credit Card holder is empowered to spend wherever and whenever he wants with his Credit Card within the limits fixed by his bank. Credit Card is a post paid card. Debit Card, on the other hand, is a prepaid card with some stored value. Every time a person uses this card, the Internet Banking house gets money transferred to its account from the bank of the

buyer. The buyers account is debited with the exact amount of purchases. The customer can never overspend because the system rejects any transaction which exceeds the balance in his account. The bank never faces a default because the amount spent is debited immediately from the customers' account.

- Smart Card Banks are adding chips to their current magnetic stripe cards to enhance security and offer new service, called Smart Cards. Smart Cards allow thousands of times of information storable on magnetic stripe cards. In addition, these cards are highly secure, more reliable and perform multiple functions. They hold a large amount of personal information, from medical and health history to personal banking and personal preferences.

E-stock trading Companies such as e-trade, datek online allow us to trade stocks, bonds, mutual funds etc. on the internet. These companies offer to trade at a small cost compared to discount brokers. The steps involved are-place a request to trade-the system responds with current prices on the web-confirm trade or cancel.

The benefits of such trading are;

- Reduced cost
- Convenience of trading from anywhere
- Access to variety of information in different sites.

E-employment Several kinds of services are provided here;

- sites give advice on developing our resumes and to post our resumes on the web
- recruiters use website to post available jobs
- match making facilities for jobs and jobseekers based on a specifications
- use of agents to do the search.

E-retailing offers the following benefits;

- Provision of online catalogue to browse different categories of goods
- Provision of search engine

- Provision of shopping cart
- Personalization of store layouts deals, promotions
- Distribute digital goods directly
- Online salesperson to help customers to navigate through the site
- An order status checking facility.

Decide Suitable Distribution Mechanism

E-stores and e-malls sell a large number of product lines rather than very few. In an e-mall, cyberspace is rented out to cyber e-stores that wish to sell their goods. Several product lines can be present in a single e-mall in an e-mall; each store is under its own management.

Mall management is responsible only for creating the cyber sites that-can be rented and can support services and marketing of the mall. It provides webhosting services. They also provide software tools, which can be utilised by a prospective e-store-to create and maintain its e-store. The advantage is that it is grouped together with other stores in a well known e-mall site.

E-brokers Brokers provide comparison shopping, ordertaking and fulfillment and services to a customer. The models of e-brokers include;

- Provide registration service
- Directory search facilities-payment facilities
- Ascertain requirement such as price
- Provide comparison-shopping between products.

E-CRM solutions can be deployed and managed to provide increased revenues and reduced costs. E-CRM goals can be achieved with internet business strategies, web based CR M specification development, web system design and project management electronic publishing and interactive interface.

They are valuable to companies face the following circumstances

- Business is driven by mission-critical customer service requirements

- Current costs for crm run high
- Large volume of information is distributed
- A complete customer care solution is required.

E-directories Telephone directories with white pages for private telephone numbers and the yellow pages for the businesses is essential to locate a person of business. Now the telephone companies allowed people to call in and ask for information. The data base is located in a single place providing a centralized functionality, offering to anyone at anytime, thus making a decentralized solution. The internet facilitates replication of phone directories without hassles. The internet makes the retrieval easier as well as more difficult.

E-engineering has also changed dramatically in the recent years. Internet changed the speed of the design. It enabled electronic collaboration to much a higher degree than n before. The location of the engineer s has become easier. The internet changed the speed of the design. It enabled electronic collaboration to a much higher degree than was possible ever before. The location of the engineers does not play a role anymore. Everyone with an internet connection is able to take part in the development. New tools concurrent development has been developed to support the possibilities of the internet. Through the internet has also become possible to develop continuous engineer ring by letting engineers participate from all overt the world. Open source development is done that way very efficiently. Anybody is able to take part and can donate a piece of code whenever there has been some time to programme it. This will vary for every person involved.

E-franchising The re-sellers are called franchising partners. By offering a set of products and brands the franchising company guarantees a certain success for the retailer as people tend to like buying these products, as the brands are well known. The advantage of the franchising companies is that they do not need to invest in shop personnel, for example, the franchising g partners is responsible or the employees and financial success of the single outlet. Electronic franchising works very similarly. It has become much easier on the internet. Moving digital products, processes and brands is extremely easy. The affiliation programmes of the large book sellers on the internet have their own store. But they allow franchising partners to exclusively distribute their products on the partner's websites. The advantage of this system is that there is no distribution costs involved. It is possible to link to the original products without letting the customers know.

E-gambling Although there is a moral issue about gambling, it is one of the most profitable businesses on the internet. In the real world gambling is restricted by many laws, making it difficult to access the casinos. The owners of the games often need to pay high taxes to the state, which makes it so difficult to create competition.

Gambling is still not legal in some states and the taxes are still high in these states, but the business has moved to places where gambling is legal and only low taxes need to paid. The companies who operate the gambling websites are able to provide the full program of games, without any restrictions. As the owners have their companies in countries where gambling is legal, they are able to operate without fearing the intervention of the state. But other than the real world casinos which are restricted to the geographical location, online casinos are able to attract gamblers from all over the world with a mouse click.

E-learning is a revolutionary way to empower, a work force with the skills and knowledge it needs to turn changes to on advantages.It is faster chapter and more productive then class room instruction.Electronic learning educating employees using web enabled materials deployed via the net offers in its most sophisticated incarnations such bells and whistles as streaming audio and video, built –in power point presentation, hot links to related information the web, animation, flipbooks and self-running screen-capture display programme. E-learning is a significantly cheaper and more protective and can be delivered with more timeliness than either classroom learning or traditional computer-enhanced teaching.

E-Marketing is a traditional marketing using electronic methods affecting traditional marketing in two ways. It increases efficiency in established marketing function and transforms many marketing strategies. Internet serves as efficient marketing tools for both secondary and primary data collection. In addition electronic technologies affect the 4ps.

- Product Internet technologies spawned a variety of innovative product for creating, delivering and reading messages as well as services such as reverse auctions, business to business (B 2 B), market exchanges and interactive games.
- Pricing The net turned pricing strategies upside down.Bartering, bidding, dynamic pricing, and individualized pricing are now quite on line.
- Place The e-marketers used the net for direct distribution of digital productsand for electronic retailing.
- Promotion The net assists with two way communication; one to one web pages-mail conversations, and e-main conferencing via news group and mailing lists. E-marketers also use the net for promotions, and sending electronic coupons and digital products samples directly to consumers.

E-Operational Resource Management Beside the goods that are needed for production, companies need to buy operational resources, these are the non production goods are services that are required and managed on a daily basis to run the day-to –day business. Operational resources allow companies to manage operational resources more strategically, by using the internet and its connectivity to provide a communication infrastructure, where buyer and supplier can together on a direct basis without losing control over the spending. E-Supply Manufacturers, logistics companies, senders, receiver and retailers all work together to co-ordinate the order generation and order taking.

The order fulfillment and the distribution of the products, services, or information are organized together by the supply chain management. By digitalizing the products, the processes and the communication the internet has a great potential linking and managing this organization.

E-Trading Before the internet, buying and selling stock war restricted to people with access to financial network. The internet has changed the way stocks are traded. E-trading also called E-brokering offers the real –time stock price to every desk throughout the world. People are able in real time to change in the stock market. Every one with on internet bank account is able to buy and sell stock. This enables anyone to participate in the stock market and earn money by investing.

The Basic E Business Models

The emerging e-business market affords companies of all sizes and types the opportunity to leverage their existing assets, employees, technology infrastructure, and information to gain or maintain marketshare. For example, in the telecommunications industry, service, rather than technology, is now the key differentiator. With lower barriers to entry, new competitors are rapidly entering the market offering new services, such as online bill presentment and payment, and leveraging their unique digital assets.

Information technology research analysts agree that e-business is any net-enabled business activity that transforms internal and external relationships to create value and exploit market opportunities driven by new rules of the connected economy. However, today's e-business requires more. Industry analysts further point out that e-business involves the continuous optimization of an organization's value proposition and value-chain position through the adoption of digital technology.

The challenge for an organization is to turn the vision and the market opportunity into a viable business. Developing the marketing strategy and plans and designing and deploying the business solution is key.

Those who successfully architect, develop, and deploy e-business solutions will need to formulate and adopt a comprehensive business plan. Because of the critical role of Internet technologies and integration requirements, it is recommended that organizations need a comprehensive planning framework—an actual e-business model. This structured planning approach enables the organization to assess, plan for, and implement the multiple aspects of an e-business.

Building an e-business (an integrated value chain) that leverages the Internet's communications capabilities is a complex undertaking. The complex integration requirements of the business solutions, all performing at extremely high levels of availability and scalability, require an e-business model architectural approach.

The value chain (comprised of the traditional supply chain management functions, planning, procurement, and inventory management, coupled with the customer-facing functions, typically referred to as customer relationship management) has integration and performance demands that exceed the requirements seen in traditional businesses. In a successful e-business, all of these areas are tightly integrated to provide an organization the ability to quickly and efficiently sell, manufacture, and deliver products or services.

Furthermore, in a successful e-business, this value chain rests on a foundation that leverages the organization's existing core operational business systems, as well as meets the new business-critical operational requirements for reliability, scalability, flexibility, and 24 × 7 × 365 availability in a highly volatile, electronic marketplace. An e-business model includes three essential elements:

- Solid strategies
- Knowledge management techniques applied to a company's information and intellectual assets
- Effective e-business processes typically grouped in the customer relationship management (CRM), supply chain management (SCM), and core business operations domains.

Solid Strategies

Strategy and execution are key to developing and sustaining a successful e-business. Only those organizations that successfully integrate key business strategies and processes dramatically increase their efficiencies. To be successful, organizations must also form the right strategic relationships and develop efficient business processes with robust backend solutions that are able to meet users' demands for real-time service today and into the future.

In the past, businesses had the luxury of developing business strategies in the boardroom and IT strategies in the IT department. They then brought these strategies together to run the overall business. E-businesses cannot afford this luxury. The ability to react and change direction is critical. Speed is everything. Grounding the organization with sound, winning strategies is key.

In the new economy's competitive electronic environment, it is easier for an organization to be global, but it is also harder to maintain consistency in the levels of services offered around the world. E-businesses must be ready and able to adjust their business and IT strategies rapidly, depending on unpredictable competitors and market pressures.

Today's e-business climate requires the continuous optimization of an organization's business and IT strategies. Because IT now has such a significant impact on every business process (from order taking to inventory to billing), both business and IT strategies are now developed in parallel.

The best example of this is Dell Computer. From the start, the company's business strategy was tightly aligned with its IT strategy, allowing Dell to successfully integrate every aspect of its business (from order taking to inventory to billing) with both its customers and suppliers. Dell vaulted to the forefront of its industry when it came to market with a winning strategy, the unique just-in-time-delivery model. Unlike traditional computer suppliers, Dell's business strategy was founded on the premise of zero inventory.

Similarly, online brokerage companies have been leaders in the area of integrating IT and business strategies. The rapid adoption of Internet technologies combined with market globalization, industry deregulation, and media convergence has afforded these companies the opportunity to gain share and create value in the e-business marketplace.

Turning an organization's intellectual assets into knowledge is a key business differentiator. In addition to a continually optimized business strategy, successful e-businesses must establish solid knowledge management practices. Knowledge management is the definitive way to leverage an organization's information and intellectual assets for business advantage. It is the formalized, integrated approach that every organization must take to "know" its business.

Knowledge Management Techniques

Every business has both tacit and explicit knowledge. One is undocumented, and the other is documented about what is "known" in the company. This knowledge may include information about products and services or information about how the company works with a particular supplier. No matter what type of knowledge an e-business has, the company must put into place processes for organizing that knowledge.

Knowledge management includes managing intellectual capital, such as best practices, critical business processes, and operating metrics. Establishing ongoing processes for acquiring, organizing, and distributing this knowledge about customers, products, and processes is critical to success. The business domains, CRM, SCM, and core business operations, are dependent on this information and these intellectual assets.

Effective E-Business Processes

In every successful e-business, the business process domains (CRM, SCM, and core business operations) are an integral part of the continuous optimization process. The advantage and, thus, the return on investment for an e-business integrating its business process domains is that it extends the organization's business directly to customers and suppliers.

When business process domains are integrated, they can increase productivity and improve customer and supplier satisfaction. For example, when a repeat customer views a successful e-business's Web site, an integrated CRM system presents that individual with offers or items of interest based on previous orders. After the customer places an order, this same e-business allows that individual to view the status of his order in real time as it moves through the supply chain.

Business process domains are aggregations of core business processes. Although there is growing popularity of business process domains as their own entities (CRM, SCM, and core business operations), they are commanding a mind-share in the marketplace (and each has attracted various vendors and products to support it). These domains must operate together as a key component to the overall e-business strategy. In a successful e-business, convergence is the driving connection of all of the business process domains. When there appears to a customer or a supplier to be no barrier between departments, the business process domains are tightly integrated with the business and IT strategies.

Customer Relationship Management

Customer relationships are becoming a more important factor in differentiating one business from another. In order to stay competitive, e-businesses in every industry have begun to analyse these relationships with customers using CRM solutions. In the past, customers would place an order via the telephone and wait until the company's purchasing department processed and shipped the order. Today's customers place an order electronically and then demand to be able to check the status of their order within minutes. CRM enables an organization to adopt a comprehensive view of the customer and maximize this relationship. These CRM systems enable a business to identify, attract, retain, and support customs centres, direct mail, and retail facilities. In an efficient e-business, there are CRM processes in place to handle:

Analytical CRM: The analysis of data created on the operational side of the CRM equation for the purpose of business performance management; utilizing data warehousing technologies and leveraging data marts

Customer interactions: Sales, marketing, and customer service (call center, field service) via multiple, interconnected delivery channels and integration between front office and back office.

Operational CRM: The automation of horizontally integrated business processes involving "front office" customer touch points.

Personalization: The use of new and traditional groupware/ Web technologies to facilitate customer and business partner communications.

Supply Chain Management

Integration of the SCM functions is emerging as one of the greatest challenges facing today's e-businesses. SCM is the integration of business processes from end user through to original supplier. The goal of SCM is to create an end-to-end system that automates all the business processes between suppliers, distribution partners, and trading partners. The new mantra for this process, according to industry analysts, is "replacing inventory with information." In an effective e-business, the following SCM independent processes must be highly integrated.

Demand management: These are shared functions, including demand planning, supply planning, manufacturing planning, and sales and operations planning.

Inbound/outbound logistics: These include transportation management, distribution management, and warehouse management.

Supply management: These include products and services for customer order fulfillment.

Core Operations

E-businesses also need to develop and operate complex transaction processing systems that support their core business operations. These core operations include the operational systems that support their particular business, such as claims processing, trade execution, enterprise resource planning (ERP), and enterprise resource management (ERM).

Whether a company is just beginning to transform its business into an e-business or is an e-business strengthening its market position, organizations must put in place architectures that support large and complex integrated solutions. E-businesses must address the performance requirements for reliability, scalability, and high availability.

These systems also require a high level of flexibility, integration, and often the added complexity of operating in a global business environment. These e-businesses need to integrate their customer relationship management, supply chain, and core business operational systems such as enterprise resource planning, accounting, and general business support systems to operate efficiently.

Marketing in the New Economy-Online Marketing

Before going into the topic let us understand the basic difference between Internet and World Wide Web.

The internet is a worldwide network of computers networks. And the World Wide Web is one of the Internet's most popular services, providing access to over two billion Web pages.

Do you think there is any difference between E-Business and E-commerce?

What is E-Business?

E-business primarily concerns the applications of digital technologies to business within the firm. E-business refers primarily to the digital enablement of transactions and processes within a firm, involving information systems under the control of the firm. It does not include commercial transactions involving an exchange of value across organizational boundaries. For example, a company online inventory control mechanisms are a component of e-business, but such internal processes do not directly generate revenue for the firm from outside business or consumers. E-business applications turn into e-commerce precisely when an exchange of value occurs. And e-commerce and e-business systems can and do blur together at the business firm boundary, at the point where internal business systems link up with suppliers, for instance.

We are living in an exciting time. The Power, capabilities, and worldwide reach of the Internet are quickly changing the way the world does business. E-business means any business conducted using electronic media such as the Internet, other computer networks, wireless transmissions, etc. It also stands for electronic business and refers to any kind of sales, services, purchasing or commerce on the Internet.

What is E-commerce?

E-commerce means the use of internet and the web to transact business. E-commerce primarily involves digitally enabled commercial transactions between and among organisations and individuals.

What is E-marketing?

Marketing deals with identifying and meeting human and social needs. One of the shortest definitions of marketing is "meeting needs profitably". The newest channels for direct marketing are electronic. E-business describes a wide variety of electronic platforms, such as the sending of purchase orders to suppliers via electronic data interchange (EDI) or extranets; the use of fax and e-mail to conduct transactions; the use of ATMs, and smart cards to facilitate payment and obtain digital cash; and the use of the Internet and online services. All of these involve doing business in a "market space" as compared to physical "market place".

The Internet today functions as an information source, an entertainment source, a communication channel, a transaction channel, and even a distribution channel. One can use it as a shopping mall, a TV set, a news paper, a library, or a phone. Users can send e-mail, exchange views, shop for products, and access news, recipes, art and business information.

The internet provides marketers and consumers with opportunities for much greater interaction and individualization. Companies in the past would send standard media –magazines, newsletters, ads-without any individualization or interaction. Today these companies can send individualized content and consumers themselves can further individualize the content; and today companies can interact and dialogue with much larger groups than ever in the past.

Very simply put, eMarketing or electronic marketing refers to the application of marketing principles and techniques via electronic media and more specifically the Internet. The terms E-Marketing, Internet marketing and online marketing, are frequently interchanged, and can often be considered synonymous.

E-Marketing is the process of marketing a brand using the Internet. It includes both direct response marketing and indirect marketing elements and uses a range of technologies to help connect businesses to their customers. By such a definition, eMarketing encompasses all the activities a business conducts via the worldwide web with the aim of attracting new business, retaining current business and developing its brand identity.

The Seven Unique Features of E-commerce Technology

1. *Ubiquity:* E-commerce liberates the market from being restricted to a physical space and makes it possible to shop from our desktop, at home, at work, or even from our car. From customer point of view, ubiquity reduces transaction costs, (the cost of participating in a market) time spend and money travelling to a market.
2. *Global reach:* E-commerce permits transactions to cross cultural and national boundaries far more conveniently and cost effectively than is true in traditional commerce.
3. *Universal standards:* The technical standards for conducting e-commerce are universal standards. The standards are shared by all nations around the world. The universal technical standards of e-commerce greatly lower market entry costs and search costs for customers by creating a single, one-world market space where prices and product descriptions can be displayed for all to see.
4. *Reachness:* During the traditional market it was not possible to reach up to the different places of the market but e-commerce enables the businessman to reach out even to the last customer living at the end of the world at any time with the development of the web.
5. *Interactivity:* E-commerce makes it possible for two-way communication between businessman and customers which was not possible in traditional market. Customers are able to get the latest of information about the product that they want to use at any time, sitting at any corner of the world.
6. *Information density:* E-commerce technologies reduce information collection, storage, processing and

communication costs. At the same time increase greatly the currency, accuracy an d timeliness of information – making information more useful and important than ever. In e-commerce markets, prices and costs become more transparent. Therefore the consumer and the merchant both are benefited by e-commerce.

7. *Personalization/Customization:* E-commerce technologies permit personalization. Merchants can target their marketing messages to specific individuals by adjusting the message to a person's name, interests and past purchases.

Types of E-commerce

There are different types of e-commerce. Following are the lists of five major types of e-commerce.

Business-to-Consumer e-commerce (B2C)

In this type, online business attempt to reach individual consumers to sell out the goods.

The most frequent online consumer purchases have been books, music, software, air tickets, PC peripherals, clothing, videos, hotel reservations, toys, flowers and consumer electronics.

Business-to-Business e-commerce (B2B)

In this type businesses focus on selling to other business. There are number of B2B business models developed, including e-distributors, B2b service providers, matchmakers, and infomediaries that are widening the use of B2B e-commerce.

Forrester and Gartner, major research firms on online commerce estimated that B2B commerce is 10 to 15 times greater than B2C commerce. Firms are using B2B auction sites, spot exchanges, online product catalogues, and other online resources to obtain better prices.

Consumer-to-Consumer (C2C)

In this type of e-commerce consumers sells to other consumers with the help of an online market maker, such as the auction site eBay. In C2C e-commerce, the consumer prepares the product for market, places the product for auction or sale, and relies on the market maker to provide catalog, search engine, and transaction-clearing capabilities so that products can be easily displayed, discovered, and paid for. The size of the market is estimate over $5 billion and is growing rapidly.

AOL boasts some 14000 chat rooms covering such topics as healthy eating, caring for your Bonsai tree, and exchanging views about latest soap opera happenings.

Peer-to-Peer e-commerce (P2P)

Peer-to-peer technology enables internet users to share files and computer resources directly without having to go through a central Web server. In this e-commerce no intermediary is required.

Examples:

1. Gnutella is a peer-to-peer freeware software application that permits users to directly exchange musical tracks, typically without any charge.
2. Napster.com established to aid internet users in finding and sharing online music files known as MP3 files.

M-commerce

Mobile commerce or m-commerce refers to the use of wireless digital devices to enable transactions on the Web. It utilizes wireless networks to connect call phones and handheld devices such as the PalmVIIx to the Web. Once it is connected the mobile consumers can conduct many types of transactions, including stock trades, in-store price comparisons, banking, travel reservations, and more. It is most widely used in Japan and Europe where cell phones are more prevalent than in the United States but it is expected to grow more rapidly.

Marketing in New Globalised Economy

Today's Companies need fresh thinking about how to operate and compete in the new economy. Today's economy is made up of old and new elements and is essentially a hybrid. We want to emphasize new elements such as the following:

* Companies are increasingly subcontracting activities to

outsourcing firms. Their principle is to outsource those activities that others can do cheaper and better but retain core activities.

* Companies are increasingly benchmarking their performance against best-of-class companies anywhere in the world.
* Companies are deepening their partnering arrangements with key suppliers and distributors.
* Companies are emphasizing interdepartmental teamwork to manage Key processes rather than relying on traditional departmental systems.
* Companies are recognizing that, much of their market value comes from intangible assets, particularly their brands, customer base, employees, distributor and supplier relations, and intellectual capital.
* Companies are making substantial investments in information systems as the key to lower their costs and gain a competitive edge.

Many standard marketing practices like mass media advertising, sales promotion, sales force calls were part of the old economy. They will continue to be important, but today's businesses will have to answer such questions as:

1. "Is too much money being spent on mass advertising and not enough on one-to-one customer relationship management?
2. "Will companies need as many salespeople as before in an information-rich economy?"
3. "Should companies reduce their huge sales promotion expenditures and move to everyday low prices?"

The Major Driver's of the New Economy

Many forces play a major role in reshaping the world economy, among them technology, globalization and market deregulation play a major role. Here we will describe four specific drivers that strengthen the new economy:

1. Digitalization and connectivity

2. Disintermediation and re-intermediation
3. Customization and customerization
4. Industry convergence.

Digitalization and Connectivity

Today most appliances and systems operate with digital information, which convert text data, sound, and images into a stream of zeroes and ones that can be combined into bits and transmitted from appliance to appliance. Software is essentially digital instructions for operating systems, games, storage, and other applications.

But bits will not reside in separate appliance unless connectivity is established. For bits to flow from one appliance and location to another, a wired or wireless communication network is necessary. The Internet, the "information highway," can dispatch bits at incredible speeds from one location to another. Much of today's business is carried over networks connecting people and companies. When they connect people within a company to one another and to the company mainframe these networks are called Intranets. Extranets when they connect a company with its suppliers and distributors; and the Internet when they connect users to a large worldwide "information repository." Connectivity is further enhanced by wireless communication. Consumers and business people no longer need to be near a computer to send and receive information. All they need is a cellular phone or personal digital assistant (PDA, such as a Palm). While they are on the move, they can connect with the internet to check stock prices, the weather, sports scores, or send and receive email messages. They can place online orders by simply using a phone or a PDA.

Disintermediation and Reinterpretation

The new technological capabilities have led thousands of entrepreneurs to launch a dotcom in the hope of striking gold. The amazing success of early online dot-coms such as AOL, Amazon, and yahoo struck terror in the hearts of many established manufacturers and retailers. For example, Compaq had its hands tied because it sold its computers through retailers, whereas Dell Computer grew faster by choosing to sell online. Established store-based retailers-notably bookstores, music stores, travel agents, stockbrokers and car dealers – began to doubt their future as more businesses went into direct online marketing. They feared, and rightly so, being disintermediated by the new e-tailers.

But disintermediation was only half the story. Re-intermediation took place on a grand scale. New online middlemen appeared such as mysimon.com, Priceline.com, lifeshopper.com, buy.com, compare.com.

As for the traditional "brick-only" firms – such as Compaq and Merrill Lynch started their own online sales channels becoming "brick-and-click" competitors.

Customization and Customerization

The old economy revolved around manufacturing companies whose main drive was to standardize production, products, and business processes. Through standardization and branding, manufacturers hoped to grow and take advantage of economies of scale. In contrast, the new economy is supported by information businesses. As companies grew proficient at gathering information about individual customers and business partners (suppliers, distributors, retailers), and as their factories were designed more flexibly, they increased their ability to individualize their market offerings, messages and media.

For example, Dell Computer invites customers to specify exactly what they want in a computer and delivers a custom-built one in a few days. The combination of operational customization and marketing customization has been called customerization. A company is customerized when it is able to dialogue with individual customers and respond by customizing its products, services and messages on a one-to-one basis.

Customization is not for every company: There are several downsides.

(a) Customization can raise the cost of goods by more than the customer is willing to pay.

(b) Some customers do not know what they want until they see actual products.

(c) Customers cannot cancel the order after the company has started the work on the product.

(d) The product may be hard to repair and have little sales value.

In spite of this, customization has worked well for some products like laptop computers, apparel, skincare products, and vitamins and is an opportunity worth investigating.

Industry Convergence

Industry boundaries are blurring at an incredible rate. Film companies such as Kodak are also chemical companies, but they are moving into electronics to digitize their image-making capabilities. Disney is not only into cartoons and theme parks, but it makes major films, licenses characters, and manage retail stores, hotels, cruise ships, and educational facilities. In all these cases, companies are recognizing that new opportunities lie at the intersection of two or more industries.

How business practices are changing ;

(a) From organizing by product units to organizing by customer segments.

(b) From focusing on profitable transactions to focusing on customers lifetime value.

(c) From focusing on just the financial scorecard to focusing also on the marketing scorecard.

(d) From focusing on shareholders to focusing on stakeholders.

(e) From Marketing being the exclusive responsibility of the marketing department to marketing being every employee's responsibility.

(f) From building brands through advertising to building brand through performance.

(g) From focusing on customer acquisition to focusing on customer retention.

(h) From no customer satisfaction measurement to in-depth customer satisfaction measurement.

(i) From over-promise, under-deliver to under-promise, over-deliver.

(j) Today's marketplace is made up of traditional consumers (who do not buy online), cyber consumers (who mostly buy online), and hybrid consumers (who do both). Most consumers are hybrid. They shop in grocery stores but occasionally order from Peapod; they buy books in Barnes & Noble bookstores and sometimes order books from bn.com.

But people still like to squeeze the tomatoes, touch the fabric, smell the perfume, and interact with salespeople. Consumers are motivated by other needs than only shopping efficiency. Most companies will need a presence of both offline and online to cater to these hybrid consumers. Companies are adjusting their marketing practices to meet new conditions. Two newer practices that companies and their marketers are getting involved are:

1. E-business and
2. Customer relationship management.

How marketing practices are changing:

E-business

E-business describes the use of electronic means and platforms to conduct a company's business. The advent of the internet has greatly increased the ability of companies to conduct their business faster, more accurately, over a wide range of time and space, at reduced cost, and with the ability to customize and personalize customer offerings. Countless companies have set up websites to inform and promote their products and services. They have created Intranets to facilitate employees communicating with one another and to facilitate downloading and uploading information to and from the company's computers. Companies have also set up Extranets with major suppliers and distributors to facilitate information exchange, orders, transactions, and payments.

E-commerce is more specific than e-business; it means that in addition to providing information to visitors about the company, its history, policies products, and job opportunities, it also offers to transact or facilitate the selling of products and services online. Amazon.com, e-plasticsnet, e-steel are examples of e-commerce sites.

E-commerce has given rise in turn to e-purchasing and e-marketing.

E-purchasing means companies decide to purchase goods, services, and information from various online suppliers. Smart e-purchasing has already saved companies millions of dollars.

E-marketing describes company efforts to inform, communicate, promote and sell its products and services over the Internet.

Customer Relationship Marketing

Customer relationship marketing (CRM) enables companies to provide excellent real-time customer service by developing a relationship with each valued customer through the effective use of individual account information. Based on what they know about each individual customer, companies can customize market offerings, services, programs, messages and media.

Examples for E-marketing

These are the examples/names of the companies and their products which sell their products through online.

Sony Company

The products of Sony Company are as under:

1. Sony cameras and optics
2. Sony digital cameras
3. Sony laptops and accessories
4. Sony TV and accessories
5. Sony LCD TV
6. Home Audio
7. Portable CD player
8. T.V. remote
9. Computer
10. Sony hardware
11. Sony mobile games
12. Walkman

13. In-car entertainment
14. Battery & charger.

IBM (International Business Machines)

The products of IBM Company are as under:

1. Punched card machinery
2. Time clock
3. Typewriters
4. Mainframe computers
5. Minicomputer
6. Softwares
7. Small business products
8. Medium business products
9. All IT services like, IT strategies, security and privacy services, integrated communication services, etc.
10. System and servers.

Nike Company

1. Watches
2. Digital sports watch
3. Compass watch
4. Clothes (men & women)
5. Bags
6. Shoes
7. Spectacles
8. Sandals
9. Sports digital audio play
10. Jackets
11. Water shoes
12. Hiking shoes.

Adidas

1. Basketballs
2. Golf

3. Tennis
4. Foot ball
5. Eyewear
6. Watches
7. Deo spray
8. Bags
9. Hats
10. Balls
11. Apparel for men and men
12. Gloves.

Pros and Cons of Online Marketing

Pros

1. *Convenience:* Customers can order products 24 hours a day wherever they are.
2. *Information:* Customers can find reams of comparative information about company's products, competitors and prices without leaving their office or home.
3. *Fewer hassles:* Customers don't have to face sales people or open themselves up to persuasion and they don't have to wait in line.
4. *Lower costs:* On-line marketers avoid the expense of maintaining a store and the costs of rent, insurance and utilities.

Cons

1. *Limited Consumer exposure and buying:* Web users are doing more surfing than buying. Only an estimated 18% of surfers actually use the web regularly for shopping or to obtain commercial services such as travel information.
2. *Chaos and clutter:* The Internet offers millions of web sites and a staggering volume of information. Navigating the web can be frustrating. Many sites go unnoticed.
3. *Security:* Consumers worry that unscrupulous interlopers will intercept their credit-card numbers.

4. *Skewed user demographics and psychographics:* Online users are more upscale and technically oriented than the general population, making them ideal for computer, electronics and financial services but less so for mainstream products.

Case Study on Ultralase Advertising

Ultralase are a company offering laser eye treatment – a high value consumer service. In 2003 their market was characterised by intense competition with other suppliers such as Optimax, Optical Express and AccuVision. Ultralase had relatively low brand awareness and was struggling with a long sales cycle and relatively uninformed customers. The main communications disciplines used were:

* Press
* Direct Mail
* PR
* Brochures
* From 2004 onwards, they increased their digital expenditure and in 2006 at Ad Tech presented their achievements through their agency, Agency.com. These included:
* 10 Million site visits per year
* 3.7 billion ad impressions (Jan to Sept 2006)
* Reach between 18M and 22M unique users per month- Now the dominant online brand with a high brand awareness and a shorter sales cycle.

To achieve this, they introduced online media channels including:

* Affiliate marketing
* Paid search marketing
* Display advertising
* Email marketing based on permission-based lead generation through offers on their website.
* DVD's.

Ultralase case study from agency Advertising.com-they are one of the largest UK Internet advertisers.

Costly product – up to four thousand plans.

Laser eye surgery clinics – 100,000 UK customersIn 2003, relatively there was low brand awareness, long sales cycle, and low brand familiarity.

Reassurance and education are important. Their advertising objectives with new agency were to improve these areas. Big Internet display ad campaign run by Agency.com more or less continuously-2006 to-date with 3.7 billion ad impressions generating 18 to 20m unique users per month. If we assume 1 visit per unique visitor I make that around 0.5% click through, so probably higher since more than one.

Ultralase use a direct response model – customers register for more information – pack and book a consultation by phone or by call-centre. All data is stored within E-CRM system. They track individual customers through their terms, e.g. Brand clicks e.g. Ultralase Generic only, e.g. Laser eye treatment When volumes highest, found increased searches on brand term, increased conversion rates on search and higher conversion rate from E-CRM/E-mail marketing activity. Shorter conversion from consultation to treatment.

Found two types of leads:

* Fast online lead – direct response – only works well over 25% of ad inventory
* Complex online lead – halo effect – longer period – works over more of network to increase leads – searches, etc. Ultralase have a deep site engages people through interactive consultation guides and consultation.

Nike Versus Adidas Case Study

Nike and Adidas are two primary footwear companies along with their competitors who have adopted an online e-commerce strategy to increase their sales and product awareness. Most importantly, companies like Nike and Adidas have invested heavily into online brand building and image development. Nike launched the nike.com web site in August 1996 primarily to provide information to its consumers. In 1996, there were no e-commerce capabilities present, however the web site served as a brand building tool for the company. In 1999, Nike redesigned their web site with expanded e-commerce functionality. Adidas launched their web site in the spring of 2000, which was later integrated with e-commerce capabilities.

In order to maximize their market share, both Nike and Adidas have placed a great importance in developing their branding and marketing strategies on the net through web appearance and user friendly functionalities such as ease of purchase, speed, and navigation.

Nike and Adidas have adopted a merchant model which encompassed three pillars of their e-commerce strategy: pure-play e-tailer, bricks and clicks, and their online store. The main purposes of acquiring relationships with pure-play e-tailers is to promote and market products; focus on the content to create new exposure and; gather, gain and transfer market knowledge to their business counterparts.

The Internet has proven to be a useful tool for firms such as Nike and Adidas by increasing sales and reducing cost.

But most importantly their web sites have provided them with an intangible asset such as market research and consumer buying behaviors. With the data retrieve from consumers, these firms are able to analyse and monitor the buying behaviors of their consumers. The data can also be used to exploit new marketing campaigns and promotions. Furthermore, the data collected can be used to produce innovative designs and improve their research capabilities.

Although, there are perceived benefits in conducting e-business over the Internet there are also potential barriers. The major barrier of e-commerce with respect to large firms such as Nike and Adidas is the technological barrier ranging from infrastructure to security. An ongoing battle the e-commerce industry faces is security. With time and additional research and resources, this problem will be mitigated. Meanwhile, both Nike and Adidas must minimize their technological risks. While both Nike and Adidas currently have an essential advantage over their rivals, but there are chances that their advantages will not last forever.

Although, Nike and Adidas have engaged in e-commerce there are apparent gaps within their e-business strategy. E-commerce is only available in restricted regions such as the United States and the United Kingdom, therefore opportunities exists within the global market to expand.

A daring dream began in 1920 when Adi Dassler fashioned his first shoe in Herzogenaurach, Germany. In 1948, Adidas was founded along with its identifying trademark, the three stripes. From its inception, Adidas has faithfully adhered to three guiding principles embedded deep into its DNA:

1. Produce the best shoe for the requirements of the sport,
2. Protect the athlete from injury, and
3. Make the product durable.

As time has passed, Adidas has evolved and is now one of the premier global leaders in sporting brands offering athletic footwear, apparel and accessories.

This feat has been cultivated through continuous innovation and a broad product portfolio. With time, Adidas discovered that in order to continue to evolve further its strategy had to include the Internet. This led to the development of www.thestore.adidas.com, an e-commerce site focused on interactively profiling Adidas's extensive product offerings accompanied by detailed product information.

Initially, what started as Blue Ribbon Sports in 1962 became Nike Inc. in 1972, based in Beaverton, Oregon. Nike was named for the Greek winged goddess of victory. The founders were Bill Bowerman, a track & field coach and Phil Knight, a runner under Bowerman.

From their modest start, Nike has grown to be a global leader in the sporting goods industry. It is recognized as the world's leading designer, marketer and distributor of athletic footwear, apparel, and accessories for a wide variety of sports and fitness activities. For Nike, an established and growing organization, a strong Internet presence felt like a natural extension to their already globally focused strategy. Today www.niketown.com, Nike's e-commerce site offers a unique experience, products and product information for its potential and existing customers.

Value Configuration The inputs to the e-commerce value configuration for both Nike and Adidas are:

1. Brand Image,
2. Price,
3. Web site design,
4. Service, and
5. Innovation.

Strengths

1. First movers advantage in e-commerce
2. Diversity and variety in products offered on the web (footwear, apparel, sporting equipment, etc.)
3. Innovative designs in footwear enabling consumers to design their own shoes online
4. Diversity and variety in products offered on the web (footwear, apparel, sporting equipment, etc.) Adidas even offers items not available in its retail stores
5. Secondary web sites (i.e. soccerevolution.com to simply promote soccer, Adidas leads the market in this sport)

Weaknesses

1. E-commerce is limited to USA
2. The direct sale to consumers is creating conflicts with its own resellers
3. Currently available supply chain, manufacturing, and fulfillment technologies aren't easily integrated with online build-to-order not known for its research and development leading to innovative designssystems
4. The e-commerce is limited to USA, however, has planned to expand to Canada and international in the near future
5. Online customer service not "helpful" or easy to find.

Opportunities

1. Increasing demand in the industry for products available online
2. E-commerce will reduce the cost of goods sold thus improving the "bottom line"
3. New technology and innovation to stay on top of market needs
4. Expand e-commerce to global markets
5. Possibility of outsourcing the web development and e-commerce to a third party developer
6. E-commerce will reduce the cost of goods sold thus improving the "bottom line"
7. Expand e-commerce to global markets
8. Collaborate with other online retailers to offer Adidas products.

Because of E-commerce

Nike's ability to realize the potential of the Internet has placed them in the e-commerce leadership position among other sporting goods companies.

Both Adidas's and Nike's strategy seem to be well ahead of their competition contributing to their e-commerce success. No other athletic footwear company is able to outshine these two firms when it comes to e-commerce, at least for now and in the near future as this task would involve large infrastructure investment and more importantly thorough commitment.

6

Economic Implications of E-commerce

The information revolution aided by the revolution in the telecommunications and institutional innovations had initially promised to change the nature of the market altogether. The market's primary role as merely a place where buyers and sellers meet (it had seemed) now has been revolutionized by the impact of the information revolution on its subsidiary role, i.e., as a transmission belt of information. Today market is a place where there is no intermediaries between a seller of a good and its final buyer to the mutual benefit of both parties (Sengupta, 2004). The Internet and its enabled technologies (especially electronic commerce) have caused the costs of many kinds of market mterachon to plummet (Saloner, 2001). Not only cost reduction, e-commerce has the potential to stimulate growth and employment in industrialized as well as developing countries. Further, e-commerce allows economics agents (both buyers and sellers) to interact more effectively by creating new market opportunities (Mukhopadhyay, 2002). Thus, e-commerce has strong economic implications at both micro and macro level.

E-commerce and Economic Growth

While e-commerce clearly has a positive impact on the business sector, doubts have been raised about its impact on the macroeconomic growth, and productive growth (2) in particular. Various studies show that e-commerce had an impressive performance particular in terms of productivity growth. The US, which leads the world in IT and e-commerce, has had a notable economic performance, particularly in terms of productive growth, since 1995. But, the same was not happened with the developing countries as they failed to catch up technologically with the industrialized world.

To assess the broader economic impact of e-commerce and the ramifications of developing countries' catching up or not, UNCTAD has conducted a quantitative analysis based on two scenario: one in which the developing countries fall behind technologically and one in which they catch up with the developed countries. The analysis is centred on cost saving and assume that e-commerce can reduce costs of services, particularly in retail and wholesale trade, transport and financial and business services. Cost savings in services are stimulated through a productive growth scenario, which allow for the analysis of such macro-economic variables as GDP, welfare, wages and terms of trade. The analysis is a unique application of a computable general equilibrium model to e-commerce at the global level.

According to the report, under the first scenario developed countries would have welfare gains of $117 billion, while the developing world (excluding Asia) would lose welfare of $ 726 million. The Asian region, on the other hand, would gain $ 802 million, largely attributable to the transport services sector. Besides welfare and GDP losses, developing countries would also experience a reduction in wages and deteriorating terms of trade.

E-Commerce could therefore end up actually widening, and not narrowing, the gap between the developed and developing countries.

Under the second scenario, however, if developing countries were to catch up with developed countries in productivity, they would increase output, wages and welfare.

A 1% productive growth m the service sector in Asia for example, would result in welfare gains of $12 billion, GDP growth of 0.4% and a 2 to 3% growth in the service exports. By reducing costs, increasing efficiency, reducing time and distance, e-commerce could thus become an important tool for development.

Impact of E-commerce on Economy

Business and the economy are inextricably linked with the development and implementation of new technology (Tassabehji, 2003). Growth and development of any modern economy has been recognized by many economic theorists, such as Kondratieff, Schumpeter, Mensch and Porter, to be based on innovation of new technology. In the early twentieth century, the economist Kondratieff introduced his 'Long Wave Theory (3)' of economic growth. He detailed the numbers of years that the economy expanded and contracted during each part of the half-century long cycle, which industries suffer the most during the 'downwave' and how technology plays a role in leading the way out of the contraction into the next 'upwave'.

Building on this theory the economist Schumpeter (1961) assigned technological innovation an almost exclusive role, as engine of economic development: the fundamental impulse that sets and keeps the capitalist engine in motion comes from the new consumers' goods, the new methods of production or transportation, the new market, the new forces of industrial organization that capitalist enterprise creates. Mensch (1979) updates the Schumpeter theory, giving it an empirical base in history, where clusters of innovation take place and generate completely new sectors. He stressed that only technological innovations can overcome depression and that government must implement an aggressive innovation policy to stimulate the search for new and basic innovation.

Further, Porter (1990), emphasizes that the prosperity and competitive advantage of a nation is no longer as a result of a nation's natural resources and its labour force, but rather the ability of its industry to innovate and upgrade. This can be seen as a disruptive technology on a macro environmental level. And today, whether economic community subscribes to these economic theories or not, the impact of new technology on the economy of a nation is indisputable. Continuous growth of e-commerce is expected to have deep impact on structure and functioning of economies at various levels and overall impact on macro-economy. Some key areas are discussed below:

Impact on Intermediation

Traditional production, transportation and distribution process is characterized by the liner-point-to-point path (4). In this process intermediaries play an important role.

In physical world, because of large distance between production units and consumer units, it is not possible for consumers to approach producers directly and vice versa. The existence of intermediaries namely, distributors, wholesalers and retailers, this increase the transaction costs for both the producers and consumers.

But in the emerging economic scenario, liner-point-to-point information and knowledge flow no longer represent the reality. In the process of e-commerce transactions, it is possible for the consumer to conduct and place an order with the manufacturer instantly and directly (Singla, 2000).

And same is possible within the various agents of this process (i.e., between producer and Retailers, Retailers and Distributors, Distributors and Retailers etc.). E-Commerce technology brings about the benefits of more accurate and timely information flow, administrative saving, lowering total distribution cost, closer trading relationship, improved cash flows, and moving closer to the end consumers. No doubt that online ordering and delivery of product is reducing the role of intermediaries. Therefore, it is also feared that intermediaries would be completely eliminated in the e-commerce economy.

However, this fear may be unfounded. In 'e-commerce economy, though it is possible to deliver a number of goods and services online, it may not be possible to eliminate the physical delivery of many goods because of their vary nature. Goods such vegetables and grocery, garments and shoes, toys etc. cannot be delivered online (they have physical existence). Though intermediaries like wholesalers and retailers can be eliminated in such transactions, it may not be possible to eliminate distributors and transporters.

The demand for distributors and transporters is in fact expected to increase tremendously (Westland and Clark). Even with the advent of e-commerce technology, the functions of intermediaries will not change, because collecting information is a labour and time intensive task. However, this group can exploit new opportunities and challenges.

Impact on Agriculture

The open access architecture of the Internet, declining information technology costs, and high volume have resulted in progressive steps forward for the entire marketing system. Parallel changes in the structure of agriculture have also contributed to the popularity of the current generation of information technology.

Chief among the changes is in the need for closer coordination of the supply chain-both upstream and downstream from the producer-and stretching' from seed, fertilizers, and machinery suppliers, to the food processors and retailers. Thus, technologies like electronic commerce have forced new relationships between and among the buyers of agribusiness to form a complex web interaction (Ehmake et al., 2001)

Various studies show that there is much about the potential success of e-commerce's in agriculture. Common agribusiness business-to-business transactions such as buying, selling, trading, delivering and contracting seem to be natural targets for conversion to e-commerce.

Many theoretical benefits of e-commerce in agriculture have been identified such as: (1) promotion of information flow, market transparency and price discovery (Poole, 2001); (2) facilitation of industry coordination (Nicolaisen, 2001); and reduction or elimination of transaction costs (Porter, 2001; Thompson, 1996).

Internet based e-commerce also offer tremendous opportunities to create collaborative marketplaces in low-cost and effective way (Nicolaisen, 2001). E-commerce in agriculture could also potentially tighten the supply chain and cut marketing margins and transactions costs in way that benefit smaller, local producers as well as local agribusinesses. It also enables a vast array of products to be transacted, usually at a price that is competitive with local retailers. E-commerce can also change the situation of hard bargain caused by scattered farmers and lack of information. At the same time, the fast and convenient electronic bargain manner can accelerate the circulation of commodities, and lessen the risk, and increase the competitions of agricultural products in the international market (Cao and Chen, 2001).

These theoretical benefits appear to be undisputed. However, these have yet to materialize into profitability. Study of Golman Sachs (2000) discussed the general barriers citied by business to Internet based e-commerce adoption and explained that these barriers also apply to agribusiness as well.

These barriers include:

(1) unclear return on investment

(2) lack of budget

(3) lack of stakeholders support and

(4) complicated technology.

Added to these, there may be some other factors (10) slowing down e-commerce adoption in agriculture. In fact, many of the issues faced by e-agribusinesses are the same as those faced by the firms in other sectors similar to changes brought by other new agricultural technologies (Hooker et al., 2001).

However, characteristics of the agricultural sector and its participants present some inherent impediments to the implementation of e-commerce practices. Nonetheless, despite these challenges, there is room for creative solutions potentially leading to successful adoption.

Those potential strategies touch on: structure of industry; market and product expertise; and organizational development. At this point of time it is not very clear-the impact of e-commerce on farms, agribusiness firms, markets, and rural communities. Are there only winners or are losers too? If so, who are they? What will government to do, with or against e-commerce in agriculture? Since e-commerce is still evolving, it is too early to definitive answer (Mueller, 2000).

An inspection of current practices; however, suggest that success of e-commerce in agribusiness is undeniable. Factors specific to agriculture will create additional challenges, which must be overcome before success may be attained. The ability of each player to work though these challenges will determine the speed of implication of e-commerce in agriculture.

Impact on Labour Market

E-Commerce, consisting of marketing and other business processes conducted over the computer-mediated networks is changing the way organizations in many industries operate. It leads to the automation of some job functions and replaces others with self service operations, raising output per worker and dampening employment requirements in some occupations, as well as in the industries in which these occupations are concerned (Hecker, 2001).

The introduction and implementation of new technologies has posed important challenges for the commercial workers and their trade unions worldwide. Among the issues that unions have to deal with are, both B2B and B2C, self-scanning, logistics system, multimedia and other in store sales support applications. In many ways, they are already deeply affecting labour market (Gottardi et al., 2004).

In contrast, e-commerce has spurred employment in industries producing software, and systems used by e-commerce and other occupations associated with websites and networks.

Various studies showed that e-commerce has a positive impact on the labour productivity. At the theoretical level, since e-commerce reduces coordination costs between different work processes, they facilitate firms to fragment tasks to enable them to improve the labour productivity. At the same time when the routine tasks can be automated, e-commerce reduces unskilled work. In a recent study, Atrostic and Nguyen (2004) considered the impact of computer networks on the labour productivity in the US manufacturing sector, using micro data predominantly for 1999.

They found a positive and significant impact of computer networks on plant level labour productivity, suggested that networks increase labour productivity by around 7.5 per cent. Motohashi (2001) provides evidence for the positive impact of different information networks on labour productivity in Japan. In the UK a recent study by Criscuolo and Waldron (2003), based on Annual Business Inquiry, shows that buying online positively affects the labour and total factors of productivity, while selling online has a negative impact on productivity.

But, perhaps the larger impact of e-commerce on labour market can be seen in the form of online job search. However, very little is known about the importance of online job applications or direct employer initiated contracts with potential candidates.

Even then, online job posting has grown spectacularly (Autor, 2001). Estimates place the number of online job boards at over 3000, the number of active resumes online at over 7 million, and the number of job posting at 29 million. Kuhn and Skuterud (2000) reported that 7 per cent of employed workers regularly use the web to search for a new job in 1998.

The leading job board, Monster.Com, offered 3.9 million resumes and 4, 30,000 jobs in August 2000. Further, the Internet is likely to change how some workers deliver labour services. For example, falling telecommunications traffic regardless of where it originates. Improvements in communication and control technology likely mean that people who monitor equipment or other workers can perform their task at the greater physical remove. Remote access to e-mail and company documents will enable many workers to perform some or all of their work from home to elsewhere.

On the flip side, it has also been feared that the reduction in number of intermediaries and sales persons due to reduction in number of supermarkets and showroom would reduce employment world over. The worst affected are expected to be the unskilled manpower.

It is true that unskilled labour is getting displaced in a big way in the e-commerce economy. Internet and e-commerce by facilitating firms to employ home-workers on a contractual basis are seen to promote insecure employment opportunities. In India, as well as in the other low-income economies, the potential of e-commerce is seen to employment from the formal sector to small firms in the unorganized sector where employment is not protected by any legislation.

Further, if this feature of e-commerce encourages the formation of small firms that are narrowly specialized, it also implies that there is less room for employee mobility within the firms, transforming the careers paths of employees (Francis, 1986). Added to this, as with other tools, the internet is not without its limitations as a means of attracting qualified candidates.

For example, companies listing opportunities on major job boards may receive applications from a much wider geographic region-and sometimes less qualified applicants-requiring additional sorting and review.

Firms are also noting that some candidates who post their resumes online may be more passive job seekers; they want to "test the waters" and wait the results, versus proactively applying for open position.

Impact on Transportation

In a very short time span common sense has emerged within the world of transport, about the assumed huge impact of e-commerce and especially the Internet on relationships between companies (and consumers). Dholakia et al, (2000) concluded that in those regions of the world where there is old, established and often congested road infrastructure, any e-commerce-based methods that could lead to trip reduction and/or trip rationalization can contribute to an improvement in the quality of life.

At least from a theoretical point of view, it seems quite clear that the online shopping could lead to reduction of transport demand. In some cases, online shopping eliminates any kind of physical transport (when goods can be dematerialized as software, books, music etc.). In other cases, a goods transport is still necessary, but the journeys to shops are eliminated or reduced. Even if the purchase is finally made at the shop, the consumer can have used the Internet, looking for information, instead of visiting different shops.

Thus, electronic commerce transactions have strong implications on transportation. In this context, numbers of studies have been conducted to measure the impact of e-commerce on the number of trips.

Browne (2001) first quoted the study made by Farahmand and Young (1998). It modelled the effects of the number of trips by switch to home shopping of 10 per cent of the customers of a grocery store and a DIY store (of a typical size) in the UK. They assumed that delivery vans would carry the loads of nine customers on each round trip.

In both the cases, the reduction in total trips is around 9 per cent. The vehicle kilometer made by the delivery vans for the 10 per cent of home shoppers suppose a reduction of 87 per cent in comparison with the vehicle kilometers previously made by car. Further, the study (Coirm, 1999) also modelled a case of grocery home delivery in UK and their result shows that if 10-20 per cent of shoppers use home shopping, the reduction in the trips could arrive to 7-16 per cent.

For the purchase made from home, the reduction in vehicle kilometers is 70-80 per cent even if each van only carries eight loads. Against this, study of Colin (2001) revealed that commerce has not had as great an impact on transport lows as some had expected, at least in terms of the volumes carried. However, some substitution effects are to be expected.

Not only on the retail transportation, e-commerce does have impact on the companies where heavy transportation is needed. E-transportation tool can enable seamless connectivity, provide dock-to-dock visibility of the supply chain, and deliver real time information that leads to better and faster decisions. E-transportation also enables shippers a choice of carriers to be used for shipments of merchandise varying in weights and service, and identifies all shipping packing, marking, labelling and communications requirements as well. (Vevaldi and Prasad, 2002).

But many shippers still are not quite ready to put their faith in this relatively new e-commerce tool. Indeed, as with the introduction of new technology, e-commerce as it relates to the transportation industry, is going to take time to catch on.

For transportation companies it is expected that, with e-commerce, a whole new market will open up for transportation and logistics companies, or whatever they may be called in the future. At present e-commerce is pursued to a fairly high degree between companies, but is still not very developed between companies and private persons.

The business-to-consumer (B2C) relation is expected to grow rapidly though, and when this happens it will result in several changes for actors in the logistics area. When delivering to private persons instead of companies, the demand for fast and accurate deliveries will increase.

This is because one or more of the physical nodes will disappear when the goods can be transported directly from the producing company to the end customer. Direct home deliveries will request shorter lead times, and more complex distribution systems will be necessary to make this possible.

Expected trends in traffic and distribution from a widely spread use of e-commerce are fewer passenger cars, an increased number of pickup trucks, and smaller consignments, especially on international transports. Further the study of Hultkrantz and Lumsden (2000) concluded that the logistics industry has to face the challenges and opportunities created by e-commerce, both from within the industry and from external players.

The industry has always been pressed to cut costs and squeeze margins, and the future will be even more formidable as competition forces most companies to continue the streamlining of their business.

Impact on Taxation

When new technologies evolve, can taxation issues be far behind? If e-commerce is being billed as one of the greatest economic developments of the 21st century the taxation issues arising there from poses the single biggest challenge of the century to both-the businesses and the taxman's. (Girish, 20001) This is particularly true in the context of digitized products because transactions of such products are not backed up by any physical of goods. As e-commerce transcends the barriers of geographical boundaries the concept like the place of transactions and place of consumption become immaterial. Therefore, it is often difficult to determine national jurisdiction and revenue rights

International tax issues in the area of e-commerce are manifold and include nexus 0fthe vendor and tax enforcement agencies. Taxing authorities may have great difficulty collecting revenue form vendors conducting commerce through foreign Internet addresses. The foremost problem associated with Internet based commerce is fixing the place of transaction.

The place where a web-server is located, the place where the user initializes the transaction and the server where payment is collected may be different. Electronic transfer of funds heightens the risk of money being sent to tax havens.

Further, many jurisdictions rely on the taxpayer to voluntarily identify himself, herself or itself as falling within its tax system.

Tax authorities may not be able to effectively enforce their rights to collect tax in such an environment, especially if a business does not consider itself to be within a tax jurisdiction and simply choose not to disclose its activities to the relevant authority. It is trite, but true, that taxation of e-commerce is a major concern for the international agencies and the tax authorities worldwide.

In Europe, North America, and Australia and in many Asian Countries (particularly India and Singapore) substantial research have been conducted on the impact of the e-commerce on taxation.

Among the plethora of books, reports, articles and papers produced on this topic however, the work of Organization for the Economic Co-Operation and Development (OECD) stands out as the most significant, given its commitment to consulting broadly with the governments worldwide as well as with the business community to develop an integrated and comprehensive approach to the taxation of e-commerce.

The identification and analysis of the inter jurisdictional measures imposed by e-commerce is one thing. The formulation of domestic and treaty policies for dealing with e-commerce is another, even more controversial challenge. Perhaps, the most fundamental threat to the international tax system is the erosion of the worldwide tax base. It is increasingly possible for a company to try to divert income to a tax haven by locating its server there. This raises issues of allocation of business profits between the residence and source countries and leakage to tax haven (Cidambi, 2000).

The debate over how international tax principles ought to be revealed and may be reformed is still in its formulative stage. It would be necessary to equip the tax administration after reviewing the entire procedure in the light of the advent of e-commerce. First, the procedures have to be simplified. Second, it would be necessary top create an environment within the tax department to ensure that the tax laws are implemented appropriately, and that integrity of the tax base is maintained. (Mantravadi and Chowdary, 2002).

For India, it is high time to learn from the experience of the work of OECD, Japan and the US to suggest a strategy to encourage e-commerce and integrate the tax system in such a way that it takes care of the twin problems of determining the sites of sales and also identifies the jurisdiction with regard to its authority to tax transactions. In doing so, we have to keep in mind the associated risk for the tax compliance.

Impact on Cost, Price and Competition

Logically, e-commerce reduces search and transaction cost (Mukhopadhya, 2002). Reducation in transaction costs are motivating businesses to incorporate e-commerce into their business strategy (Garcia, 1995 and Kambil, 1995) The net impact of e-commerce on UK Economy has been estimated to be between 2% to 3% of GDP. It has also been estimated that improved demand forecasting and stock management as a result of e-commerce will enable reduction in overall inventories by as much as 25% in the US.

At the micro level, there is evidence that this will provides an one-off sustainable improvement in the profitability by an average of 5% or more for the enterprises currently working with low margin (Goldman Sachs, 1999). The e-commerce lowers costs because, the Internet lowers selling search costs as well as, by allowing seller to communicate product information cost effectively to potential buyers, and by offering sellers new ways to reach buyers through the targeted advertisement and one-on-one advertising.

Thus it is helpful in reducing the search costs on both the sides. By reducing search costs on both sides of the market, it appears likely that buyers will be able to consider more product offering and will identify and purchase products that better match their needs, with a resulting increase in economic efficiency.

But the reduction in the cost combined with new capabilities of technology can set off more complex market dynamics (Bakos, 2001). The lower search and information cost should push markets towards a greater degree of price and competition, and this outcome is certainly possible, especially for the homogeneous goods. On the other hand the use of Internet technology to provide differentiate and customized products, and thus avoid competition purely on the price.

Lower search costs in the digitized markets will make it easier for the buyers to find low cost sellers and thus will promote price competition among the sellers. Thus e-commerce economy comes quite close to the features of the prefect competition, as larger numbers of buyers and sellers can instantly interact with each other. Many characteristics of e-commerce should increase competition because buyers will have access to a global marketplace and the ability to easily compare price and product features (Fletcher et al., 2000).

E-Commerce technologies have the potential to significantly increase competition by increasing consumers' choice of products and traders (ACCC, 2001). However, some of the distinguishing characteristics of the e-commerce set up also have the potential for creating the monopoly power in the certain lines of products. The e-commerce set up has negligible distribution cost for the intangibles and therefore marginal cost of the production and distribution is almost nil for these goods.

Sales of these goods to a particular customer does not reduce its availability to the other potential customers. Economies of scale arising out of negligible marginal cost, along with network externalities and consumer preference for the already acquired skills, provide natural monopoly power to some of the products in the e-commerce set up. Early birds are thus expected to reap the benefits in these lines of production. Therefore, in the e-commerce environment, monopoly is expected to exist along with the prefect competition. Competition would be especially seen in those areas where goods and services cannot be digitized and economies of scale are not very prominent. Breaking the monopoly power to remain in the competition would require high speed of innovation and making the product visible all the time, whether there is a demand for the products or not. Competition would be basically in the forms of converting ideas, knowledge and brain power into innovation.

Impact on Money

With the new economic landscape now outline, let us return to the money. Not surprisingly, in the intangible (e-commerce based economy) economy, money is also becoming increasingly intangible. The relative weight on non-cash monetary transactions now exceeds the value of cash money by the factor often (Goldfinger, 2002).

Money and payments are delivered via electronic networks as data bits and database entries. At the wholesale level, money representation and manipulation are fully automated. Beyond the alteration of the appearance and mechanics of money, there are deeper structural changes. The triumph of markets means that money is increasingly used to settle multilateral transactions rather that the bilateral commercial transactions.

The functional evolution in turn leads to profound modification in the design of the clearing system and networks, which need to handle large volume, work in real time, and offer more open access. Growth of e-commerce and development of various payment alternative channels (i.e.. Debit and Credit Cards, E-Cheque, Digital Purse, E-Cash etc.) assist payment channels.

The delivery channels greatly impacted the retail banking and the wholesale markets of banks. And today, these new technologies have transformed the banking business almost beyond the belief in the last decade and the half. Most of all the customers have benefited, as have the bank themselves. Added to this, digital currencies have many other advantages; some of the important are: cheaper, faster, safer, global, and more private than traditional credit cards and bank wires. In other words, digital currencies will prove to be as world-changing as the invention of the printing press and gunpowder. Digital currencies link together financial institutions and markets across the globe in a way that allows instantaneous value transfers with a mere fraction of the cost associated with traditional bank wires and credit cards. But, this new forms of money has also posed certain challenges before the banking sector, most of them are related to IT plans (Kamesan, 2003). Many schemes have been piloted or rolled out but the use of e-money is still tiny. This raises the question why e-money has not been more successful. One explanation may be that there is not sufficient demand. Another explanation is that we are merely observing the slow start that is typical for many inventions. Once critical mass has been reached, e-money will take off. Finally, the problems of e-money may stem from regulation.

No doubt, these changes make money more visible and pervasive but also less stable, more volatile in its value and more elusive. Therefore, in the new economy, monetary policy become more important as a lever of economic management at the same time that the classical monetary aggregates—lose their reliability as signals of the future economic growth and inflation' (Goodhar, 1984). Nevertheless, one thing appears certain, electronic money will continue to emerge, rendering the overall money landscape more intricate and multifarious. To facilitate the emergence of electronic money, it is important to be open minded, to accept innovate vision of money and money transaction. At the same time it is also essential to recognize that many of these visions will either never be implemented or fail the critical test of customer acceptance.

Concluding Remarks

The emergence and rapid growth of Internet and E-Commerce has strong implications on economic and social actitivities. It is quite possible that these new technologies might transform the future of economic and societal landscape. At the economic front, there is a clear evidence that E-Commerce and Internet techonolgy have positive impact (UNDP, (2003), Pohjola (2000), Dewan and Kramer (2000), Kraemer and Dedrick (2000)}. To study the economic implications of e-commerce, few areas of economy (transportation, Intermediation, Agriculture, Labour Market, Taxation, Cost, Price and Competition, and money) has been selected. On the basis of various studies it is revealed that e-commerce technology have strong economic implications. At the general level, there are two types of potential economic gains from the use of E-commerce and IT enabled technologies. First, are the gains in efficiency, both in static and dynamic.

Static gains are one-time, and come from more efficeint use of scarce resources, allowing higher consumption in the present. Dynamics gains come from higher growth, potentially raising the entire future stream of consumption and population. Efficiency gains of e-commerce also come about through the enabling of new digitized goods and services. The second type of potential benefits comes from cost reduction. Studies indicates that e-commerce is helpful in reduction of search cost, administration cost, distribution cost and even the labour costs. However, all these opportuities are yet to materlize in to profitability i.e. in agricultural sector, benefits of e-commerce exists, but, only theortically; not practically, as the implemetnation of e-commerce technolgy in agricultural sector has certin challenges. Addes to this, e-commerce based economic models has also posed number of challenges before the concerned people and community.

The area of e-taxation is one of the best example and most controversial issue all over the world. As e-commerce transaccends the barriers of geographical boundaries, the concept like the place of transactions and place of consumption become immaterial. With the emergence and growth of digital money in the economy, the chances of frauds have also incresased. Another most difficult issue is the planning regarding the adoption and implemetation of e-commerce technology in the various economic activities. In nutshall, with the e-commerce based economic models, there is little to lose and more to gain.

The Internet Intermediary: Gateway to Internet Commerce Opportunities

Given the projections that internet commerce will grow astronomically over the next four years, firms of all sizes must become proactive in not only seeking out Internet opportunities, but in determining ways to exploit this revenue generating medium. The environment presents such opportunities right now in the form of the Internet intermediary.

Trends indicate that firms should already be involved in Internet commerce. At minimum, firms should be beyond the information-seeking only stage and actively involved in Internet commerce to some extent.

They should already be experimenting with the Internet as a medium for conducting business transactions. Although the possibilities of being an industry leader have already passed, there still is time to become an active player in Internet commerce. That entry point could easily be the use of Internet intermediaries to acquire the non-production consumable materials/services, a segment of every firm's operational, repair, and maintenance materials and services needs (ORM/MRO).

The clock is ticking and necessity seems to be clearly dictating that Internet commerce needs to become part of one's business thinking now and woven into the fabric of the firm's strategic business plan.

Internet Commerce

Depending on which trade journal one picks up and to whom you make reference, Internet commerce is predicted to have tremendous growth into the 21st century. Even as far back as late 1997 Blane Erwin, director of Forrester's Business Trade & Technology Strategies authored a report with highlights in the September 1997 "Computer Dealer News" that predicted I-commerce growth to rise from $8 (U.S.) billion in 1997 to $327 billion (U.S.) by the year 2002. At the same time International Data Corporation (IDC), Framingham, MA., provided a more conservative projection of electronic commerce being $10 billion in 1997 rising to more than $220 billion by the year 2001. More recent predictions, September 1998, John Gantz, IDC senior vice president, announced his projection that this number will approach one trillion dollars by 2002. It is also felt that 80% of that volume is business-to-business transactions with expectations of that growing to 92% by 2003. Regardless of which projection one values, the reality is a significant increase of Internet commerce activity within the next two to three years. The bottom-line is that substantial growth in Internet commerce is inevitable.

It is suggested that an evolution not unlike that of EDI when it first evolved is taking place but with the emphasis on the buyer and not the seller. It is also clear that the opportunity to be a player does not carry the same restrictions of EDI, nor is one limited by current participation in EDI. Generating revenue on the Internet is much more opportunistic. This trend is re-affirmed in a study done by Forrester Research, Inc., where they predict the growth of Internet commerce as a channel of revenue to increase from 15% in 1997 to 42% in 2001.

Research shows that most sellers will be dragged into Internet Commerce by their customers [Gurley 1997]. There is a fast growing interest to have options for both on-site and off-site transactions with the expectations that off-site will include Internet commerce. Several models are put forth as having potential, but the most pertinent deals with automated purchasing; it prescribes the use of the Web as a medium to acquire non-production goods and services through established business partners, not unlike current EDI methods. Another model suggests a more anonymous exchange where the product is considered homogenous.

In this model, decisions will be based on the information and not on the identity of either the seller or the buyer. Current trends also suggest that Internet commerce is clearly dominated by the buyer, making it a buyer's market (buyer-centric). However, the ground rules for leveraging the new buyer-centric model have yet to be established.

Internet commerce is past the experimental stage and it may even be past the early-adopter stage in spite of the continued threat of prohibitive technology barriers and operational problems. Although ongoing discussions on standards, interoperatability, security, bandwidth, intellectual property protection, content regulation, fraud, import/export controls, taxation etc. continue to happen, it is recognized that their impact has an overall global effect on Internet commerce. As such the impact will be felt as a whole and will thus require ongoing tweaking by developers of any solution application(s) put into use as regulations and standards are enacted.

Even after considering all of the valid issues that the use of technology imposes, there is another possible non-technology threat that certainly needs to be taken into consideration. One must take into account the threat to the current reseller-intermediary "middle-man".

The question is raised as to whether one can expect resellers to take this predicted shift of manufacturer-to-consumer buying in stride (dis-intermediation). It is believed that any significant migration of consumer to manufacturer activity is a good reason for resellers to penalize web-based manufacturers for abandoning the traditional reseller by threatening with a possible move to their competition. This has serious impact when it is based on the perception that the majority of the public does not buy over the Web yet, and therefore manufacturers cannot afford to alienate traditional resellers.

In spite of the above concerns and issues, Internet commerce continues to grow and solutions are being developed to address most of the identified problems. This is recognized as a continuous effort as new issues surface. Experts agree that Internet commerce is fast becoming a popular medium in which to conduct business-to-business transactions. At minimum the Internet will be evaluated as to how it can bolster the firm's competitive edge. Research addresses this in particular by presenting the discussion that firms need to use technology as a means to expand their "bounded rationality" [Bakos & Treacy 1986], more specifically, technology will allow a firm to go beyond its information processing limitations by using what technology and now the Internet have to offer.

Considering the projections for Internet commerce and the observed growth of the Internet itself, there are reasonable expectations that Internet commerce is more than a fad. In addition, the adoption of the Open Buying Internet (OBI) standard further supports that big firms who are EDI players now are looking at ways to utilize the Internet for more commerce. It becomes a safe assumption that Internet commerce must be incorporated into the business strategy of all firms. It is also predicted that once the use of Internet commerce becomes a commonplace activity, the advantage quickly switches to a strategic necessity [Green et al. 1998, Bakos 1991]. Firms can no longer ignore this means of potential revenue-generating medium. All firms must look for the most efficient mechanism to enter into the Internet commerce market whether they intend to buy or sell.

The Internet Intermediary

One can ask how a firm might make the transition from predominately retrieving information from the Internet to actively using it for commerce. The novice is being cautioned not to just jump in and attempt to partake without some planning and a strategy. A possible solution that already exists is in the form of currently available Internet intermediaries. The intermediary concept is not new to the Internet, and it is far from being fully exploited. Players are moving in and out of this market niche as opportunities permit. Besides providing an entry point of access to Internet commerce, the Internet intermediary provides a multitude of critical benefits. To formulate an action plan, an organization needs to have a strategy based on key factors which can be supported by the roles of an Internet intermediary.

Whether one intends to buy, sell or take on the function of the Internet intermediary, the roles are important factors against which to measure business strategies. To get a better understanding of these roles, the beneficial attributes can be categorized under each defined role stated above which provides further clarification and definition. The roles of the Internet intermediary can then be further refined by their corresponding benefits as follows:

Access: Provides access 24 hours, 7 days/week, 365 days/year. Prohibits movement of unwanted information (junk mail). Serves as a means to curtail information overload. Provides, establishes, and enhances communications standards. Provides for a secure channel to transact business.

Extends business from local to global market. Promotes the use of new technology. Makes available a scalable architecture. Takes care of the infrastructure needs for all clients (guaranteed uptime). Provides a training ground for the novice firms entering the Internet. Authenticates and validates genuine business users.

Aggregation: Provides a forum for transactions of multiple products from multiple sellers. Ongoing recruitment of clients (buyers & sellers). Ongoing search for new potential markets/ products. Bundles multiple services/products into a single priced package. Allows for side-by-side product comparison.

Costs: Reduces Costs: Coordination of players (link buyer & seller), Searching (looking for best fit, product features), Processing transactions (quicker and less resource consuming), Information gathering to determine product prices (includes manufacturing costs and all distribution costs), Helps to avoid "Deadweight" costs (lost costs due to unsuccessful searching), Provides for economies of scale investing in technology.

Facilitation: Provides a dictionary of terms for merchandise/ services. Improves chances for linking best fit for buyer & seller. Facilitates information exchange between producer and end-user. Collects information on buyers' preferences. Tracks market information and transaction data. Provides for a controlled information link from end-user back to manufacturer. Handles the interfaces for accounting and financial. Provides the forum which relieves the manufacturer from the obligation of dealing directly with the end-user. Provides forum for end-user to avoid having to sift through large quantities of information to determine important decision factors.

Trust: Prevents opportunistic behaviours & unfair trade practices. Buffers/mediates interests of buyers against interests of sellers. Assures against transaction failures. Allows for the complete processing of business transaction(s). Enhances business activity by reputation. Provides some commerce regulation where there is none now. Extends credibility to products/service.

Value-Added: Introduces/identifies uniqueness of services & products. Enhances product-line with differentiation. Informs buyers about availability. Provides detailed product specifications. Makes available a forum for advertising and marketing new or existing products.

It is also understood that the intermediary will avoid limited partnerships which lock out potential clients. Some of the additional benefits include the direct involvement to risk aversion, tracking of market information, providing product information, providing a forum for multiple products from multiple sellers, monitoring of transaction data, and promoting new technology after being tested.

What one sees is that the Internet provides for additional options and/or enhances the role of the intermediary in dealing with the attributes of the functions prescribed. Action on the part of either the buyer, seller, or a third party can become the first step in the foundation upon which firms can begin to exploit what the Internet has to offer.

Intermediaries are already well-entrenched in the business model of most firms where they play an active role in the supply chain. This is also supported by a survey conducted by "Purchasing Online" magazine in May 1999 [Avery 1999], where the respondents affirmed the ongoing interest in using distributors (intermediaries) to continue to acquire the supplies/materials which fall into the category of maintenance, repair, and operations. The acceptance of the potential role of the intermediary leads us into determining what type of products can and should be made available over the Internet. If the products/services are simple to describe and/or they can be described via industry standards, or more specifically if products/services are not asset specific, and are low in description complexity, then these products/services will tend towards the Internet which promotes an open market [Williamson 1991, Malone et al. 1987]. It is from this theory that the suggested area of concentration be the non-production consumable materials and services that are traditionally categorized in the MRO.

This category of expenses is grouped in the operating resources budget of the firm and can include such commodities as: office supplies, travel, electronics, groceries, apparel, audio/video equipment, computers, gifts, etc. This category of merchandise, which is low in complexity and low in asset specificity, and viewed as meeting the conditions prescribed above, are a very likely channel for Internet commerce [Peterson et al. 1997].

This is already being observed by the research of Forrester Research, Inc. where they have captured and compiled a listing of the high revenue generators in the Internet commerce market to date.

It is further suggested that efforts in capturing savings by improving efficiencies in the managing of operating resources which includes the MRO categories can be realized and that these savings can affect the profit line directly [Killen & Associates 1997].

The value of these operating costs is identified by a corporate cost breakdown developed by Forrester Research and Killian.

Speculation on what type of firm would be the best intermediary is another item for further discussion. Time is already proving what research has proposed, that new ventures will be formed and/or existing institutions will step up to fill the gap in Internet commerce [Galbraith, 1977].

Simply stated, new entities form to fill information gaps and needs. Possible entities that could easily become the intermediary are unlimited. There is however a natural attraction to this role for existing non-Internet intermediaries, financial institutions, parent corporations of conglomerates, governmental agencies, and consortiums of buyers or sellers.

Conclusion

The conclusion that can be drawn from the discussion is that firms must take immediate action and get involved with Internet commerce. However, one should do so prudently and with a defined business strategy. One such entry point is via intermediaries.

The Internet intermediary provides an immediate opportunity for most firms to engage in Internet commerce. The Internet intermediary in turn becomes a business partner dealing with the specifics of transacting business via the Internet. In the business-to-business market, it is also believed that one of the initial market areas that will be influenced is the maintenance repair and operations (MRO) type of products and services. It behooves those firms which are not actively engaged in Internet commerce to not delay their entry for much longer or risk missing the boat.

A note of caution is advised that one should address Internet commerce based upon identified benefits which can be attributed to specific Internet intermediary roles. The concern is no longer whether the time has already come and gone for the industry leaders; instead the focus is now on Internet commerce for future business survival. As the Internet opens what once were restricted geographical markets to what is now being viewed as a global playing field, delaying entry into Internet commerce could prove to be fatal regardless of the type or size of the firm.

7

Securing E-Commerce: A Systematic Approach

Introduction

Electronic commerce, or simply e-commerce, is changing the way in which banks and consumers interact and transact. E-commerce provides consumers the ability to bank, invest, purchase, distribute, communicate, explore, and research from virtually anywhere an Internet connection can be obtained.

Given the explosive growth of the Internet, most e-commerce providers are migrating from proprietary networks and dial-up servers to the Internet in order to capture larger market shares. The World Wide Web, or simply the Web, has become the vehicle of choice for conducting commerce over the Internet because of the user-friendly and rich multi-media interface provided by Web browsers.

The vast growth potential for e-commerce in the banking and financial services industry is tempered by legitimate concerns over the security of such a system. Most diners are not too concerned about the possibility of a waiter keeping an imprint of their credit card number. Similarly, most of us feel comfortable about giving our credit card numbers over the phone to an operator.

Why should e-commerce be any different? The answer lies in the scale by which fraud or theft can be perpetrated by flaws in the software systems that facilitate e-commerce transactions. The very nature of computing has the ability to amplify many-fold the effect of a simple error in e-commerce software into large-scale fraud, theft, or security intrusions. A simple error in configuring a commerce site's Web server can lead to the compromise of thousands of credit card numbers which can be quickly and widely distributed.

A recent criminal case illustrates this vividly. Carlos Felipe Salgado Jr. pleaded guilty to have been paid $260,000 in an FBI sting for a diskette containing personal information for over 100,000 credit-card holders. The data was allegedly obtained by Salgado hacking into company databases through the Internet. To protect e-commerce systems from these types of abuses, the systems must be secured systematically.

Securing e-commerce must occur on four fronts: (1) securing the Web clients, (2) securing the data transaction, (3) securing the Web server, and (4) securing the network server operating system. To date only the data transaction protocols have gained recognition and development of secure properties. The security of e-commerce systems, though, are only as strong as their weakest component. A failure to secure any one of these four components of electronic commerce may result in the entire system being insecure. If one component is much more secure than others (e.g., the data transaction protocol versus the network servers), then criminals will attack the weakest component (the path of least resistance).

The benefits of providing goods and services over the Internet are immediately apparent. However, placing a server on the Internet also opens the potential for malicious criminals to break into systems, steal files, deny service and possibly destroy the host systems. Erecting firewalls can prevent attacks against internal computer systems (at least initially); however, firewalls can only provide trivial security assurance against data-driven attacks through the Web.

This article highlights critical vulnerabilities in Web security that providers of e-commerce will find invaluable. First, the security issues for banks and other providers of e-commerce have in using the Internet and the Web are discussed. These issues include: setting up and maintaining a secure Web server, vulnerabilities in web servers, and the dangers of CGI scripts and Web applications in general. Also addressed are the client-side security issues in e-commerce transactions for consumers as well as for employees who use the Web. Security and privacy breaches are a concern when using commercial Web browsers, downloading programs, viewing images, and surfing to Web pages with active content applications. Future articles will address the data transaction security and network server operating system security.

Web Server Vulnerabilities

What are the security issues that companies must be concerned about in using the Web for electronic commerce? First, the setup and configuration of a Web server can be complex and the security implications of a misconfigured server are severe. Take as an example a system administrator who installs and configures a Web server. The system administrator knows that the server must start up as the super user in order to listen to the privileged HTTP port. Without necessarily thinking of the security implications, the system administrator sets the executing privilege of the Web server to the super user. Now, any actions the server takes will have the weight and privilege of the super user. So, if an attacker is able to subvert the server, the attacker will now have super user privileges.

Flaws, shortcomings, or even features in a Web server can provide a gateway for a malicious intruder to break into corporate systems. The Web server is responsible for accepting and responding to requests over the Internet—similar to other network programs which allow users to remotely log into systems. However, the range of functions handled by the Web server is quite large. An axiom of software development is that the more complex the software, the more likely flaws exist in the software code.

Security professionals are now beginning to recognize and embrace the idea that most security breaches are made possible by flaws in software code. As an example, the HTTP Web server version 1.4 released from the National Centre for Supercomputing Applications (NCSA), which is popularly used at many sites, contained a software flaw that has been a favourite target of many computer crackers. The flaw is in a software routine that is intended to remove possibly malicious input characters in Web server requests. However, when the routine was coded, an ASCII character was omitted from the list of possibly malicious input. This particular character can be used in a simple attack that enables an intruder to execute arbitrary commands on the server. Given this ability, a hacker may retrieve files, write files, and possibly erase files, depending on the privilege with which the Web server is executing. A patch for this problem has since been released; however, the extent to which the vulnerability has been patched in installed versions is unknown.

Web Client Vulnerabilities

Equally important to e-commerce security is the security of client-side software, specifically Web clients. Active content applications such as Java applets, Active controls, Java Scripts, VBScripts, browser plug-ins, and e-mail attachments all pose potential security and privacy hazards for e-commerce end-users.

The first issue companies must wrestle with is whether or not to trust the Web browser itself. Most browsers are given the privilege to execute programs locally, to write to user disks, to upload and download files and programs from the Internet. Since the source code is usually not distributed with the browser, the consumer must trust that the browser software is not performing any malicious actions such as corporate espionage on a file system. Often times, when installing the software, the user must agree not to hold the browser vendor responsible for any damages resulting from use of the browser. Netscape Navigator versions 2.x, 3.x, and 4.1 as well as the Internet Explorer versions 3.x and 4.0 browsers have all had serious flaws that have permitted complete security violations.

Beyond the issue of the browser source itself, companies must be concerned with the features that many browsers provide. The most popular browsers come with options for plug-ins that automatically execute files viewed from remote Web sites. Certainly, this provision makes surfing the Web interesting as far as multimedia presentations; however, executing an untrusted application opens the door for malicious attacks.

Perhaps the most popular form of active content available on the Internet is Java applets. When viewing a Web page which has a Java applet attached, the Java applet is downloaded to the client's disk and automatically executed unless this default feature is disabled in the browser. While Java was designed with security measures to prevent unauthorized access to client file systems, this security model has been repeatedly violated. Java Script has also been shown to contain very serious security holes in previous releases. Corporate users should not download active content unless the source is trusted—and even then, no assurance of security is provided.

In order for corporations to begin to address the security concerns of Web browsing, a security policy must be established and enforced at corporate sites regarding downloading files from the Internet. It is easily conceivable that an employee could unknowingly download a virus, a malicious program that opens a backdoor in the system, or even images which have programs encoded in them that are executed once downloaded. This malicious use of images to store programs is a focus of a field of research called steganography. Java security is expected to improve over the long term, but until the security issues are resolved, it is safest to disable Java and Javascript unless you are viewing trusted applets. System-wide filtering solutions are also available for preventing executable content from being downloaded over the Internet.

The Internet today is a vast frontier of unknown elements including new types of software, new discoveries of security flaws, and unfriendly neighbours. The most secure technical solution to preventing attacks launched from the Internet is to unplug the network from the computer. This solution is not viable in today's business climate.

Rather, the components that comprise e-commerce systems must be adequately secured. Two components of e-commerce that are often overlooked in security are the network server software and the Web clients. For mis-configured servers (mail, news, Web, FTP, and others), breaking into a site becomes as simple as following a recipe (usually published in underground sites). Armed with the facts about security, corporate MIS managers and system administrators can begin to make appropriate decisions to secure e-commerce.

The Risks and Rewards of Electronic Commerce

The "Economist" magazine notes that technological turning points are difficult to spot. The publication pointed out that at the turn of the century when Studebaker switched from making horse-drawn carriages to making cars, the move was not obvious because in the previous five years New Yorkers had bought 350,000 carriages and only 125 cars.

Now we are entering a new century, and the information age is about change and about achieving new impossibilities. This change will affect businesses. They need to understand it and, more importantly, take advantage of it.

Businesses of all sizes need to understand the role that telephones, computers, networks, and technology can play in creating new impossibilities. And if they can harness this potential, they will be the successful entrepreneurs and business persons who will bring new products to the market, increase consumers' choices, lower costs, and improve national economies.

Just consider for a moment the changes that have taken place in the telecom and information sectors in the last several decades. The global network of computers, telephones, and televisions has increased its information-carrying capacity a million times over.

In 1960, a transatlantic telephone cable could carry only 138 conversations simultaneously. Today, a fiberoptic cable can carry 1.5 million conversations at one time. Today's laptop computers weigh as little as 1.85 pounds (0.83 kilograms) and are many times more powerful than the $10 million mainframe computers of the mid-1970s. Twenty-five years ago there were only about 50,000 computers worldwide; today that number is estimated at 140 million. And no communications medium has ever grown as fast as the Internet, which has an estimated 50 million users worldwide.

Two key issues are emerging as increasing numbers of individuals and companies use electronic networks to engage in commerce: (1) the need for companies to focus on their value-added; and (2) the need to delineate the appropriate roles of the private sector and the government.

The Risks and Rewards for Businesses

The explosive pace and unpredictable nature of the technological developments make any attempt to engage in electronic commerce a bit like betting on a long-shot in a horse race. Even industry leaders don't always make it to the winner's circle.

The Internet, Intranets, extranets, and other communications networks are lowering entry barriers to commerce, enabling both small and large firms as well as consumers to engage in and benefit from electronic commerce. Electronic commerce is already generating important sales and savings for businesses.

For example, the on-line bookseller Amazon.com's increasing share of the bookstore market (by offering discounts up to 40 percent) forced major bookstore chains like Barnes & Noble and Borders Books to go on-line. Federal Express delivery service saved as much as $10,000 a day in 1996 by moving some of its customer service to its Web site. Dell Computer now sells $1 million worth of PCs every day on the Web. General Electric buys $1,000 million in materials from suppliers on-line and saves money by streamlining the process and opening it up to more competition.

Keep in mind that it is not simply a matter of creating a Web site. Amazon.com is a success, now valued at $500 million. Interestingly, a British businessman pursued the same idea at the same time – but his company is only worth $3 million today. Why the difference? Jeff Bezos, the American owner of Amazon.com, researched the industry and relocated to be near one of the world's biggest book warehouses. Mr. Bezos also raised $11 million from venture capitalists at the outset and heavily marketed his business. And he learned how to market effectively worldwide – Amazon.com sales outside the United States are 10 times the British company's sales outside of Britain.

Electronic commerce is not just for big corporations. In fact, it provides exciting possibilities for small companies and entrepreneurs to tap into markets around the world. Moreover, it enables the sharing of valuable information and resources. Recently, Women Inc. (a non-profit organization devoted to helping women business owners succeed) and AT&T announced a partnership that will greatly help women entrepreneurs and could serve as a model for other groups. AT&T has provided Women Inc. with a $25,000 grant to develop and host a Web site that will give Women Inc. members data space for business transactions, space to sell their products and services, the opportunity to "ask the expert" business-related questions, and the ability to register for conferences. Through the Web site, members also have access to a host of services.

The Internet is causing a lot of businesses to rethink how they do business. Business owners and executives should ask themselves: "If the Internet, in its current state, had been around when the enterprise was founded, would you be running your business the way you are doing so today?" If the answer is no, why not change now? Can you develop a niche market? How can you compete effectively with off-line companies as well as other on-line companies?

Private Sector, Government Roles

The Clinton administration believes that the private sector can and should develop many of the solutions to emerging legal, policy, and technical challenges with respect to electronic commerce, particularly activities on the Internet. When activities on the Internet raise new issues, the government should first turn to the private sector to see if a solution can be crafted without government action. The Internet community has a demonstrated record of expanding the Internet, successfully managing its operation and growth, and developing policies and mechanisms to govern its use without government regulation.

Many of the solutions to emerging Internet-related concerns lie with technology, and in turning to the private sector we can take advantage of its entrepreneurial energy. The private sector has already demonstrated its ability to develop new technology tools, such as screening software to address concerns about children's access to adult material on the Net, as well as standards that would give individuals the ability to control the disclosure and use of their own personal profiles generated when using the Web. The U.S. federal government does have a valuable, and at times critical, role to play with respect to the development of electronic commerce. The federal government should be engaged in:

(1) promoting a market-driven environment;
(2) creating a predictable legal environment governing electronic commerce transactions, and
(3) building business and consumer awareness about externalities that undermine healthy markets.

Even as the government takes steps to fulfill this role, we must ensure that any government action is the minimal necessary to achieve goals and one that allows competition and innovation to flourish.

A Market-Driven Environment

The federal government has a valuable role to play now to preserve the global environment in which a contract-based, market-driven model of commerce can emerge. Increased commercial activity on the Internet makes it an increasingly attractive target for government regulation to address concerns about fraud, content, and competition, as seen by recent state and foreign government action. Consequently, the federal government has two distinct, but complementary, roles:

(1) U.S. leadership is needed to preserve the Internet as an unregulated, contract-based, market-driven environment internationally as well as interstate.
(2) In some cases concerted international, intergovernmental action will be needed to facilitate electronic commerce and protect consumers. In these cases, U.S. leadership is needed to promote a minimalist approach designed to ensure competition, prevent fraud, foster transparency, and facilitate dispute resolution.

The Clinton administration believes that government should minimize regulations and let technology blossom and grow. The administration's approach to the Internet is that, in general, our first instinct should be to refrain from regulation. No form of electronic media has grown as fast as the Internet, and the Net has grown precisely because it is not regulated.

We are very concerned that a number of nations have taken steps or are contemplating action to censor information received by their citizens via the Internet. We believe that freedom of speech applies in cyberspace and that laws censoring the information that flows over the Internet are both misguided and impractical, especially given the global nature of the Internet.

We strongly believe that the best way to fight misinformation is with more information. To quote actress Mae West: "Too much of a good thing is wonderful." Moreover, the best guarantee of democracy and stability are informed citizens.

Obviously, on certain issues such as pornography and children's access to adult material, the U.S. government is concerned. But even here, we are looking to industry to self-regulate and to develop technological tools that parents and Internet service providers, not the government, can use to filter out material inappropriate for children.

The good news is that the computer industry and the on-line service industry have been moving quickly and responsibly to develop new products and services to make the Internet "family-friendly." These technologies enable parents — not governments — to determine what is appropriate for their children. The Internet and its products also are generating new competition for traditional telecommunications and media companies. The Clinton administration is concerned with recent attempts by other nations to ban or block telephone calls on the Internet to protect their state-owned phone companies.

A Predictable Legal Environment

The U.S. government has an important role to play as facilitator and catalyst for electronic commerce. We need to examine whether existing governing standards should continue to apply and whether new ones are needed. The major issues include data security, intellectual property, privacy, and financial issues.

The United States recognizes that other nations are facing these same issues, yet often with a different historical and cultural perspective as well as different legal and regulatory frameworks. Given the global nature of the Internet and other networks, a consensus regarding governing standards needs to be developed on both national and international levels.

Is SET Really the Answer to E-Commerce?

For the past two years, the Secure Electronic Commerce protocol (SET) has been promoted as the answer to safe and secure e-commerce. But the acceptance of SET has been slow to happen with US banks. Meanwhile, electronic commerce continues to grow in its absence. Consumers believe they are already making purchases in a secure environment with SSL (Secure Sockets Layer protocol). By the time we get around to a version of SET that s workable on a broad scale, it may be too late to sell it to the general public.

The latest version of SET promised to be the catalyst that would jump-start widespread commerce on the Internet. To date, some SET pilots are being conducted, primarily in Europe, Asia and Latin America. Only two US banks have agreed to a SET pilot so far; and at least one of those tests has been delayed until 1998. Even with the latest version of SET, lack of interoperability among software remains an issue. Why has the acceptance of SET been so slow to happen?

The complexity and the cost of making SET work are just beginning to be realized. While SET addresses the specifications for cardholder-merchant-acquirer transactions, it does not address the many operational requirements for card issuers to make it work on a large scale.

Cardholder certificates are the cornerstone to providing the real value of SET, but the infrastructure has not yet been developed to manage them on a day-to-day basis. Many bank executives don t understand certificate authorities and digital signatures; and according to SET, it is the banks that are responsible for issuing cardholder certificates. It is not likely that the funding for this is included in many banks business plans for 1998.

What is the Difference Between SET and SSL?

Unlike SSL, SET does solve the issue of identifying the cardholder in electronic transactions. But there s a real cost involved in doing that, and is it really the area of greatest risk? It is generally agreed that the greatest risk with e-commerce is catastrophic losses from large-scale theft of credit card numbers. If that occurred, it would more likely happen with break-ins to file servers, and not during the transmission of transactions through a secure pipe. SET does not protect against that-SET begins and ends with the individual credit card transaction.

How are they Alike?

Secure electronic commerce is happening today with SSL encryption (Secure Sockets Layer), in spite of all the press about the lack of security on the Internet. SSL does some things as well as SET, and it s already available to consumers through their browsers.

Let s take a look at SET versus SSL. Both SET and SSL solve the following issues:

- Confidentiality of information, and protection against; hacking; or other interception during transmission across a public network, through the encryption of data.
- Integrity of data (like SET, SSL has the capability to determine if messages have been altered).
- Verification that the merchant has been certified by a trusted Certificate Authority. (While it may not be widely known, this capability exists today with SSL for the cardholder to verify that the merchant site is legitimate. If merchants want to conduct transactions in a secure environment, they must provide business licenses and other notarized proof of ownership to be certified by the CA.)

How Realistic is SET Implementation?

SET is working today in limited pilot tests, which are controlled environments. The issue really lies with widespread implementation and acceptance by the general public. Certainly, in an ideal world, SET could be the protocol of choice to ensure absolute security of transactions. But does the incremental benefit provided by SET justify the cost of its implementation? What is the fraud potential for Internet transactions with SSL, as compared to the fraud potential that exists today with MO/TO transactions going across phone lines?

I m not sure that even those who developed SET believe it can be fully implemented. SET specifies that cardholder certificates are optional at the payment card brand s discretion. This may be an out if all else fails, but in the absence of cardholder certificates, who needs SET?

Nothing Fails Like Success: Online Growth in the Offshore World

The 1950s and 1960s saw the emergence, from some tax haven jurisdictions, of the offshore financial centre (OFC). The need for a new type of offshore institution was matched by technological developments which helped bring it into being and gave it shape and form.

For example, the technologies of jet planes and advanced airport infrastructures meant that clients could do business in the Channel Islands and be back in London the same day. The same technologies worked for Canadians and Americans and various Caribbean destinations. As telecommunications technology grew in sophistication geographical proximity to onshore clients became less important. Clients began to use secure, reliable and high capacity phone lines to conduct a variety of banking and commercial services with OFCs. With the Internet, the picture changes again. As we shall see, the technology of the Internet transforms the potential of online economic activities. It has special implications for the offshore world. It promises to change the role of the offshore financial centre.

This century has seen communications technologies link the economic centres of the world as never before. Wiring up the world has brought global integration or globalization.

Globalization rests on an infrastructure of inexpensive, reliable and accessible digital networks. These networks carry sound, pictures, text or numbers, as a stream of digitized 'bits' of information. A series of 1s and 0s.

As networks become more secure, commercial opportunities expand. Products are bought and sold over networks.

Currently, most net-based merchants follow the same taxation rules that apply to mail-order purchases. There is little difference if a product is ordered through the Web or via a 1-800 toll-free number.

But what happens when the product isn't shipped to the buyer, but is delivered electronically as a digital bit-stream via the Internet? With a typical mail-order purchase, the product is shipped somewhere. But the design of the Internet makes it nearly impossible to determine the location of the buyer. With digital distribution, the seller is likely to have no idea of where the product ends up.

Where does the seller reside? Geographical location or where the computer server is located?

What happens when the electronic product is downloaded from a server located offshore? What happens when other transactions, including financial flows of all types, take place over the net and those transactions are from anywhere to anywhere and anywhere just happens to be an offshore low or no tax jurisdiction?

With encryption tax avoidance becomes easier. The technology that protects buyers and sellers can also keep secret the transaction itself from government tax authorities.

Secrecy is made more effective when payment is not via a charge card such as Visa or Mastercard, rather payment is via digital cash. An anonymous payment from one person to another without a third party intervention.

With computer software, music, movies, magazines, business services including banking and financial transactions—all headed for electronic distribution governments everywhere are facing the threat of tax erosion.

In the online trading environment how will taxes be collected? Who will collect taxes? On whose behalf will taxes be collected and where will they be sent? With little evidence of a papertrail—what a job for the tax collector! Digital networks are distance insensitive. Digital data can be stored anywhere, sent anywhere, manipulated anywhere, sold anywhere. Payment can be from anywhere to anywhere on earth.

Little wonder that the major trading nations are worried about their tax base. Participation in low tax jurisdictions is growing "exponentially." Investment by G7 countries in offshore jurisdictions increased by more than 500 percent between 1985-1994. One web site interested in locating new businesses offshore estimates 60,000 offshore businesses were incorporated in the Caribbean in 1995 and—over 130,000 offshore companies were formed worldwide in the same year. Over the next three years they estimate another 500,000 offshore companies will have been incorporated worldwide.

Offshore entrepreneurs are showing the way to those who want to do business from a low tax location. Consider the web site of Hansa.net. Hansa.net offers "location optimized commerce on the Internet" so that "taxes are an option." Hansa.net offers a wide range of services to those who want to avoid taxes by locating offshore, but do business anywhere.

Each day the Net carries more offers to "get rich by moving offshore." The web site "escapeartist" has a page "One Thousand and One Offshore Tax Havens and Banks." (Which also tells how to acquire a 2nd passport.) Or consider "The Offshore Money Book: How to move assets offshore for privacy, protection and tax advantage" available from the web site of offshore-net.com. And if clicking through web pages to find a tax haven is too onerous don't worry, every few days an unsolicited email arrives. The most recent one offers a guide to offshore riches for US20 dollars. Caveat emptor!!

The promise of tax avoidance is not restricted to exotic islands. In December 1997, the US State of Montana completed regulations on a new law that would allow non-residents to protect their assets in Montana. The first state in the US to have such a law!

Muscovitch of Osgoode Hall Law School in Toronto in his Internet article, Taxation of Internet Commerce makes the point of tax avoidance as a growing part of everyday life. Companies in Canada or other treaty countries will add the relevant taxes to Internet sales. But what happens when the web site is located in a tax haven? Sales from servers in low or no tax jurisdictions are likely to grow, while sales from servers in other jurisdictions are likely to lag.

Either directly, through offshore banks or other financial intermediaries, the Internet will allow more people everywhere to participate in offshore commerce. The net and encryption clears the way for average citizens of OECD countries to use OFCs.

Numbered bank accounts and on-line payment options open the prospect of tax avoidance to many. A change in quantity leads to a change in quality. So too with tax avoidance. When relatively few people had the skills and legal advice to benefit from an OFC link, onshore governments seemed to look the other way. But what happens when the dam threatens to burst, when the trickle to offshore threatens to become a flood?

The success of the OFC, coupled with the future promise of Internet commerce is leading onshore governments to react. To deny the growing movement to restrain or control offshore activities is likely to be a strategic error.

The OECD has underway a major review of tax avoidance. It is designed "to counter the distorting impact of harmful tax competition on investment and financing decisions and the consequences for national tax bases." It plans to convene a Forum on Harmful Tax Practices and will issue a report listing those countries deemed to be tax havens. At least twelve OECD countries have Commissions, Committees or Ad Hoc Groups looking at the tax implications of the Net.

The UK government has announced a wide-ranging review of the financial systems of the Channel Islands (Man, Jersey and Guernsey). Other EU countries are also taking aim at tax breaks and tax havens. A single market and a single currency seems to be leading the way to tax harmonization.

In November, 1997, the Swedish government asked European finance ministers to "get tough" with tax havens. The Swedish tax minister said "tax havens are a threat to fiscal stability." The US Treasury has noted the problem and say they will act in time. In a parallel move, US officials have acted against offshore gambling via the Internet. US Attorney General Janet Reno (NY Times, March 5, 1998) said "The Internet is not an electronic sanctuary for illegal betting...To Internet betting operators everywhere we have a simple message: You can't hide on line and you can't hide offshore."

The Canadian and Australian governments have gone public with their concerns. An official of Revenue Canada in a public speech (February 11, 1998) said, "The fear is that electronic commerce will gravitate to offshore jurisdictions to take full advantage of corporate and bank secrecy laws, encryption and electronic cash to avoid and evade taxation in other jurisdictions."

Of course it is the existence of tax (and interest) differentials that causes wealthy individuals and many multinationals to shop around for a low-tax location. And the OECD countries have been part of the problem—with tax concessions of all types offered by member countries. But the OECD is concerned that the Internet and links to offshore centres will make tax avoidance much more widespread.

As the OECD has stated;

> ***"Governments cannot stand back while their tax bases are eroded through the actions of countries which offer taxpayers ways to exploit tax havens and preferential regimes to reduce the tax that would otherwise be payable to them."***

The offshore has benefitted from a range of technologies and with the technology of the Internet the OFC stands to benefit again. Offshore commerce is a truly successful venture. To deny the success of the OFC is to invite retaliation and the possibility of eventual failure. Hence the title of my presentation, Nothing Fails Like Success.

Success leads to complacency. We see it over and over again in the affairs of people, companies and nations. A recent Wall Street Journal op-ed article describes the success of McDonald's—

and the problems raised by that success—in just this way, "McDonald's seems to have fallen into the hell that traps many of the best companies at some point in their lives. Having established a dominant position under a previous generation, it is bedeviled by a reverence for the old formulas, while its leadership takes weak steps and then denies all problems."

Success carries with it responsibilities. Here it is the responsibility to protect the place of OFCs. Albert Camus, the French philosopher said "Freedom is not constituted primarily of privileges but of responsibilities." To protect the future freedom of the OFC there is a need to act responsibly.

A crasser way to put it is to quote some folk lore from Guernsey, one of the Channel Islands. "All that comes with the flood will return with the ebb. Riches too rapidly acquired, or ill-gotten, will disappear as quickly as they came." Your job is to act responsibly, even if it involves some enlightened self-interest, so that OFCs can participate in on line commerce now and in the future.

How to do this?

We have seen that more and more ecomm transactions are likely to migrate to OFCs for a variety of reasons. Tax avoidance by buyers and sellers being the major reason. We have seen that onshore governments are watching and will not long tolerate tax erosion.

As tax avoidance grows and threatens tax bases in jurisdictions around the world it might be wise to suggest a defensive move by offshore jurisdictions. The best defence is an offence. Why not mount an offence without being offensive?

I am suggesting that a way of countering any international attempt to control OFCs is to say;

> *"We have seen the future and it is one of net commerce. It is a world where attempts by one jurisdiction or another to impose a tax will fail because of the nature of the net itself and because of the various tools available to encrypt and keep secret these transactions. Yet a tax base is essential if governments of the world are going to be able to provide the range of infrastructure and*

> *public goods that citizens in jurisdictions around the world have come to expect. We therefore suggest a modest turnover tax on net traffic."*

I am here to suggest to you today, for your consideration, one such tax. A bit tax. A tax on each interactive digital bit of information. While many will find it odd that I propose such a tax at such a meeting in this jurisdiction I am confident that those concerned with the longer term implications and governance of OFCs will see this as a useful strategic move.

An official from one of the OECD countries said "...if the OFCs suggest an online Internet transaction or bit tax it would set back efforts to regulate the OFCs by a decade..."

Over two hundred years ago Adam Smith wrote his classic book— The Wealth of Nations. He concluded that wealth was based on the division of labour and the extent of the market. Today we can add to society's production function: knowledge, information, and communications. The new wealth of nations can be found in the trillions of digital bits of information pulsing through global networks. These are the physical/electronic manifestations of the transactions, conversations, voice and video messages and programs that, taken together record the process of production, distribution, and consumption in the new economy.

Digital networks provide a place to create a new indirect tax, a tax not on the wealth being created but, rather a turnover tax for using the information highway. (I would like to add at this point that the tax is fiscally and economically sound and more detail can be found in a book that I co-authored called The New Wealth of Nations: Taxing Cyberspace.)

While there are few kudos for proposing a new tax, there is a strategic reason for offshore jurisdictions to propose a new indirect tax on interactive digital traffic. The time is ripe to suggest positive and constructive ways of dealing with the fiscal realities created by more and more shopping, banking and trading moving online and offshore. The move to cyberspace suggests consideration of a new and growing tax base. A tax that is difficult to avoid, where collection is in few hands. A tax that can be collected by many jurisdictions.

How do we do this? Consider a turnover tax on digital traffic. This would be similar to a gasoline tax or a bridge toll or license plate fees for a car. These current excise and indirect taxes apply by weight of vehicle, and amount of gas used, not on the value of the commodity carried by the truck or automobile. So why not examine a possible tax on the digital traffic of the Information Highway? Why not tax each digital bit of information?

Imagine a "bit tax." I am proposing that we tax each digital bit of information flowing in global networks. And with convergence, all information—data, voice, images—will be in digital form.

The digital bit may be part of a foreign exchange transaction, a business teleconference, an Internet e-mail or file transfer, electronic check clearance, or an ATM transaction. The tax can be levied on fibre optic, micro-wave, cable or interactive satellite traffic. The bit tax as a new tax is congruent with a new economy based on digital networks.

The bit tax offers a way for Offshore Financial Centres to say to the rest of the world, "Fear not for your financial future, there is a way to conduct commerce in cyberspace and still maintain a tax base, a tax base that is growing." Say the tax is.000001 cents per bit. Collected automatically it will cause fewer problems than most other direct or indirect taxes. If collected by the telecom carriers, satellite networks, and cable systems, the revenues would flow directly to the national revenue service of the respective country.

The bit tax would be applied to all interactive digital transactions. Interactivity makes the transaction valuable. A conversation, data search, accessing an ATM, shopping on the net, banking via the net—is an activity you choose to do because it does something for you. You get something for doing it, you get something out of doing it— otherwise you wouldn't be doing it. It is this new value, this new productivity that is creating so much new wealth in networks.

The tax would apply to all interactive digital traffic. Digital broadcast ("one-to-many" broadcasts) would be exempt. But broadcasts of one-to-few, eg., TV broadcast to a few stations for later rebroadcast, or newspaper transmission by satellite to remote printing plants are interactive (because they are "addressable") and would be subject to the bit tax.

Research is needed on many aspects of the tax. For example, two pricing models have been proposed. One is the "letter model." This would operate in a similar way as today's postal system. Here the digital message would carry a further piece of information: an electronic franking mark. The electronic frank would consist of changing one bit in the header of the message. The metaphor is to today's postage stamp and franking by the local post-office which indicates the postage has been paid and the letter can be delivered anywhere in the world. Member countries would have a settlement mechanism, similar to the Universal Postal Union, to assure that revenues are equitably distributed.

Another pricing model is based on the turnpike or the toll road. Here the digital message would be subject to a number of (lower) bit taxes as it travels through the network. With collection taking place at each node in the network, countries would keep what they collect. Here there is no need for an electronic franking mechanism.

Pilot studies are needed on how to impose the tax. User-pay or applied at a regional level, say, by area code, metro area, province or state? Or some combination of both? Part of the tax in the customer's base rate and the rest based on actual use.

Note the implications of including area code or other region as part of the taxable base. If transactions greatly increase in one region, new network investments and operations would likely take place in a lower bit tax rate region.

Research must be done on the burden or incidence. Is it progressive or regressive? Will it be absorbed by carriers, or passed on to consumers, or both? Should lower rates apply to very large files such as digital movies downloaded to the home?

Leased or private lines would be charged a fixed rate depending on the bit-carrying capacity of the line. Thus a 1-800 number or other leased line would have a bit tax rate of, say, 70 percent of the carrying capacity. With no built-in meters in these lines and because the traffic fluctuates, it is easier to settle on a fixed percentage of capacity.

It is unlikely that any single country could institute a cybertax such as a bit tax. It is equally unlikely that I can clearly see as of this day in 1998 when and how a global bit tax would be fully implemented. But it is quite clear to me that if offshore jurisdictions suggest a constructive and responsible way to deal with the world of online transactions, then direct notice will be taken. And direct notice will be taken almost immediately. Those concerned with global governance, those who have been worrying about tax erosion will take notice of any suggestion by OFCs to dialogue on cybertaxes. This suggestion to look at cybertaxes. From offshore jurisdictions! Imagine!

To speed things along there may be merit in establishing a leadership position. Set in motion some pilot projects among a number of offshore jurisdictions to lead by example. Maybe the bit tax as outlined is too difficult to implement, maybe it will be a modified bit tax or some other form of cybertax. What is important is that offshore jurisdictions will be seen to be sensitive to the issue, will be seen to acting in a responsible way to deal with the challenges and opportunities posed by online commerce.

And what about the tax rate itself? Is it too high or not high enough? If.000001 cents per bit yields too much revenue, it can always be adjusted. As network-based commerce expands, the number of bits increases. During peak periods in North America 1 trillion bits per second (bps) are transferred on telephone networks. In the future, with fibre optic networks the capacity will be expanded to a peta bps. A "1" followed by 18 zeros! The bit tax rate will have to be adjusted for changing times.

Some oppose the tax, arguing that a tax on this new area of economic activity risks slowing its introduction. My answer is: did the imposition of the gasoline tax slow the development of the automobile industry?

Other opponents are those want to decrease the power of the nation state. To do this they would choke off all its taxing powers.

They see the bit tax as a sort of stealth tax. To this group I can only say that I take a different view. From my perspective, I offer a quote from US Supreme Court Justice Oliver Wendell Holmes, Jr., who wrote in a decision in 1904 that "taxes are what we pay for civilized society."

As more and more commerce takes place on global digital networks it is important to develop new fiscal tools that are effective in the digital environment.

I am sure that most can recall the mantra of "thinking globally but acting locally," an idea that came from the environmental movement. It may be that globalization is leading to a reversal of the mantra: it may be that the new reality is one where acting globally and thinking locally is all that nation-states can effectively manage.

One step in global action could be the bit tax. It could supplement the revenues of nations everywhere. As an additional source of tax revenue it could have applications locally. While the economy has gone global, the nation state is the place where citizens turn for a host of services: from education to medical care to income support when jobs are lost. The nation state provides the social and physical infrastructure in which individuals come into the world, are educated, raise families, find meaningful work, and finally leave the world.

While the role of the nation state is undergoing a re-evaluation—there are bills to be paid!

How does the nation meet the fiscal challenge in a globalized economy? How does the nation maintain its tax base in a porous globalized world? How do the developed countries of today avoid becoming part of the "third-world" of tomorrow's information-based global economy?

Today I have suggested one way. A cybertax—a bit tax or some variant offers a way for nations to maintain their tax base.

And it could be, as we peer into a still somewhat murky future, that the bit tax itself—once implemented—could be but the basic turnover tax on the information highway. It could be that somewhere out there we will see the development of a range of bit taxes. Bit tax, bit tax plus and bit tax plus-plus. Might this be one way that low, medium and high tax jurisdictions distinguish themselves in the future?

This line of speculation is for another time, for another venue.

The title of my talk is Nothing Fails like Success. I hope I have offered to this group some thoughts on how to deal with the present and projected success of the OFC in a positive and responsible way. A way that can ensure the continuing success of the offshore environment.

E-commerce Awareness Program for Regional Communities

Increasing the levels of awareness of e-commerce in regional and rural areas has been identified as a major catalyst to encourage the usage of online technologies in rural communities. E-Comm AWARE! is one such pilot project focusing on providing rural communities in Australia the opportunity to develop expertise in online technologies to become 'smart' communities and more competitive in the global marketplace.

Electronic Commerce is fast becoming the catch-all phrase for electronic means of communicating information and business transactions. The fastest growing area of electronic commerce in Australia and the rest of the world is the use of the Internet and online services for exchanging knowledge, for advertising and marketing, for selling and buying, for banking, and for the emergence of entirely new ways of doing business and communicating with individuals and organisations. Electronic commerce is levelling the playing field for small companies to trade as if they were much larger corporations, in a global marketplace, and for regional businesses and communities to participate in cultural, social and commercial networks in a seamless and borderless way.

E-Comm AWARE! is a project that will prepare regional communities to understand the possibilities, to use the technologies and to then participate in local, state-based and federal government electronic communications and commerce initiatives. The project will support sustainability of regional communities and be a model electronic community awareness program that can be transposed to other regional areas across Australia.

The project is funded by the Commonwealth government of Australia, with a local government organisation (La Trobe Shire) and a major educational institution (Monash University) providing cash and in-kind support. The project will be piloted in the La Trobe Shire in Gippsland in the South Eastern corner of Australia, and is managed by the Monash Centre for Electronic Commerce.

Background

The Commonwealth of Australia through the Department of the Communications and the Arts have introduced a five year $250 million Networking the Nation Regional Telecommunications Infrastructure Fund (RTIF) to assist Australian regional, rural and remote communities to identify their communications needs, and develop and implement telecommunication, communication and infrastructure projects that meet the needs of regional communities. This fund is the major cash contributor to the project.

La Trobe Shire Council, (a local government organisation) in conjunction with Monash University Centre for Electronic Commerce, has adopted as a key strategy, the development of electronic commerce and communications in the La Trobe region as a means of enhancing community collaboration and development.

The shared vision for electronic commerce is also consistent with La Trobe Shire's drive for a clever, greener future for the region. Monash University Centre for Electronic Commerce was the first Centre of its kind in Australia, and provides leadership and expertise in the area of e-commerce.

E-Comm-AWARE! will support a primary objective of the La Trobe Shire Council's Strategy for the development of Electronic Communications and Commerce. That objective is to improve the social and economic environment of the shire, which has been impacted greatly by unemployment and social dislocation following the restructure of the Power Industry in Victoria. E-Comm-AWARE! will also facilitate equality of access and opportunity for La Trobe business and citizen communities, and, flowing from this, the mitigation of greater Gippsland's traditional isolation.

It is against this background of groundswell toward adopting new and emerging technologies to facilitate improvement in public sector management and community development that the La Trobe Shire Council and the Monash University Centre for Electronic Commerce formed a strong partnership to initiate electronic communications related projects, of which E-Comm AWARE! is one. Other projects include the GI Extranet, which is a pilot project to establish an Extranet between 16 engineering SMEs and the GippsComm project which is a telecommunications audit project that will recommend and implement a set of telecommunications solutions to increase connectivity of business and citizens throughout the Gippsland region.

What is E-Comm AWARE! ?

The aim of E-Comm-AWARE! is to raise the level of awareness and encourage the development of the Regional Electronic Community. The project will establish a "network" of e-commerce aware business and citizens as a model community which may be transposed in similar regional communities across Australia.

It is a comprehensive programme of awareness, training, community skills-audit and live project involvement, through the development of a number of products and services to support this aim.

The project commenced in April 1998 and is expected to be launched in April 1999. A comprehensive project plan and business plan has been completed, with the training needs analysis and database components of the project currently underway. The training needs analysis includes conducting extensive business and community surveys and consultation, and analysing existing research of similar projects being undertaken nationally and internationally. A number of databases are being developed to capture information on alliance organisations, potential distribution channels and product developers which will assist a number of processes throughout the project. An online skills database of regional e-commerce and IT skills will be developed as a regional skills resource, to attract business and investment to the region and market the skills of the region globally. The products produced throughout the life of the project will be piloted on 20 regional SMEs, with results feeding into the refinement of the end products and services.

The results of the research will form the basis of the program design which at this stage may include:

- Video
- CD Rom
- Web Site
- Starter Pack (hard copy information on what e-commerce is, where to get further information, initiatives, ISP contact details in region, free ISP sample kit etc.)
- Regional seminars (12)
- Train the trainer pack, and
- "How to" guide (for other regional areas).

These products will be packaged and distributed throughout the pilot region, La Trobe Shire and the wider Gippsland region, and then extensively throughout regional Australia at the end of the project. Summative and formative evaluation and marketing will be undertaken throughout the project. E-Comm AWARE! will prepare regional communities in Australia to understand the possibilities, to use the technologies, and to then participate in local, state-based and federal government electronic communications and commerce initiatives and will assist the community to move toward internetworking the region with its constituents and the rest of the world.

The Electronic Commerce Challenge

One of the biggest challenges in the development of electronic commerce has been for banks and merchants to overcome the issues of customer identification and account verification for online purchases. While the credit card systems have a process in place to verify and authorize transactions, the Internet poses challenges for merchants to not only validate that funds are available in an account, but to positively identify that the customer is in fact authorized to use that account for purchases. Early in the life of eCommerce, this situation led to the development of the SET protocol (Secure Electronic Transactions). While the initial version of SET was written in 1995, it has yet to be implemented for a number of reasons.

More recently, there has been a standard proposed called x9.59 (Account Authority Digital Signatures, or AADS), which recognizes the necessity of binding a certificate to an account number. Lynn Wheeler, the author, appropriately summarizes the current situation in his document: "To make electronic commerce real, it will be necessary to demonstrate integration of public-key bindings into the core account-based business processes. This requires changes to the installed data processing implementations. Without this integration, there is little hope of deploying electronic commerce on a large scale."

One of the biggest challenges in the development of electronic commerce has been for banks and merchants to overcome the issues of customer identification and account verification for online purchases. While the credit card systems have a process in place to verify and authorize transactions, the Internet poses challenges for merchants to not only validate that funds are available in an account, but to positively identify that the customer is in fact authorized to use that account for purchases.

In the physical world, merchants can validate the identity of the accountholder by comparing the signature on the credit card with the signature on the sales slip. But in a virtual world, where the customer is not present, the merchant does not know if that person is authorized to use the account number provided for the transaction. The danger in the eCommerce environment is that without some additional controls, the exposure to losses from fraudulent usage is exponentially greater.

The Development of SET

Early in the life of eCommerce, this situation led to the development of the SET protocol (Secure Electronic Transactions). While the initial version of SET was written in 1995, it has yet to be implemented for a number of reasons. But the catalyst for SET was the realization that there must be a way to positively identify individuals in an online environment, and that the identification process must include the binding of the individual to a specific transaction. This is absolutely critical to the effective management of credit card and debit card account usage. The implementation of the SET protocol has been challenging for a number of reasons, and as time has passed there have been other standards and solutions proposed as alternatives. No doubt there will be many more, as eCommerce is still in its relative infancy. But with each iteration of SET or other proposed solutions, it's clear that the industry has recognized the major obstacles, both technically and operationally, and is working to overcome them.

When the first version of SET was released in 1995, it became clear to me that there were monumental operational issues related to its implementation which were not addressed in the specification. Most notably, I saw two major obstacles:

- While the role of a Certificate Authority is to guarantee the identity of an individual, in the case of financial transactions, it must extend far beyond that — it must also link the identity of that individual to a certain account number. This greatly increases the issue of liability for the CA.
- The linking of digital certificates to specific account numbers would require an overhaul of the mainframe systems and operational functions that manage credit cards or other transactional accounts, and the cost of implementation could be significant.

An Alternative Solution

More recently, there has been a standard proposed called x9.59 (Account Authority Digital Signatures, or AADS), which recognizes the necessity of binding a certificate to an account number. It was developed by Lynn and Anne Wheeler, a husband-and-wife team of computer scientists who work at First Data Corp. Their understanding of credit card processing and account management is reflected in this proposed standard, as it addresses three major issues:

- The fundamental concept of AADS is that it limits the scope of a digital signature to a specific account, so that the CA's liability is limited as well. In this case, it would be far more attractive to the banks to issue digital certificates; and they would be in the best position to do this since they would have both the customer and the account information.
- Since a digital certificate is tied to a specific account, it makes the operational process for the bank or card company manageable. If a card is reported lost or stolen, or if there is a credit problem with the account, both the account number and the certificate can be blocked at the same time to limit liability.
- The customer's public key would reside with the account record, eliminating the need for a parallel system and the associated operational issues and costs.

AADS advocates the use of public key cryptography, yet it incorporates business operational considerations that are necessary to the cost-effective implementation of electronic commerce. This viewpoint is critical for widespread acceptance and every-day use.

Lynn Wheeler appropriately summarizes the current situation in his document: "To make electronic commerce real, it will be necessary to demonstrate integration of public-key bindings into the core account-based business processes. This requires changes to the installed data processing implementations. Without this integration, there is little hope of deploying electronic commerce on a large scale."

AADS advocates the use of public key cryptography, yet it incorporates business operational considerations that are necessary to the cost-effective implementation of electronic commerce.

8

Electronic Marketing: Yesterday, Today and Tomorrow

Electronic market is relatively new concept and has crept into business vocabulary around 1970s. Electronic commerce denote the seamless application of information and communication technology from its point of origin to its end point along the entire value chain of business processes conducted electronically and designed to enable the accomplishment of a business goal. These processes may be partial or complete and may encompass B2B as well as B2C and C2B transaction (Wigand, 1997).

The E-commerce further leads to the emergence of the "market space"-a virtual world of information paralleling the real marketplace of goods and services-enables marketers to manage content, context, and infrastructure in new and different ways, thereby providing novel sources of competitive advantage. With electronic marketing one can think for business across the globe that was not possible earlier.

Traditional way of market segmentation with an internet audience may not be fruitful. In electronic marketing, segmentation can be done effectively by considering two key dimensions i.e. potential value of the segment to the particular market sector and comparative attractiveness of the channel to the customer (Hymas, 2001). The 4Ps frame work of traditional product marketing is not appropriate for electronic marketing due to unavailability of demographics and psychographics of electronic customers. Booms and Bitner (1981) considered 7Ps frame work for electronic

Marketing. All most all the product can be made available for customer via electronic marketing but few product categories like Software, music, reports, games, videos etc., products can be delivered online at the same time, for other products it can be delivered later at the doorstep of the customers. It was initially believed that the Internet could benefit organizations because of the decreased costs involved with distribution, hence improving profit margins if they chose not to pass these benefits on to customers. But there are some electronic marketers like Amazon.com, have also contributed to price competition, effectively forcing the competitors to reduce the price. But same time Bromage (2001) argued that online customers buy online for convenience rather than for price advantages.

Regarding place, electronic marketing offers potential to shift from a non-virtual marketplace to a market-space instead, incorporating virtual transaction/distribution spaces. Websites have the potential to give information, to entertain and be interactive in their communication. Internet can take over some of the activities offered by the personal sales person (e.g. accepting purchase orders), but some of the activities undertaken by sales representatives cannot be replaced by technology.

The Internet allows organizations to make their service delivery system flexible. Because of the lack of physical proximity in electronic marketing, marketers make use of "virtual evidence" in the virtual environment. Lack of the personal interface may result in customer distrust of first-time interaction with electronic channels. It is also more difficult for marketers to build a relationship with customers whom they never see (Dobie et al., 2001); in such a situation trust (to reduce transaction cost) can be generated by other means, such as communication messages and brands.

Electronic marketing proved its effectiveness by reducing the time of shopping and made it easy for the people to shop. Most of the business houses adopted electronic marketing so far and many more are in pipe line.Although electronic marketing has proved its success in facilitating communication and exchange but still it has long way to travel.

E-Commerce and its Application in Indian Industries

Many international business researchers are of the opinion that increased globalization of markets and increasing international competition imply that firms in all nations will face similar, if not identical, competitive environments. In India due to liberalization of economy, the companies are facing acute competition in the international markets.

In the new millennium, the internet-based way of doing business has certainly changed many industries and has influenced many customers and businesses. It has changed the shapes of whole set of industries and markets and has already had a great impact on consumers and is all set to have a very exciting future. It has improved services, reduce costs, open new channels and transform the competitive landscape.

This paper is divided into two parts. First part deals with how E-Business is changing business environment. Second part of the paper is designed to examine the application of E-Commerce in selected Indian industries. For the purpose of the study, the e-business applications are divided into three categories:

* E – Commerce
* E – Procurement
* E – Collaboration.

E-commerce

E-Commerce, which primarily refers to buying, selling, marketing and servicing of products or services over internet. Business on the net is classified into B2B (Business to Business), B2C (Business to Consumer) and C2C (Consumer to Consumer).B2B transactions are largely between industrial manufacturers, partners, and retailers or between companies.B2C transactions take place directly between business establishments and consumers.

B2B sites are essentially the net meeting points for buyers and sellers of the industrial world. They serve a limited number of customers. Thė Turnover would be many times that of the most B2C sites and most importantly they make profits.

B2C sites are offering low value items CDs, Cassettes, Food, Toys, Flowers, and Cards etc. because no complicated logistics are involved.

C2C sites don't form a very high portion of web-based commerce. Most visible examples are the auction sites. Basically, if some one has something to sell, then he gets it listed at an auction sites and others can bid for it.

E-procurement

The Internet offers a natural platform to facilitate efficient procurement as numerous buyers and sellers find each other and transact according to some pre-specified protocols. The following are the procurement strategies available for a manufacturer.

* Strategic Partnership
* Online Search Strategy
* Combined Strategy.

1. *Strategic Partnership:* Strategic partnership strategy is to develop a long-term supply relationship with a specific supplier.
2. *Online Search Strategy:* Online Search Strategy is to shop online for a better price.
3. *Combined Strategy:* The combined strategy is to combine both – sign a long-term purchase contract with a supplier up to a certain level, but if necessary additional quantity may be purchased online.

E-collaboration

We define e-collaboration as business-to-business interactions facilitated by the Internet. These include information sharing and integration, decision sharing, process sharing and resource sharing. There are many new cases that examine different elements of collaboration from information sharing and integration to process and resource sharing.

E-commerce Application in Banking Industry

New information technologies and emerging business forces have triggered a new wave of financial innovation – electronic banking (e-banking). The banking and financial industry is transforming itself in unpredictable ways (Crane and Bodie 1996), powered in an important way by advances in information technology (Holland and Westwood 2001).

Since the 1980s, commercial banking has continuously innovated through technology-enhanced products and services, such as multi-function ATM, tele-banking, electronic transfers and electronic cash cards. Over the past decade, the Internet has clearly played a critical role in providing online services and giving rise to a completely new channel. In the internet age, the extension of commercial banking to the cyberspace is an inevitable development (Liao and Cheung 2003).

E-banking creates unprecedented opportunities for the banks in the ways they organize financial product development, delivery and marketing via the internet. While it offers new opportunities to banks, it also poses many challenges such as the innovation of IT applications, the blurring of market boundaries, the breaching of industrial barriers, the entrance of new competitors and the emergence of new business models. Now the speed and scale of the challenge are rapidly increasing with the pervasiveness of the internet and the extension of information economy (Holland and Westwood 2001).

Products Offered: All of the major banks in India have an internet presence offering a range of products directly to consumers by way of proprietary internet sites. While the initial focus of the banks has been in the retail-banking sector, there is a growing range of small to medium enterprise ("SME") and corporate banking products and services being offered. The products available include

Funds Transfer and Payment Systems: The major banks offer a range of online financial services including;

(i) Payment of bills;

(ii) Transfer of funds;

(iii) Remittances;

(iv) Applications for letters of credit; and

(v) Settlement through the MAS Electronic Payment System.

B2B E-Commerce: At least one of the major commercial banks offers an integrated B2B e-commerce product directly through its website, involving product selection, purchase order, invoice generation, and payment. However, integrated B2B products and services are not as yet generally available directly from the banks.

Securities Placement and Underwriting/Capital Markets Activities: Most commercial banks offer securities services such as online payment for shares and subscriptions for initial public offerings directly though their websites. However, more sophisticated online brokering services are generally only available through the banks' share-broker subsidiaries.

Securities Trading: A full range of online securities services are provided by the specialist securities subsidiaries of the major commercial banks including online trading.

Retail Banking: All of the major commercial banks have established websites for retail services. Typically such sites will offer the following services:

(i) a full range of personal account services, including foreign currency accounts;

(ii) funds transfers;

(iii) Bill payments;

(iv) Credit card services;

(v) Investment services; and

(vi) Online application for loan services including

(a) Car loans;

(b) Renovation loans;

(c) Home loans; and

(d) Personal credit lines.

E-Commerce has provided the platform that enables the implementation of core banking solutions (CBS). Today all the major banks have gone on to implement CBS. And with time being a premium among bank customers, banks have been ideating and developing newer modes of delivering banking services. Today there is a whole plethora of such platforms available ranging from the ATM to the mobile.

Banks like State Bank of India and its associates are recording over 100,000 transactions on a daily basis through their 5,000 plus network of ATMs. Incidentally the profile and usage pattern of ATMs in India matches that of ATMs abroad with an overwhelming (more than 80%) being used for cash withdrawal. Today with over 20,000 ATMs, India is recording one of the fastest growth in terms of ATM proliferation, though the per capita availability of ATMs doesn't compare anywhere to markets like Japan or the US.

With most banks now providing Internet banking facility, bankers say that customers are using the bank for a variety of purposes. One commonly used service being booking of rail tickets. Bankers also say that customers are using bank networks for online shopping. Most of the online banking channels are linked to major retailers. Estimates also indicate that today over 40% of the share transactions are being put through the internet.

E-commerce Application in Travel Industry

In India e-commerce is being driven by the growing online travel industry and online travel bookings have increased substantially after the entry of low cost carriers. Currently, online travel industry is contributing 50% to the revenue generated by e-commerce in India. To boot, online travel industry is growing at 125% (compounded annual growth rate) annually. Generating revenues of around $300-500 million (Rs.1,350-2,250 crore) currently, the size of the online travel industry is around 2% of the entire travel industry. Online travel industry is expected to become a $2 billion industry by 2008. In India, it is basically low cost carriers like Air Deccan and the Railways, which have significantly led to increased use of e-commerce.

However airline industry is still exploring the advantages of e-commerce. Currently e-commerce is being used mostly for e-ticketing among the domestic airlines though e-ticketing penetration in India is as low as 17% against the world average of 49% and 42% in Asia Pacific. But according to the UN's International Telecommunication Union, about 400 million travellers worldwide are expected to book tickets on-line this fiscal.

Air Deccan launched its operations with a 100% web enabled ticketing service and in no time became India's largest e-commerce site, with Rs.30 million worth transactions per day. Electronic ticketing now accounts for 35%-40% of tickets sold by Air Deccan. E-ticketing not only make tickets more accessible for travellers 24/7 but also eliminates the need to invest in ticketing offices and other related infrastructure reducing operational costs. Also travellers could avoid the long queues and save the service charges payable to travel agents.

Being a 100% e-ticket enabled airline, Kingfisher not only offers e-ticketing but also electronic check-in, wherein after printing the boarding card on-line the customer can use web-enabled check-in on the airline's website and board the plane directly passing through only mandatory security check at the airport. One of the biggest advantage of e-ticketing is that one can neither lose an e-ticket nor destroy it by leaving it accidentally in the pocket. Also e-ticketing environment offers much better degree of connectivity and reachability.

E-commerce Application in Government

India is now getting used to e-tendering. The Andhra Pradesh government's initiative is now a model for other states. It began in the year 2002 in Andhra Pradesh State government projects had been stalled by delays in awarding tenders. Cartels regularly cornered the bulk of government contracts and bids were tampered with after closure. For N.Chandrababu Naidu, the tech-savy chief minister in a hurry, this was unacceptable. He needed a way around the mess and predictably by use of technology. Now, 90% of all the tenders in Andhra Pradesh are completed online. Last year, orders worth Rs.15,000 crore were placed. While it earlier took anywhere between 90 and 135 days to finalise a tender, today it takes only 35 days. Northern Railway is planning to implement E-Procurement (E-Works contracts) System from December 2006.

Globally, e-commerce growth has been led by the popularity of online shopping portals like amazon.com and ebay.com but in India that has not been the case. It is mainly driven by the online travel industry and banking sector. For instance, 29% of Indian Internet users book airline tickets online and the figure is expected to touch 46% next year. Online rail ticket booking stands at 39% of the total bookings. As far as banking is concerned, there are 4.6 million online banking users in India. This figure is expected to go up to over 16 million by 2007-08 that will include both internet and mobile banking users. According to the Internet and Mobile Association of India (IAMAI), the e-commerce industry in India is expected to grow to a size of Rs.2,300 crore by 2007 against the Rs.1,200 crore. The total number of internet users which right now is 38.5 million is expected to reach 100 million by 2008.

E–Business and Supply Chain Management– A New Methodological Approach

Supply Chain Management has generated substantial interest in recent years for a number of reasons. Managers in many industries now realize that actions taken by one member of the chain can influence the profitability of all others in the chain. Many international business researchers are of the opinion that increased globalisation of markets and increasing international competition imply that firms in all nations will face similar, if not identical, competitive environments. In India due to liberalisation of economy, the companies are facing acute competition in the international markets. Many manufacturing companies are forced to improve the quality of their products and reduce their manufacturing costs.

This paper is divided into two parts. First part deals with how e-Business is changing supply chains. Second part of the paper is designed to examine the related research in this area. For the purpose of the study, the e-Business applications are divided into three categories:

* E – Commerce
* E – Procurement
* E – Collaboration.

E-commerce helps a network of supply chain partners to identify and respond quickly to changing customer demand captured over the Internet. E-procurement allows companies to use the Internet for procuring direct or indirect materials as well as handling value-added services like transportation, warehousing, customs clearing, payment, quality validation and documentation. E-collaboration facilitates coordination of various decisions and activities beyond transactions among the supply chain partners, both suppliers and customers over the Internet.

The main objective of Supply Chain Management is 'Customer Satisfaction' and to achieve this, all roadblocks are eliminated in between ultimate customer and the raw material supplier.

Features of Supply Chain Management

* Customer focus
* Retaining existing customers
* Streamlining of operations
* Minimum Fixed Cost
* Elimination of paper work
* Just in time
* Transparency at all levels
* Developing multiple supply sources for a multiple components
* Customer value enhancement and cost reduction.

E-commerce

Buying and selling on the Internet is known by the generic term e-commerce, just like e-mail, which is the way of sending mail through the net. Business on the net is classified into B2B (Business to Business), B2C (Business to Consumer) and C2C (Consumer to Consumer).

B2B transactions are largely between industrial manufacturers, partners, and retailers or between companies.

B2C transactions take place directly between business establishments and consumers.

B2B sites are essentially the net meeting points for buyers and sellers of the industrial world. They serve a limited number of customers. The Turnover would be many times that of the most B2C sites and most importantly they make profits. B2C sites are offering low value items CDs, Cassettes, Food, Toys, Flowers, and

Cards etc. because no complicated logistics are involved. C2C sites don't form a very high portion of web-based commerce. Most visible examples are the auction sites. Basically, if some one has something to sell, then he gets it listed at an auction sites and others can bid for it.

E-procurement

The Internet offers a natural platform to facilitate efficient procurement as numerous buyers and sellers find each other and transact according to some pre-specified protocols. The following are the procurement strategies available for a manufacturer.

* Strategic Partnership
* Online Search Strategy
* Combined Strategy.

1. *Strategic Partnership:* Strategic partnership strategy is to develop a long-term supply relationship with a specific supplier.
2. *Online Search Strategy:* Online Search Strategy is to shop online for a better price.
3. *Combined Strategy:* The combined strategy is to combine both – sign a long-term purchase contract with a supplier upto a certain level, but if necessary additional quantity may be purchased online.

E-collaboration

We define e-collaboration as business-to-business interactions facilitated by the Internet. These include information sharing and integration, decision sharing, process sharing and resource sharing. There are many new cases that examine different elements of collaboration from information sharing and integration to process and resource sharing.

Several cases have highlighted the impact of information integration on some particular aspect of the supply chain. Some of the cases are focused on managing supply while others are more focused on the customers. For example, the Solectron case focuses on how the use of information has transformed Solectron from a simple contract manufacturer into a full service supply chain integrator General Motors and Lufthansa cases illustrate how information can be used to increase customer loyalty and manage the prices.

Research in Supply Chain Management

Research in Supply chain management has identified twelve distinct management areas that are associated with the subject. Each area represents a supply chain issue facing the firm. For each area, we provide a brief description of the basin content and refer the reader to a few articles that apply. The twelve categories are,

* Location
* Transportation and logistics
* Outsourcing and logistics alliances
* Sourcing and supplier management
* Marketing and channel restructuring
* Inventory and forecasting
* Service and after sales support
* Reverse logistics and green issues
* Product design and new product introduction
* Information and electronic mediated environment
* Metrics and incentives
* Global issues.

Location: Of the twelve categories, decisions in this area have perhaps the longest time horizon. Decisions at this level set the physical structure of the supply chain and thus create constraints for more tactical decisions such as transportation, logistics and inventory planning. Engineering tools such, as mathematical models of facility location and geographic information systems are very useful in sorting the location choices.

Transportation and logistics: It includes all issues related to the physical flow of goods through the supply chain, including transportation, warehousing and material handling. This category addresses many of important choices related to transportation management including vehicle routing, dynamic fleet management with global positioning systems and merge-in-transit.

Outsourcing and logistics alliances: It examines the supply chain impact of outsourcing logistics services. With the rapid growth in third party logistics providers, there is a large and expanding group of technologies and services to be examined. These include fascinating initiatives such as supplier hubs managed by third parties.

Sourcing and Supplier management: This category addresses the issue of outsourcing components and the management of the suppliers who provide them. Make/buy decisions fall into this category. These decisions should involve top managers and strategic thinkers because they can literally define the future of the firm. For example, IBM to outsource its PC operating software to Microsoft and its central processing unit to Intel.

Marketing and Channel restructuring: It includes critical decisions related to getting the products from a firm's factories all the way into the customer's hands. As with facility location, these decisions impact the supply chain structure as well as define an interface with marketing.

Inventory and forecasting: It includes techniques for ongoing inventory management and demand forecasting. Industrial engineers and operation managers have employed statistical models for forecasting and inventory planning. Stochastic inventory models can identify the potential cost savings from sharing information with supply chain partners, but more complex models are required to coordinate multiple locations.

Service and after sales support: This category covers the important issue of providing service and service parts. Some leading firms, such as Saturn and Caterpillar, build their reputations in this area, and this area and this capability generates significant sales.

Reverse logistics and green issues: This area examines both reverse logistics issues of product returns and environmental impact issues. Growing regulatory pressures in many countries are forcing managers to consider the most efficient and environment friendly way to deal with product recovery. Product recovery includes the handling of all used and discarded products, components and materials.

Product design and new product introduction: It deals with design issues for mass customisation, delayed differentiation, modularity and other issues for new product introduction. Traditionally, products destined for world markets would be customized at the factory to suit local market tastes. The customized product is desirable and managing worldwide. Thus if the French version selling well, but the German version is not, German products can be quickly shipped to France and customized for the French market.

Information and electronic mediated environments: This category addresses the impact of information technology to reduce inventory and the rapidly expanding area of electronic commerce. It focuses attention on integrative ERP software such as SAP and Oracle as well as supply chain offerings such as Manugistics, i2's Rhythm and Peoplesoft's Red pepper.

Metrics and Incentives: It refers to the measurement of both engineering and organisational processes and the related economic motivations. Several recent articles concentrate on the link between performance management and supply chain management.

Global issues: It considers the issues beyond local country specific operating environments to encómpass issues related to cross-border distribution and sourcing. For example, currency exchange rates, duties and taxes, freight forwarding, customs issues, government regulation and country comparisons are all included.

Supply chain management is indeed a large and growing field for both engineers and managers. Nearly all major manufacturing consulting firms have developed large practices in the supply chain field and the number of books and academic research papers in the field is growing rapidly. In fact, each of the twelve areas covered in our treatment of supply chains are important in themselves. Finally, the Internet continues to change many fundamental assumptions about business, pushing managers to continue to evolve their supply chain practices or find themselves driven out of the market.

Customer Relationship Management

We all know the meaning of customer, relationship & management, but by compiling these three words it is defined as

C.R.M., which is a tool used by businesses in order to increase profitability, revenue & also customer satisfaction by segmentin the customers, then finding customer satisfying behaviour, and also implementing the process to satisfy the customers. C.R.M. technology should have the potential to seek the customer's satisfaction and which increases customer access and leads to deep and strong interactions. Take it like this: we all live in a society and we all are surrounded by some relationships. But, if these are having some grievances then our performance will be hindered.

Evolution of C.R.M.

With the very emergence of needs C.R.M. took birth and with the passage of time it has been coloured as per the market requirements.

1. *Traditional marketing:*-C.R.M. took birth, when people started exchanging goods to satisfy their needs and wants. This was the time of barter system.
2. *Mass marketing:*-At this time barter system became obsolete and industrial revolution took place and sellers were engaged in mass production, mass distribution. At this time production was given emphasis.
3. *Value-based marketing:*-At this time producers lay emphasis on offering better value to customers money by improving quality of products and services offered to customers.
4. *Relationship marketing:*-The scenario changed and producers started feeling the importance of customers and tried to build long-term relations either by providing free gifts, or various services like guarantees etc. This was the time of customer-centred marketing.
5. *Marketing on web:*-This is also known as E-SHOPPING and is itself diversified in its nature. Doing just few clicks of mouse purchase variety and number of products. This is the most convenient and comfortable way of shopping. Many co. like Amazon, embay are the best-suited examples.
6. *Customized marketing:*-With the advancement in technologies this very advancement in marketing has

become possible. Software database is used for this. Software databases help in providing & storing customers' information. Softwares like:-Sap, Siebel, Broadvison, Chordiant, Onyx, Selligent, Silknet, Lucent, Inference, IBM, Goldmine etc. are being used by the companies. Aircraft parts distributor Aviall, consumer product giant Kimberly-Clark, Lakme, Mattel's 'My Design Barbie', Dell computers, Nike shoes, electronic connector manufacturer Molex, and McDonald's are enhancing their sales, revenue and customer's loyalty with the implementation of this technology. Harvard business review depicts that by the end of 2010 almost 30% of U.S. commercial activity will involve customized marketing.

Types of C.R.M.

C.R.M. allows a company to address all types of customers at different points in its life and choose the market program that best fits a customer's attitude.

There are basically four types of C.R.M.:-

1. *Win back customers:*-This is the way of convincing the costumers to stay with the company at that point of time when they discontinue with the company. Coke, Pepsi and others soft drinks are the best-suited examples of this type.
2. *Prospecting:*-This is an effort to win new, first time customers. In this company needs to segment the market which helps organization to affectively target the offer.
3. *Loyalty:*-This is an effort in which company tries to prevent customers to leave the company. It is very difficult to gain it accurately. It uses two elements:-
   (a) *Value based segmentation:*-it helps in determining that how much company is willing to invest in retaining its customer's loyalty.
   (b) *Need based segmentation:*-after determining its investment power, company can determine its customer loyalty program means either to use relationship marketing or marketing on the web or customized marketing.

4. *Cross sell/Up sell:*-In this company provides value addition in its product. In cross sell after getting customer data the value means offer to be provided is considered. And in up selling the product or service offered is an enhanced one means innovated.

Importance of Retaining Customers

Strong bonds provide that loyalty that turns out to be everlasting. Helps in recovering customer acquisition cost and also benefits by 'word of mouth' as it is more fruitful than television, direct mail and press put together. Harvard research also depicts that 5% increase in customer retention increases NPR by 20%-120%.

Why C.R.M.

Despite having best manufacturing capabilities, best marketing approach, best business strategy the organizations use C.R.M. WHY? Because each and every tool or strategy of a business can be copied by anyone but one's soft skills, one's way of handling relations can't ever be copied by anyone.

Because of all these advantages it is being use by many co. like Lakme employed 'Computer Touch Screen', Ponds Institute has a customer response center, HLL-Surf received 'Open Customer Feedback' and Surf-Excel is the result of that, Apollo Tyres offered 'Dia-a-Tyre, Asian paints is also providing home solutions.

In short the CRM is a process enabled by technology to know your customers well and use the database to retain profitable relationship with high life time value customers. Retention of good customers and maximizing revenue through them is at core of CRM.

E-Commerce: Challenges and Opportunities

E-commerce as anything that involves an online transaction. This can range from ordering online, through online delivery of paid content, to financial transactions such as movement of money between bank accounts. This paper has analysed some of the challenges and opportunities of e-commerce.

Elizabeth Goldsmith and others (2000) reported that the general category of e-commerce can be broken down into two parts:

1. E-merchandise: selling goods and services electronically and moving items through distribution channels, for example through Internet shopping for groceries, tickets, music, clothes, hardware, travel, books, flowers or gifts.
2. E-finance: banking, debit cards, smart cards, banking machines, telephone and Internet banking, insurance, financial services and mortgages on-line (Elizabeth Goldsmith and others, 2000).

Farooq Ahmed (2001) reported that the enormous flexibility of the internet has made possible what is popularly called e-commerce which has made inroads in the traditional methods of business management. All the facets the business tradition with which we are accustomed in physical environment can be now executed over the internet including online advertising, online ordering, publishing, banking, investment, auction and professional services. E commerce involves conducting business using modern communication instruments: telephone, fax, e-payment, money transfer systems, e-data interchange and the internet. The WTO has recognized that commercial transactions can be broken into 3 stages. 'The advertising and searching stage, the ordering, and payment stage, and the delivery stage.'

Growth of E-commerce

Electronic commerce or e-commerce encompasses all business conducted by means of computer networks. Advances in telecommunications and computer technologies in recent years have made computer networks an integral part of the economic infrastructure. More and more companies are facilitating transactions over web. E-commerce provides multiple benefits to the consumers in form of availability of goods at lower cost, wider choice and saves time.

People can buy goods with a click of mouse button without moving out of their house or office. Similarly online services such as banking, ticketing including airlines, bus, railways, bill payments, hotel booking etc. have been of tremendous benefit for the customers. Most experts believe that overall e-commerce will increase exponentially in coming years. Business to business transactions will represent the largest revenue but online retailing will also enjoy a drastic growth. Online businesses like financial services, travel, entertainment, and groceries are all likely to grow.

Factors Influencing the Distribution and Forms of Global E-commerce

Nir B. Kshetri (2001) reported that the twin forces of globalization and the Internet have the potential to offer several benefits to individuals and organizations in developing as well as developed countries.

Apart from economic benefits such as more choices and the convenience of shopping at home, the twin forces can make progress on educational and scientific development, mutual aid, and world peace; foster democracy; and offer exposure to other cultures.

To fully exploit the potential of the Internet and e-commerce, policy makers in developing as well as industrialized countries are taking initiatives to develop the global information infrastructure (GII) and connect their national information infrastructures to the GII (Gore 1996).

All countries are not likely to benefit equally from the virtuous circle of Internet diffusion created by globalization and multiple revolutions in Communication technologies (ICTs). Forces influencing the distribution of global e-commerce and its forms include economic factors, political factors, cultural factors and supranational institutions.

Economic factors mainly influence perceived relative advantage of Internet use whereas political and cultural factors influence the compatibility of the Internet with a society. Supranational institutions' initiatives are influencing the price, quality and availability of ICT products and services, mainly in developing countries, thereby increasing relative advantage of Internet use.

Moreover international institutions are influencing laws, regulations and policies in developing countries making them more compatible with Internet use.

Brief Review of Literature on E-commerce: Challenges and Opportunities

An attempt has been made to put forward a brief review of literature based on few of the related studies undertaken worldwide in the area of e-commerce as follows.

Elizabeth Goldsmith and Sue L.T. McGregor (2000) analysed the impact of e-commerce on consumers, public policy, business and education. A discussion of public policy initiatives, research questions and ideas for future research are given.

Andrew D. Mitchell (2001) examined the key issues that electronic commerce poses for Global trade, using as a starting point the General Agreement on Trade in Services (GATS), the World Trade organization (WTO) agreement most relevant to e-commerce.

Nir B.Kshetri (2001) This paper attempts to identified and synthesized the available evidence on predictors of magnitude, global distribution and forms of e-commerce. The analysis indicated that the twin forces of globalization and major revolutions in ICT are fuelling the rapid growth of global e-commerce.

Jackie Gilbert Bette Ann Stead (2001) reviewed the incredible growth of electronic commerce (e-commerce) and presented ethical issues that have emerged. Security concerns, spamming, Web sites that do not carry an "advertising" label, cybersquatters, online marketing to children, conflicts of interest, manufacturers competing with intermediaries online, and "dinosaurs" were discussed.

Mauricio S. Featherman, Joseph S. Valacich & John D. Wells (2006) examined whether consumer perceptions of artificiality increase perceptions of e-service risk, which has been shown to hamper consumer acceptance in a variety of online settings.

Young Jun Choil, Chung Suk Suh (2005) examined the impact of the death of geographical distance brought about by e-marketplaces on market equilibrium and social welfare.

Prithviraj Dasgupta and Kasturi Sengupta (2002) examined the future and prospects of e-commerce in Indian Insurance

Industry. (Arvind Panagariya, 2000) examined Economic issues raised by e-commerce for the WTO and developing countries. E-commerce offers unprecedented opportunities to both developing and developed countries.

Opportunities for E-commerce

Young Jun Choil, Chung Suk Suh (2005) reported that the development of the internet in the 20th century led to the birth of an electronic marketplace or it is called e-marketplace, which is now a kernel of electronic commerce (e-commerce).

An e-marketplace provides a virtual space where sellers and buyers trade with each other as in the traditional marketplace. Various kinds of economic transactions and buying and selling of goods and services, as well as exchanges of information, take place in e-marketplaces. E-marketplaces have become an alternative place for trading. Finally, an e-marketplace can serve as an information agent that provides buyers and sellers with information on products and other participants in the market. These features have been reshaping the economy by affecting the behaviour of buyers and sellers.

E-business

E-business affects the whole business and the value chains in which it operates. It enables a much more integrated level of collaboration between the different components of a value chain than ever before. Adopting e-Business also allows companies to reduce costs and improve customer response time. Organizations that transform their business practices stand to benefit immensely from innumerable new possibilities brought about by technology.

E-commerce as anything that involves an online transaction. This can range from ordering online, through online delivery of paid content, to financial transactions such as movement of money between bank accounts. One area where there are some positive indications of e-commerce is financial services. Online stock trading saw sustained growth throughout the period of broadband diffusion. E-shopping is available to all these who use a computer. Over the past year Amazon.Com, ebay India, Indiatimes have seen a rapid growth in categories such as mobile handsets, jewellery, fashion apparel, books, gift items and other items.

Naukri.com – India's premier recruitment site has captured around 50% of the recruitment market.

Icicidirect.com-Stock trading simplified, Icicidirect.com is today the country's premier trading portal.

Baaze.com the country's premier shopping site started as an auction site and graduated to be the most popular platform-shopping site.

Irctc.com-One of the best things about this site is that a credit card is not an essential requirement for buying tickets here. Instead the site offers a direct debit facility having tied with most of the popular banks.

It is being estimated that the online travel market in India was estimated at $300 million in 2005 and has crossed $750 million in 2006. By 2008, it is expected to exceed $2 billion.

Young Jun Choil, Chung Suk Suh (2005) reported that the economic consequences of the death of geographical distance due to the emergence of e-marketplaces. It has shown that overcoming spatial barriers by means of e-marketplaces lowers the price level. Since e-marketplaces achieve economies of scale by aggregating dispersed demands, they allow the economy to have more varieties that did not exist before their emergence.

E-commerce Integration

Zabihollah Rezaee, Kenneth R. Lambert and W. Ken Harmon (2006) reported that the rationale for infusion of e-commerce education into all business courses is that technological developments are significantly affecting all aspects of today's business. An e-commerce dimension can be added to the business curriculum by integrating e-commerce topics into existing upper-level business courses. Students would be introduced to e-commerce education and topics covered in a variety of business courses in different disciplines e.g. accounting, economics, finance, marketing, management, management information systems. To help assure that all related business courses in all disciplines such as e.g., accounting, finance, economics, marketing, management, information systems pay proper attention to the critical aspects of e-commerce, certain e-commerce topics should be integrated into existing business courses.

Open and Distance Learning

Diana Oblinger (2001) reported that one is that education and continuous learning have become so vital in all societies that the demand for distance and open learning will increase. As the availability of the Internet expands, as computing devices become more affordable, and as energy requirements and form factors shrink, e-learning will become more popular. In addition to the importance of lifelong learning, distance education and e-learning will grow in popularity because convenience and flexibility are more important decision criteria than ever before. E learning will become widely accepted because exposure to the Internet and e-learning often begins in the primary grades, thus making more students familiar and comfortable with online learning. In fact, for many countries, distance education has been the most viable solution for providing education to hundreds of thousands of students.

E-commerce and E-insurance

Prithviraj Dasgupta and Kasturi Sengupta (2002) reported that the recent growth of Internet infrastructure and introduction of economic reforms in the insurance sector have opened up the monopolistic Indian insurance market to competition from foreign alliances. Although the focus of e-commerce has been mainly on business to consumer (B2C) applications, the emphasis is now shifting towards business to business (B2B) applications. The insurance industry provides an appropriate model that combines both B2C and B2B applications.

Traditional insurance requires a certificate for every policy issued by the insurance company. However, paper certificates encumber problems including loss, duplication and forging of the certificate. The conventional certificate is now replaced with an electronic certificate that can be digitally signed by both the insurer and the insurance company and verified by a certifying authority. Online policy purchase is faster, more user-friendly and definitely more secure than the traditional processes. Therefore it is more attractive to the insurer. At the same time it incurs less cost and requires fewer resources than traditional insurance and is therefore more profitable for the insurance company.

E-insurance also makes the insurance procedure more secure since the policy details are stored digitally and all transactions are made over secure channels. These channels provide additional market penetration that is absent in traditional channels and help in earning more revenue than traditional insurance processes.

Future Media of E-commerce

Patric Barwise (2001) reported that Probability 99% of e-commerce today is done using PCs either desktops or laptops. For B2B e-commerce this is unlikely to change.For B2C e-commerce however, things will be more complex.

There will be wider range of relevant media, including interactive digital TV, and a range of mobile and wireless services.

There will be huge difference between different consumers' ownership of equipment and access technology. Some will have broad band access and others have no digital communication at all.

Current and Future B2C Digital Media

Digital media able to support consumer e-commerce can be grouped under five main headings, with in the home PCS, IDTV and with in next five years a range of other online device such as games, computers, utility meters etc. In summary, the online PC is well established while the other B2C digital media are still emerging. Economic issues raised by e-commerce for the WTO and developing countries.

Arvind Panagariya, 2000) reported that access to e-commerce, which in the WTO parlance often means access to e-exports, has two components that must be distinguished sharply: access to internet services and access to services that can be traded electronically. The former deals with to access to Internet infrastructure while the latter relates to specific commitments in electronically tradable services. E-commerce offers unprecedented opportunities to both developing and developed countries.

In the short run, the gains are likely to be concentrated in developed countries have more to benefit. This is because, in the short run, developing countries lack the infrastructure necessary to take full advantage of Internet. For many countries, especially developing ones, in these countries, most consumers do not have computers or Internet access. A likely scenario, therefore, is one in which a handful of independent entrepreneurs will receive the product by Internet, convert it into physical form such as CDs and sell the latter to consumers.

But this activity may itself be costly, using up real resources. But in the long run, they can leapfrog, skipping some of the stages in the development of information technology through which developed countries have had to pass. Some efficiencies issues must be addressed. The issue of tariffs, which are applicable to products imported in physical form but not when transmitted electronically. As long as the cost of electronic transmission is lower than that of physical delivery, the presence of tariffs on the latter poses no problem. Effectively, the electronic transmission offers the product to the country at a price lower than that available through physical delivery.

Challenges for E Commerce

Internet based e-commerce has besides, great advantages, posed many threats because of its being what is popularly called faceless and borderless.

Some examples of ethical issues that have emerged as a result of electronic commerce. All of the following examples are both ethical issues and issues that are uniquely related to electronic commerce.

Ethical issues: Jackie Gilbert Bette Ann Stead (2001), reported the following ethical issues related to e-commerce.

1) *Privacy:* Privacy has been and continues to be a significant issue of concern for both current and prospective electronic commerce customers. With regard to web interactions and e-commerce the following dimensions are most salient:
   - Privacy consists of not being interfered with, having the power to exclude; individual privacy is a moral right.

- Privacy is "a desirable condition with respect to possession of information by other persons about him/ herself on the observation/perceiving of him/herself by other persons"

Security concerns: In addition to privacy concerns, other ethical issues are involved with electronic commerce. The Internet offers unprecedented ease of access to a vast array of goods and services. The rapidly expanding arena of "click and mortar" and the largely unregulated cyberspace medium have however prompted concerns about both privacy and data security.

Other ethical issues: Manufacturers Competing with Intermediaries Online. "Disintermediation," a means eliminating the intermediary such as retailers, wholesalers, outside sales reps by setting up a Website to sell directly to customers.

Disintermediation include (1) music being downloaded directly from producers (2) authors distributing their work from their own Web sites or through writer co-operatives.

Dinosaurs – "Dinosaurs" is a term that refers to executives and college professors who refuse to recognize that technology has changed our lives. When an executive speaks in terms of the Internet being the "wave of the future," it is a sure sign of "dinosaur.

Perceptions of Risk in e-service Encounters

Mauricio S. Featherman, Joseph S. Valacich & John D. Wells (2006) reported that as companies race to digitize physical-based service processes repackaging them as online e-services, it becomes increasingly important to understand how consumers perceive the digitized e-service alternative. E-service replacements may seem unfamiliar, artificial and non-authentic in comparison to traditional service processing methods. Consumers may believe that new internet-based processing methods expose them to new potential risks the dangers of online fraud, identity theft and phishing swindles means schemes to steal confidential information using spoofed web sites, have become commonplace, and are likely to cause alarm and fear within consumers.

E-commerce Integration

Beside many an advantages offered by the education a no of

challenges have been posed to the recent education system.

Zabihollah Rezaee, Kenneth R. Lambert and W. Ken Harmon (2006) reported that E-commerce Integration assures coverage of all critical aspects of e-commerce, but it also has several obstacles. First, adding e-commerce materials to existing business courses can overburden faculty and students alike trying to cope with additional subject matter in courses already saturated with required information. Second, many business faculty members may not wish to add e-commerce topics to their courses primarily because of their own lack of comfort with technology-related subjects. Third and finally, this approach requires a great deal of coordination among faculty and disciplines in business schools to ensure proper coverage of e-commerce education.

Online Advertising

A company needs to make marketing decisions not only in the areas of segmentation, product offerings, pricing and distribution but also in the areas of promotion. The successful promotion of a produce requires that, at a minimum, a positive message be received by potential customers. And advertising is the main and most commonly used source of communication to convey the message to the ultimate customers. Advertising is not a new concept. The principles of advertising have their root going back very deep into the history of man. About 3,000 years ago in Thebes, an advertisement was written on papyrus calling for information regarding a runaway slave.

This was not the first advertising, merely one of the first examples, which has survived. Pompeli is rich in advertisement scratched and painted upon its wall. But time changes; so do we. And the way people advertise their product or a service is no exception either.

Online advertising is the latest addition in this genre. Online advertising is also known as Web advertising, Internet advertising and e-advertising. But whatever be the name, in essence, it is all advertising. In a very simple sense online advertising can be defined as the use of electronic communication resources (especially Internet and its enable technologies) to engage in the activities of advertising.

The realm of which is a relatively new, un-researched area with a huge untapped potential. What fascinates me about this topic is the fact that in the information age, the growing accessibility of the Internet among diverse sections of consumers, can become a powerful tool for endorsement and hence sale of products. What is unique and defining about this medium is that, the advertiser reaches only those who are interested (a focused audience), and more cost-effectively than with conventional advertising.

With the new focused channels, the Advertiser can concentrate on timely and customized announcements, rather than the relatively static and mass appeal approach in conventional media. On an individual level, for example, the marketer may use the technology to make himself more accessible to the consumer thus adding to his service levels through interactive marketing.

The introduction of interactive marketing and specifically interactive advertising heralds the beginning of an era where customers will choose the advertising they wish to see, when they want to see it. The Web can be transformed into a research tool, a brand builder and an advertising medium in one swoop, something not offered by other media. Furthermore, unlike other media where the advertising agency is the only link between the client and the media-owner, the Web allows the client to become the media owner. The assortment of features of web advertisement notwithstanding, it provides a special challenge to marketers and planners due to its relative infancy, which brings previously un-encountered circumstances to the fore.

Why Online Advertising?

The Internet has produced a revolutionary new way for business to communicate and interact with customers. Everyone from small businesses to fortune 500 company's are racing to make their mark in cyberspace with their own "Home Pages" on the world wide web (www). The reason it presents great advertising opportunities for marketers because of its continuing growth. The number of Internet users around the world is constantly growing. The computer industry almanac has reported that by the year 2005, 118 people per 1000 around the world will have Internet access. As Internet users are growing day by day; so are Internet advertisers because they can easily, effectively and efficiently communicate their products or services to targeted mass audience. Add to this the fact that Internet users are well educated with high incomes, it is only logical to conclude that Internet surfers are a desired target for advertisers.

Other reasons why online advertising is growing rapidly are:

* Advertisement can reach very large number of potential buyers globally.
* Web superiority over other advertising medium.
* Web page (advertisement) can be updated any time and changes or corrections are painless.
* Online advertisement works 24 hours a day, 7 days a week, 365 days a year.
* In online advertisement specific interest groups or individuals can be targeted.
* Online advertisement can effectively use the convergence of text, audio, graphics, and Animation.
* Online advertisements are cheaper in comparison to traditional advertisement. There is no printing costs, no postage costs etc.

Forms of Online Advertising

The Internet is a great place to advertise. There are many forms of online advertising. Some of the main ones involved:

* E-mail sponsorship advertising
* Newsletter and E-zine advertising
* Rich media advertising (flash ads, Interstitials & Superstitials, streaming audio/video, etc.)
* Pop-up/pop-under advertising
* Online banner advertising
* Sponsorship (web sites, e-mails, sweep stakes)
* Advertorial (Paid-for editorial) placements.

Sector wise online advertising trends in world:

* Around 1/3 of net advertising is from FMCG Companies.
* Around 15% comes from finance companies.
* Around 11% from technology companies.

* Around 7% comes from communication a publication etc.
* And the rest from other sectors.

Online Advertising: Indian Scene

Online advertising is still in the embryonic stages in India, while in other parts of the world it has already taken deep roots. The share of India's online advertising in world pie is almost negligible.

But developing countries like India; where Internet users are growing very rapidly, it has huge potential. India's leading advertisers are starting to advertise online, but at a very slow pace. Indian companies are also showing keen interest in promoting their products or services online. Currently finance sector is most dominating sector in online advertising and accounted about 40% of total online advertising in India. Some of the leading companies from this sector are HDFC, Citibank, SBI, and UTI etc. FMCG goods have just started to come in led by companies like Hindustan Lever, Procter and Gamble etc.

FMCG accounted about 20% of total online advertisement spending in India. Consumer durables companies are also coming and accounted 15% of total online advertisement. Share of media sector is about 10% and rest comes from other. In India, most popular form of online advertising is banner advertising.

The reason, it is easy to create, place and use. E-mail advertising follows it. India has to cover a lot of grounds to come up to the level of online advertising as, say, a country like U.S. There are many stumbling blocks in the growth of online advertising in India like, psychological fears of IT, high cost, low education and above all low awareness level. Still many Indian companies are hesitant, anxious and doubtful about the potential it offers. Unless these are dealt with online advertising can't really take off in India.

Benefits of Online Advertising

The Internet has great potential as media carrier compared to traditional media. It offers higher selectivity which is tailored to the user's profile. The customer can also customize the adverts as he/she is in charge of his own navigation. Through the online advertising the advertiser can get quick, easy and inexpensive feedback in real time, which no other media offers, providing a higher feedback rate. Some other benefits of online advertising are as under:

* Online advertising facilitates the advertiser to reach an absolutely pinpointed and targeted audience.
* "Traditional advertising is usually a one-way mechanism there is no way for customers to act on the information in the advertisements. On the Internet, however, interested customers can click on a banner, learn more, and actually make purchase on the spot," states Arti Dwarkadas, business director, Ogilvy Interaction.
* The Internet as a medium knows no demographic boundaries and gives the advertiser a huge audience to tap and build brand image if not sell products.
* Internet's interactive nature allows for greater flexibility than traditional media in the type of information transmitted and the method of transmission.
* Online advertisement can facilitate purchase decision.
* Enhance customer company relationship.
* Protection of environment.
* Online advertisement expands the company's market to global market.
* It is easy to create, and place, it saves time, labor and money.
* No loss of quality even after a very long period of time.

Limitations of Online Advertising

Research, reveals that not many companies take advantage of online advertising opportunity. There are many reasons behind it. Some of the most common are as under:

* Online advertising is not simply a "Customer oriented" medium; it is a customer-dominated medium
* Online advertising is not emotional medium like T.V.; it is a cognitive medium
* Mindset shift in using online advertising
* Psychological fear of IT

* Infrastructure inadequacy
* High cost
* Limited space
* Limited information
* Users work on the net for a specific purpose; they are not interested in other things like advertising.

Company can't target all the potential customers like those who are not Internet;

* Too many companies are trying to slice up a tiny online advertising pie, resulting in Commoditization of the business and leading to extreme competition pressure.
* Suggestions for online advertising
* Understanding the right way to advertise on the Internet is extremely important as the negative or downside potential is extremely great for a small startup or medium sized firm.

Ethics in Social Marketing

Problems faced by marketers in non-profit organizations are among the most important and interesting issues in marketing today.

For marketers in commercial organisations, ethical considerations are non-essential constraints. The ultimate aim is to make profits for shareholders, and ethical considerations may limit the methods employed to achieve this aim. For social marketers the situation is different. By definition, their ultimate aim is ethical, and for them the question of whether the ends justify the means is real and challenging. For social marketers, therefore, ethical issues are fundamental.

Unfortunately, most social marketers, believe that it is important to define just what social marketing is, the different types of social marketing that exist, and how social marketing differs from commercial marketing.

Some of these points seem quite appealing at first as some social marketers typically believe that they have only limited resources for achieving such impressive objectives. However, a moment's thought would show that this is not true. Some government agencies in India, for example, have comparatively large promotional budgets that would exceed those of many commercial marketers, particularly those who work in small companies. Thus, the overlap between commercial and social marketing is arguably much greater, and it would be helpful to explore common ground rather than create dubious distinctions.

Although it is worthwhile to argue that these concerns attached with the nature of social marketing are misplaced, it is still not clear whether these are the exclusive domains of social marketers. It is sometimes quoted that "Thoughtful social marketing practitioners are faced all too frequently with ethical dilemmas". This is clearly true, but the same is true of all marketers, who must make personal decisions regarding their activities and the implications these have for others. For example, commercial marketers have to decide whether it is appropriate to market products rich in highly processed carbohydrates while the social marketers have to decide whether it is appropriate to promote immunisation knowing that a very small proportion of children will suffer adverse effects to the vaccines. So, at times it becomes very difficult to demonstrate the ethical problems of social marketers from those faced by marketers in general.

Furthermore, it has been observed that both social marketers and commercial marketers have the same compelling interest; hence it is not surprising that social marketers borrow concepts first developed and applied in commercial marketing. However, it is surprising that there is little discussion of how social marketers can apply this commercial knowledge to the behavioural objectives they wish to tackle.

Ultimately, marketers interested in problems that involve social behaviours want to learn more about the options available for changing or reinforcing those behaviours, and the relative effectiveness of those options. These are difficult questions, as little has been empirically established. However, for social marketing to progress, these questions, as well as their ethical implications, need to be explicitly acknowledged and discussed, and actively researched.

Bibliography

Bhushan Ekta : *Developing Professionalism in Hospitality : Aviation Sector,*, Rajat Publications, Delhi, 2010.

Coccosis, Harry and Nijkamp, Peter: *Sustainable Tourism Development,* Aldershot, Avebury, 1995.

Cukier, J. : *Tourism Employment in Bali: Trends and Implications,* London: Thompson, 1996.

Daniel Minoli : *A Networking Approach to Grid Computing,* Wiley, Delhi, 2010.

Digumarti Bhaskara Rao: *International Meetings on Human Rights,* Discovery, 2001.

Donald E. : *Public Personnel Management: Contexts and Strategies,* Upper Saddle River, NJ: Prentice Hall, 1998.

Eckel, Peter J.: *College & University Foodservice Management Standards,* Westport, AVI Pub. Company, 1985.

Elio, C.: *The Hospitality Law Desk Reference,* Miami, Southern Beverage Journal, 1994.

Foster, Douglas: *Travel and Tourism Management,* London, Macmillan Educational, 1985.

Frechtling, Douglas C: *Practical Tourism Forecasting,* Oxford, Butterworth Heinemann, 1996.

Gopalkrishnan: *Brand Alliances : New Models of Networking,* ICFAI, 2007.

Graham M S: *Language of Tourism,* The, Wallingford, CAB International, 1996.

Gunn, Clare and Var, Turgut: *Tourism Planning,* London, Retailed, 2002.

Hays, Judi Radice: *Restaurant & Food Graphics,* Glen Cove, PBC International, 1994.

Her Majesty's : *Higher Education in the Polytechnics and Colleges, Hotel, Catering and Tourism Management*, London, DES, 1992.

Horner, S. and Swarbrooke, J.: *Marketing Tourism, Hospitality and Leisure in Europe*, London, International Thomson Business Press, 1996.

Karski, A: *Urban Tourism* - A Key to Urban Regeneration?, 1990.

Klein, S. : *Information & Communication Technologies in Tourism*, Springer-Verlag, Wien-New York, 2000.

Kotler, Philip: *Marketing for Hospitality and Tourism*: New Jersey, Prentice-Hall, 1998.

Labarge, Margaret Wade: *Medieval Travellers: The Rich and Restless*, London, Hamish Hamilton, 1982.

Larkham, P J: *Building a New Heritage: Tourism, Culture & Identity in the New Europe*, London, Routledge,1994.

Lawrence, E.: *Technology of internet business*, Wiley, Australia, 2002.

Laws, Eric: *Tourist Destination Management: Issues, Analysis & Policies*, London, Routledge, 1995.

Maitland, R: *Tourism Destinations, London*, Hodder and Stoughton, 1997.

Medlik, S. : *Tourism, Past, Present and Future*, London, Heinemann, 1981.

Pearce, Douglas: *Tourism Today: A Geographical Analysis*, Harlow, Longman, 1995.

Peter J.: *College & University Foodservice Management Standards*, Westport, AVI Pub. Company, 1985.

Peters, M: *International Tourism*, London, Hutchinson, 1969.

Robert C.: *Cases in Hospitality Marketing and Management*, New York, John Wiley, 1997.

Rocco, M.: *An Introduction to Hospitality Today*, Orlando, Educational Institute, 1998.

Rue, Nancy N.: *Choosing a Career in Hotels, Motels, and Resorts*, New York, Rosen Pub. Group, 1997.

Sharma Jitendra K. : *Contemporary Tourism and Hospitality Management*, Kanishka, Delhi, 2006.

Shaw, G and Williams, A: *Tourism and Tourism Spaces*, London, Sage, 2004.

Index

□□□